PARTY DEVELOPMENT
AND
DEMOCRATIC CHANGE
IN
POST-COMMUNIST EUROPE

The First Decade

edited by

PAUL G. LEWIS

The Open University

FRANK CASS
LONDON • PORTLAND, OR

First Published in 2001 in Great Britain by
FRANK CASS PUBLISHERS
Crown House, 47 Chase Side, Southgate,
London, N14 5BP, England

and in the United States of America by
FRANK CASS PUBLISHERS
c/o ISBS
5824, N.E. Hassalo Street
Portland, Oregon 97213-3644

*Website:*www.frankcass.com

British Library Cataloguing in Publication Data

Party development and democratic change in post-communist
  Europe : the first decade. – (Democratization studies)
  1.Political parties – Europe, Eastern 2.Representative
  government and representation – Europe, Eastern 3.Europe,
  Eastern – Politics and government – 1989–
  I.Lewis, Paul G. (Paul Geoffrey), 1945–
  324.2'47

    ISBN 0714651559 (cloth)
         0714681741 (paper)

Library of Congress Cataloging in Publication Data

Party development and democratic change in post-communist Europe : the
first decade / edited by Paul G. Lewis
    p. cm. – (Democratization studies, ISSN 1465-4601)
    Includes bibliographical references and index.
    ISBN 0-7146-5155-9 – ISBN 0-7146-8174-1 (pbk.)
    1. Political parties–Europe, Eastern. 2. Political parties–Former
Soviet republics. 3. Post-communism–Europe, Eastern. 4.
Post-communism–Former Soviet republics. I. Lewis, Paul G., 1945-
. II. Series.
    JN96.A979 P384 2001
    320.947–dc21
                                             2001028202

Typeset in Times New Roman 10.5/12 by Frank Cass Publishers

Printed in Great Britain by
MPG Books Ltd., Bodmin, Cornwall

PARTY DEVELOPMENT

AND

DEMOCRATIC CHANGE

IN

POST-COMMUNIST EUROPE

Of Related Interest

PARTY POLITICS IN POST-COMMUNIST RUSSIA
edited by John Löwenhardt

THE RESILIENCE OF DEMOCRACY
Persistent Practice, Durable Idea
edited by Peter Burnell and Peter Calvert

DEMOCRACY ASSISTANCE
International Co-operation for Democratization
edited by Peter Burnell

THE INTERNET, DEMOCRACY AND DEMOCRATIZATION
edited by Peter Ferdinand

DEMOCRATIZATION AND THE MEDIA
edited by Vicky Randall

FACTIONAL POLITICS AND DEMOCRATIZATION
edited by Richard Gillespie, Michael Waller and Lourdes López Nieto

Contents

Preface

During the last decade the task facing scholars who study political parties comparatively has come to resemble that of an inadequate juggler. Having learnt earlier the equivalent of juggling five balls successfully, it has now become necessary to be able to juggle ten, if one's peers are to judge one competent. Until the end of the 1980s the would-be comparativist had to have a – working knowledge of the western European democracies, have enough familiarity with the United States so as not to misunderstand its parties, and be able to find his or her way round the parties of the Westminster democracies. Parties outside the liberal democratic were so different from both each other and also from those in the democratic world that much less familiarity with these regimes was necessary in most comparative studies. Those who focused on east-central Europe or South America, for example, may have engaged in comparative studies within their own regions, but often they were regarded as simply 'area studies' experts whose work did not impinge that much on those who studied liberal democratic regimes.

Even studies of the democratic world were not always complete; often there were problems of how to incorporate the rather unusual cases of India and Japan. Thus, while it might helped to have that knowledge of other systems, few scholars apart from Giovanni Sartori attempted world-wide comparisons of political parties. There was the real danger that one's knowledge of particular systems might be revealed to be rather thin. It was bad enough if, as a comparative analyst of the democratic world, one was not always able to explain adequately the basis of the two-party system in Malta, it was that much worse if one claimed familiarity with Syria's Ba'ath Party or Bulgaria's Communist Party, but then demonstrated in print that one's understanding was faulty or wholly inadequate. For that kind of reason most comparative studies were restricted to the three groups of democratic regimes. This was the equivalent of keeping five balls in the air, it was not that easy, but it was feasible and it was possible for someone to believe that they had become the equivalent of the competent juggler.

During the 1990s it became evident that the equivalent of 'five-ball jugglers' were becoming obsolete in political science. Re-democratization in Central and South America, and democratization in east-central Europe, meant that the democratic regimes in these regions had to be embraced within comparative politics, at least if one assumes that comparative politics was to mean something more than 'area studies' even worse 'foreign countries about which we don't usually study on their own'. For those who hoped to retain their credentials as comparativists, studies of the emerging parties and party systems in these areas were becoming of crucial importance. Consequently, for their future work, comparativists must draw on specialist studies of these systems to help them develop a sufficient understanding of the parties there, in order their own work not seem merely parochial. For that reason, research on the parties of east-central Europe has become of great interest and significance even to those who are not part of the community of scholars who work on the region. No longer can that region be dismissed, as it could during the cold war era, as the preserve of a particular group of area specialists who would be largely talking to each other in academic debates.

The research by Paul Lewis and his colleagues fills an important gap in our understanding of how parties have developed under the constraints of electoral competition. It is itself a comparative study – not only is it informed by the political literature on parties in the older democracies, but a number of its essays are explicitly comparative in their approach. Moreover, the book has the great merit of not concerning itself with just the large democratic systems in the region, such as Poland, it also includes studies of the smaller democracies – such as Slovenia and the new Baltic democracies. It is precisely this kind of study that will prove so crucial in the transition from the more restricted comparative analyses of political parties in early decades to the more fully comparative research that will develop in the present century. The comparative analyst can but hope that collections of essays like this, based on high quality research, continue to be published regularly in the future; east-central Europe is of central concern to all those of us who engage in research on political parties.

Alan Ware
October 2000

Introduction: Democratization and Political Change in Post-Communist Eastern Europe

PAUL G. LEWIS

Democratization and Party Developments in Eastern Europe

The emergence of independent, competitive parties, a sequence of properly conducted and fully contested elections, and the development of democratic party government have been the most significant aspects of the first decade of political change in post-communist eastern Europe (by this I mean all European countries formerly subject to communist rule with the exception of Russia, but inclusive of the countries many people prefer to call central European; some chapters of this book take a yet broader comparative focus and also consider related developments in Russia). Political parties appear as one of the most prominent institutions of modern liberal democracy. It is hardly possible, in practice if not in theory, to conceive of a functioning representative democracy without some kind of competitive party system. The development of a range of reasonably effective parties is a prime indicator of the democratization of the former communist countries and the progress they have made towards joining the broad European community of established democratic nations. Parties help anchor the recently established democratic regimes in a broader society and contribute to their stability amidst multiple processes of rapid social and economic change. Effective constitutions and the diverse processes involved in the rule of law are strengthened by the possibilities parties offer for the development of a more active citizenry and the emergence of a robustly democratic political culture. There are also strong reasons to believe that such conditions are conducive to stable processes of economic development and the development of market economies. Views differ, however, about the importance of the contribution made by political parties to post-communist democratization and the role they play in the different phases of the process.[1]

An initial focus on electoral activity is of particular importance in the context of post-communist Europe. Participation in competitive elections is a major feature of party identity formation and party development. Electoral competition is a prominent feature of the contemporary regimes that distinguishes them from the single-party dictatorships of the communist period and provides a natural focus of attention at the present juncture. The end of the first decade of post-communist change offers it own perspective on a period that can be divided into several distinct electoral phases, while the sequence of elections held towards the end of this period – 12 in total between September 1997 and March 1999 – presents a further basis for evaluating levels of party development and the emergence of pluralist party systems.

Entry into parliament brought 'some order out of chaos' in early post-communist Europe by introducing a measure of consistency in relations between the major parties and clarifying the identity of the different political organizations.[2] A focus on elections is a prime component of what has been identified as the process approach to new party systems in post-communist Europe, which places major emphasis on the developmental patterns emerging in the region and the dynamic properties of the transition process. Electoral and parliamentary activities thus 'serve as a filter for the management of political space, acting as a screening device that elevates some political contenders to prominent roles, marginalizes other party formations, and eliminates altogether most aspiring parties'.[3]

This prime aspect of democratization under contemporary conditions was established quite successfully during the first decade of post-communist change in eastern Europe. Multi-party elections have been held regularly throughout the region and mostly conducted according to agreed constitutional procedures, although major disputes emerged over these matters in Belarus and some other countries subject to authoritarian rule. Three reasonably standard elections have been held in most countries, a situation that permits an overview of party development and electoral practice under the new conditions. A relatively small number of parties have emerged as the major players in the new political order and only a few are real contenders for governmental power, although there are important differences between the different countries and broad areas of the region.

The process has, not surprisingly, advanced furthest in the more developed countries of east-central Europe. In Hungary, Poland, the Czech Republic and – in 1998 – Slovakia two major parties or electoral unions emerged as the leading contenders for power with the capacity to mobilize the support of around 30 per cent of voters, with one or more second-rank parties establishing themselves with sufficient parliamentary strength to present themselves as viable coalition partners for the formation of reasonably stable governments. In these countries at least, a situation that approaches a reasonably balanced competitive party system has emerged following the acclamatory elections of the early years that in many countries just endorsed broad anti-communist forces and newly organized but only loosely structured democratic organizations (see Table 1). Slovenia, formerly part of federal Yugoslavia, has also developed quite stable patterns of

TABLE 1
ELECTION RESULTS IN EAST-CENTRAL EUROPE
CZECH REPUBLIC 1992–98 (PERCENTAGE OF VOTE FOR PARTIES
REPRESENTED IN 1998):

	Party	1998	1996	1992
CSDP:	Czech Social Democratic Party	32.3	26.4	6.5
CDP:	Civic Democratic Party	27.7	29.6	29.6
CPBM:	Communist Party of Bohemia and Moravia	11.0	12.3	14.0
CDU:	Christian Democratic Union	9.0	8.1	6.3
FU:	Freedom Union	8.6	–	–

HUNGARY 1990–98 (PERCENTAGE OF FIRST ROUND VOTE FOR PARTIES
REPRESENTED IN 1998):

	Party	1998	1994	1990
FIDESZ	(Alliance of Young Democrats)/			
	Hungarian Civic Party	28.2	7.5	8.9
HSP:	Hungarian Socialist Party	32.3	32.6	10.9
ISP:	Independent Smallholders' Party	13.8	8.5	11.8
AFD:	Alliance of Free Democrats	7.9	19.5	21.4
HJLP:	Hungarian Justice and Life Party	5.5	1.6	–
HDF:	Hungarian Democratic Forum	3.1	12.0	24.7

POLAND 1991–97 (PERCENTAGE OF VOTE FOR PARTIES REPRESENTED IN 1997):

	Party	1997	1993	1991
SEA:	Solidarity Electoral Action	33.8	–	–
	– ChNU: Christian National Union			
	(Fatherland/CEA)		6.4	8.8
	CIP: Confederation for Independent Poland		5.8	7.6
	NBSR: Non-Party Bloc to Support Reform		5.4	–
	S: Solidarity			
	CA: Centre Alliance		4.4	8.7
DLA:	Democratic Left Alliance	27.1	20.4	12.0
FU:	Freedom Union (Democratic Union)	13.4	10.6	12.3
PPP:	Polish Peasant Party	7.3	15.4	8.6
MPR:	Movement for Polish Reconstruction	5.6	–	–
	German Minority	0.6	0.7	1.5

SLOVAKIA 1992–98 (PERCENTAGE OF VOTE FOR PARTIES REPRESENTED IN 1998):

	Party	1998	1994	1992
MDS:	Movement for Democratic Slovakia	27	35.0	37.3
SDC:	Slovak Democratic Coalition	26.3	–	–
	– CDM: Christian Democratic Movement		10.1	8.9
	DU: Democratic Union		8.6	–
	DP: Democratic Party		3.4	3.3
	SDP: Social Democratic Party		(PDL)	4.0
	GPS: Green Party of Slovakia		(PDL)	2.1
PDL:	Party of Democratic Left	14.7	10.4	14.7
HC:	Hungarian Coalition	9.1	10.2	7.4
SNP:	Slovak National Party	9.1	5.4	7.9
PCU:	Party of Civic Understanding	8.0	–	–

TABLE 2
ELECTION RESULTS IN SLOVENIA AND THE BALTIC STATES
SLOVENIA 1992–96 (PERCENTAGE OF VOTE FOR PARTIES REPRESENTED IN 1996):

	Party	1996	1992	1990
LDS:	Liberal Democracy of Slovenia	27.0	23.5	14.5
SPP:	Slovene People's Party	19.4	8.7	12.6
SDPS:	Social Democratic Party of Slovenia	16.1	3.3	7.4
SCD:	Slovene Christian Democrats	9.6	14.5	13.0
ULSD:	United List of Social Democrats	9.0	13.6	17.3
DPRP:	Democratic Party of Retired People	4.3	(ULSD)	0.4
SNP:	Slovene National Party	3.2	10.0	–

ESTONIA 1992–99 (PERCENTAGE OF VOTE FOR PARTIES REPRESENTED IN 1999):

Party	1999	1995	1992
Estonian Centre Party	23.6	14.2	–
Estonian Reform Party	16.0	16.2	–
Fatherland Union	16.0	(as alliance) 7.8	–
– Fatherland (Isamma)			22.0
National Independence Party			8.8
Moderates (SD and Rural Centre)	15.1	6.0	12.9
Coalition Party	7.6	(with Country People's) 32.2	17.8
Country People's Party/Rural Union	7.2	–	–
United People's Party	6.1	(Rightists: 5.0)	–

LATVIA 1993–98 (PERCENTAGE OF VOTE FOR PARTIES
REPRESENTED IN 1998):

Party	1998	1995	1993
People's Party	20.2	–	–
Latvia's Way	18.1	14.6	32.4
Conservative Union for Fatherland and Freedom	14.2	–	–
– National Conservative Party		6.3	12.4
Fatherland and Freedom		11.9	5.4
National Harmony Party	14.2	5.6	12.0
Latvian Social Democratic Alliance	12.8	4.6	–
New Party	7.3	–	–

LITHUANIA 1990–96 (PERCENTAGE OF VOTE FOR PARTIES
REPRESENTED IN 1996):

Party	1996	1992	1990 (% of seats)
Homeland Union - Lithuanian Conservatives	29.8	18.4	63.8
Lithuanian Christian Democratic Party	9.9	12.0	1.4
Lithuanian Democratic Workers' Party	9.5	46.6	22.0
Lithuanian Centre Union	8.2	–	–
Lithuanian Social Democratic Party	6.6	5.7	6.4

democratic government. It, too, can be counted as part of a contemporary east-central Europe with a substantial level of democratic achievement, most of whose members are well advanced in accession negotiations with the European Union.

The first election with a major competitive element was held in Poland during June 1989, when Solidarity was permitted to contest 35 per cent of seats in the lower house and all in the newly established Senate. The first democratic multi-party election of post-communist eastern Europe was held in Hungary during March 1990, and in the following nine years most other countries also held three or more competitively organized elections. The main exceptions have been the countries of the former Soviet Union, where the early elections were pre-transitional and the population's experience of competitive party politics has been decidedly more limited. Their sparser electoral record is certainly reflected in a lower level of pluralist party development and the general absence of anything like a stable party system. But party development has also been limited in some of the other countries of eastern Europe, not least because formally organized groups have not always been prominent in the competitive political process and ruling cliques based on the old establishment have been quite successful in holding on to power in some countries.

Four Phases of Electoral Politics

With the exception of Hungary, initial elections hinged on the contest between communist forces and the anti-communist opposition as representatives of different systems rather than as expressions of discrete interests or conflict between actual parties. In 1990 independence movements or anti-communist coalitions prevailed in Czechoslovakia, Lithuania, Latvia, Slovenia, and Croatia, and made a strong showing (and thus exercised a determinant influence on the political outcome) in Estonia and Moldova. The nationalist Internal Macedonian Revolutionary Organisation achieved a similar victory in its homeland, while an equivalent ethnic-based outcome was reached in Bosnia. The same year the existing establishment won some kind of popular mandate in Ukraine, Belarus, Montenegro, Serbia (with a second round in January 1991), while rapidly recast communist forces were victorious in Bulgaria, Albania (in March/April 1991) and (in the ambiguous guise of the National Salvation Front) Romania as well. These were the dominant forms of conflict during the early post-communist elections, which can be termed *Phase One*.

In the early post-communist period, then, only Hungary saw an electoral contest between major independent political parties and one which, moreover, produced a relatively stable and effective form of party government that lasted its full constitutional term of four years. Reference in the general literature on democratic transition is often made to the early formal contests in the post-authoritarian countries as 'founding' elections which set the scene for subsequent development of a pluralist order and broadly identify the main players in the newly liberated political arena. In eastern Europe, however, the idea of such founding elections needs rather to be extended to encompass second, third or even subsequent ballots as the complex process of post-totalitarian pluralization and institutional development slowly progressed.[4]

A multiplicity of elections then contributed to the unfolding process of democratization. A second wave of elections, some in 1991 (Poland and Bulgaria) but most in 1992 (Czechoslovakia, Romania, Albania, Slovenia, Croatia, Serbia, Estonia and Lithuania) now followed. In some cases they pointed to a new direction of political development, in others they confirmed the line already taken. New elections were held just one year after the initial ballot in Bulgaria (in October 1991) and Albania (March/April 1992) that reflected a shift to right-wing, anti-communist forces. In 1992 further elections were held in the now independent states of Slovenia and Croatia, which confirmed respectively the essentially pluralist and national populist regimes in the two countries. A nationalist victory was also secured in Latvia during 1992, while in Lithuania a post-communist Democratic Workers' Party was propelled to power by popular dissatisfaction with declining living standards and the social upheaval that characterized the early transition period. Strong socialist majorities were again confirmed in Serbia and Montenegro, and an equivalent victory obtained for President Iliescu's portion of the NSF in Romania. Further elections were also held in Czechoslovakia, as provided for in the 1990 agreement, and produced a decisively right-wing oriented government in the Czech lands and a more ambiguous form of post-communist nationalist domination in Slovakia – an outcome that led directly to the break-up of the federal state at the end of the year. By the end of 1992 considerable diversity was evident throughout the region and different kinds of parties were clearly emerging – and indeed, a large number of them. This was the major outcome of the *Phase Two* elections.

Whether this period represented the 'freezing moment' of the new, post-communist party systems may be questioned, but the statement that the typical result of the second elections was a fragmented party system was certainly close to the mark.[5] In 1990 the 25 per cent of the vote taken by the Hungarian Democratic Forum appeared rather a modest accomplishment beside the 46 per cent cast for Civic Forum and Public Against Violence in Czechoslovakia and 55 per cent of DEMOS in Slovenia, let alone the 78 per cent of the relatively unreconstructed Socialist Party of Serbia and similar outcomes for the other communist parties of Ukraine, Belarus, Albania and

Montenegro whose position was so far relatively untouched by the ongoing regional regime transformation. The political supremacy implied by these high totals turned out to be of strictly limited duration. By 1992 Civic Forum and Public Against Violence in Czechoslovakia, Solidarity in Poland, DEMOS in Slovenia and the Popular Front of Estonia had already fragmented and largely passed from the scene. The ambiguous NSF had split in Romania and it was the fraction strengthened by links with President Iliescu that remained in control of parliament. The proportion of votes or seats now taken by virtually all parties or groups at the top of the electoral lists – anti-communist and post-communist alike – was considerably lower than that gained in the first election.

Fragmentation was most pronounced in Poland following the election of 1991 conducted without a threshold, where the largest parliamentary group was the Democratic Union with only 12.3 per cent of the vote. But even the entrenched conservative regimes of Serbia and Montenegro saw a decline in their previous dominance. Although the situation was fluid and highly differentiated, there were also signs that a new pattern of party forces was emerging. Parties of a recognisable liberal or conservative character that bore a resemblance to those in the west could be identified on the right wing of the party spectrum in some countries and were becoming more influential in the pluralist states of east-central Europe.

Elsewhere, parties that sprang directly from the communist establishment were prominent. In some countries, particularly those of the former Soviet Union and the residue of the old Yugoslav federation, their direct successors still ruled. In others, former communist organizations had been taken over by reformist groups and were being reconstructed along authentically social democratic lines to provide the kind of left-wing alternative prevalent in western Europe. This was most obviously the case where the former communists had lost power and had to win back power in a multi-party election, as happened in Lithuania and was soon to be the case in Poland and Hungary. It was, too, becoming apparent that the revived 'historical' parties had little prospect of becoming a dominant force, playing at best a marginal role in the new democracies. The bigger players were increasingly either new parties or different kinds of ex- or post-communist party.[6]

But the precise nature of the parties was open to considerable doubt. The degree to which communist parties had indeed reformed was a matter of some controversy, while the nature of the growing range of right-wing parties also diverse. After further elections in 1993 and 1994 the number of east European governments formed by parties deriving from the former communist establishment rose yet further. Social democrats and socialists returned to power in Poland and Hungary respectively, while ex-communists of a less definitively reformed character took office in Bulgaria and

Macedonia. By the end of 1994 (and leaving to one side Bosnia, where all normal political life was now engulfed by fierce warfare) the decided majority of 'post-communist' states were actually governed by communist-successor parties – eleven were ruled by various forms of socialist or communist administration, and seven by various forms of liberal or nationalist party. This was the major development in *Phase Three* of the post-communist elections.

In some cases this simply reflected the slow pace of political change and the reluctance of influential groups to move away from earlier patterns of authoritarianism. In others, though, it represented a shift away from the dominance of the early anti-communist movements and the relative weakening of the largely right-wing parties they had formed. Different explanations have been offered for this distinctive tendency during the early years of political change in eastern Europe. Factors held responsible by various analysts include: the influence of forces generated by the major process of economic transition and the systemic transformation seen to some extent in all countries,[7] disillusion after early post-communist euphoria and the continuing strength of a socialist value system,[8] the overall dynamics of the transition period in junction with the differing capacity of parties to adapt to a changing environment,[9] varying levels of organizational strength and contrasting leadership skills,[10] and the capacity of parties to strike a politically rewarding balance between the benefits of transition and the costs voters have to pay.[11]

Phase Four of the electoral sequence was evident by the end of 1998, when three or so reasonably competitive elections had taken place in most countries of eastern Europe. By this time a range of identifiable parties not wholly dissimilar from their western counterparts could often be detected, and something like a party system or relatively stable pattern of party relations was emerging. In the more developed countries of east-central Europe and Lithuania there were signs of a two-party, or two-bloc, system coming into existence. Of course, it takes more than that for a fully-fledged party system to be identified. But by the end of the first decade of post-communist rule in eastern Europe early forms of party system in some countries gave a clear indication of democratization and signs of the establishment of a solid basis for party development. Nevertheless, the emergence of broad patterns of party representation was not the only way in which the political impact of successive elections could be assessed. Measures of electoral 'volatility' (reflecting the fluidity of voting patterns and the extent to which parties command a steady level of voting support), estimates of the number of 'effective' parties (those that could reasonably be expected to form a stable government and escape the weaknesses associated with excessive parliamentary fragmentation), as well as levels of party

8

membership and estimates of party support, were all measures of political maturity that could be used to gauge the formation of stable patterns of democratic political life and pluralist party development.[12]

Party Development in Eastern Europe

Party development and the establishment of stable patterns of interaction suggestive of proper party systems is most advanced in the more solidly established democracies of eastern Europe.[13] Parties developing on the conventional left-right lines characteristic of western Europe and showing some capacity for stable alternation in government have stronger roots in the more democratic states of east-central Europe and the Baltic region than in the Balkans and other countries of the former Soviet Union. By the end of the first post-communist decade the countries of eastern Europe showed considerable variation in terms of democratic development as measured by the establishment of a range of fundamental political rights and civil liberties. Seven countries of east-central Europe and the Baltic region scored high by such measures, with other post-communist states showing a range of democratic achievement and tailing off to the authoritarian rule of Lukashenka in Belarus, and the aggressive dictatorship of Milosevic in Serbia and the rump Yugoslavia.

The seven countries identified as leading in terms of democratic

TABLE 3
COMBINED FREEDOM RATINGS IN EASTERN EUROPE, 1998–99 (SCALE OF 1 TO 7)

1.5	Czech Republic
	Estonia
	Hungary
	Latvia
	Lithuania
	Poland
	Slovenia
2	Slovakia
2	Romania
2.5	Bulgaria
3	Macedonia
	Moldovia
3.5	Ukraine
4	Croatia
4.5	Albania
5	Bosnia
6	Belarus
	Yugoslavia (Serbia and Motenegro)

9

indicators had all, by March 1999, held three multi-party elections that showed distinct signs of party development and party system formation. In east-central Europe by 1998 two parties dominated the parliaments of Hungary, Poland and the Czech Republic and two alternations of government had taken place in Hungary and Poland (in the Czech Republic, the Civic Democratic Party won the election of 1996 and only lost power in 1998). Slovenia's Liberal Democracy remained the core of several governing coalitions throughout the 1990s, although its dominant position crumbled in April 2000 when it lost the support of one of its coalition partners. But in several countries a more structured parliamentary landscape only emerged or was maintained with the formation of new parties. Solidarity Election Action was only established in 1996 to overcome the chronic fragmentation of the Polish right wing, while the Hungarian Civic Party arose from the former FIDESZ to restore the fortunes of the right after the demise of the HDF as a major political force. Party development was far from stable and, while more identifiable patterns of left-right representation were emerging, the institutional form they took remained fluid.

The instability of party forms was even more pronounced in the Baltic states. The Lithuanian scene showed greater stability and had developed more of a bipolar model of party representation. In the other two states party structures were less stable and more fluid. Electoral alliances broke and reformed with startling regularity. Two of the parties elected to the 1998 Latvian parliament were new creations, and the status of electoral alliances and inter-party agreements were the subject of hot debate prior to the 1999 Estonian election. Even in the more democratic states at the end of the first post-communist decade in eastern Europe, then, party development showed distinct limitations. The institutionalization of party systems is by no means a foregone conclusion, and preliminary analysis suggests that electoral volatility in the new east European democracies is not declining anything like so fast as it did in western Europe after 1945.[14] Party membership and overall levels of support also remain quite low although this, too, is a feature by no means restricted to the eastern democracies.[15]

Whatever their levels of democratic achievement, then, party development in the countries of eastern Europe is advancing only gradually and the nature of any party system that might be emerging remains quite uncertain. The process overall is a complex and highly differentiated one, and the chapters that follow below examine a number of different countries and a range of dimensions of party development. Most of them are based on papers presented at the joint sessions of the European Consortium for Political Research held in Mannheim during March 1999, and thus reflect the particular enthusiasms and insights of participants in the original workshop I organized at that time. They do not – and could not – cover all possible countries or examine all conceivable dimensions of party development and democratic change during the first decade of post-communist politics. All, however, are informed by a strong comparative interest and most of the country studies raise strong analytical concerns that bear on developments throughout the post-communist region.

The first two chapters concern issues that link directly with the legacy of communist rule, the impact of past practices on contemporary patterns of party allegiance and the extent to which the former ruling parties now contribute to processes of democratic consolidation. Oates, Miller and Grødeland thus seek to establish the level of support that continued to exist for communist parties in a range of east European countries and identify the factors that help sustain their capacity to survive and operate (with considerable success in some contexts) in a competitive political environment. John Ishiyama then draws a rather broader focus and directs attention to the larger population of 'successor' parties – the wide range of contemporary actors with roots in the ruling parties of the old communist regime. Only some of those studied (in Ukraine, Russia and the Czech Republic) have continued to identify themselves as communist, and most now fall into a more general socialist or social democratic camp. By changing their ideology and political objectives, they have also moved closer to the values and operating principles of the liberal-democratic regimes that have been developing in most countries of eastern Europe. They have increasingly evolved a capacity not just to operate within the new democratic environment but also to contribute to its consolidation. Ishiyama's chapter seeks to identify the factors that differentiate between the successor parties in this respect, and to chart precisely the implications for democratic consolidation of electoral performance and the contrasting organizational paths followed by the range of successor parties.

The next two chapters look at developments in parties and party systems in Poland, but also raise questions about the general processes of party development and the overall dynamics of democratic evolution. On the basis of Polish experience Radoslaw Markowski raises broad questions about the relationship between party system institutionalization and democratic consolidation. While the conventional (and intuitively obvious perspective) might indicate that party system institutionalization is likely to occur first and provide the basis for subsequent processes of democratic consolidation, Markowski argues differently and provides important evidence to support the view that broader processes of democratic consolidation actually precede those of party and party system development. Next, Aleks Szczerbiak identifies issues fundamental to the development of modern parties in terms of the formation of a bureaucracy to direct the activities of the emerging organization and the professionalization of the staff assembled to run it –

particularly in the critical area of political campaigning. He undertakes an exercise still quite rare in the study of party development in eastern Europe, and actually seeks to establish empirical parameters of an aspect of party development in terms of the precise number of people working in the headquarters of the main Polish parties. This he uses as a basis for making general statements about processes of bureaucratization and professionalization.

Aspects of party development and organizational consolidation in another of the more successfully democratized countries of east-central Europe are examined by Alenka Krasovec, who focuses on relations between party and state in Slovenia. She examines in particular another critical dimension of party development, and outlines the main sources of funding for Slovenian parties and patterns of campaign expenditure. As in other east European countries, Slovenian parties are strongly dependent on the state for their funding, and this leads her to draw tentative links between the new democracies and developments in western Europe that have given rise to discussion of the cartel party. A comparative view on another area of successfully democratized eastern Europe is presented by Vello Pettai and Marcus Kreuzer, who direct attention to institutions and party development in the Baltic states. They outline a framework that emphasizes the role of institutional variables in party development, and examine the role of the different varieties of representative institution that have been established in the three Baltic countries. Certain differences in terms of electoral institutions like ballot structure, candidate recruitment, and district size are identified and linked with possible party outcomes, although the full range of relations and linkages will only emerge after more exhaustive research.

Further chapters direct attention to countries where the level of democratic development has been more patchy than in the core countries of east-central Europe or, in the case of Belarus, hardly been raised at all since Soviet times. Gordon Wightman examines the more ambiguous case of Slovakia which, having started out on the same democratic path as the rest of Czechoslovakia, diverged after the establishment of an independent state at the beginning of 1993 to develop a pattern of politics characterized until 1998 by strong features of one-party rule and the personalized leadership style of Vladimír Meciar. Slovakia's party system was strongly polarized and produced conditions generally less favourable to democratization than other countries of the region, although decidedly more prospects of development opened up following the elections of 1998. Belarus on the other hand, a former republic of the Soviet Union with little capacity or experience of independent statehood of any kind, had one of the weakest bases for democratization and party development in the entire region. The establishment of an independent parliament did not take place until 1995 but was then suspended the following year by a president clearly committed to the extension of his own powers over those of either a freely elected parliament or a competitive party system.

Kenneth Ka-Lok Chan and Geoffrey Pridham pursue themes that cut across the different countries of the region and raise broad comparative questions about the nature and direction of party development. Kenneth Chan focuses on issues of conservatism and discusses what this well-established current, a common coin in the political currency of established democracies, means in countries subject to the dual transformation of democratization and capitalist restructuring. Its meaning, he argues, cannot fail to be more differentiated in post-communist eastern Europe and less closely identified with the traditional 'right' of the party spectrum seen in the west. Three variants of post-communist conservativism are identified and defined as communist/ex-communist conservatism, traditional conservatism and a neo-liberal variant. But changes in these three party types have already been taking place with some intensity under pressures of electoral competition and the Europeanization that is a primary component of the overall process of post-communist transformation.

Geoffrey Pridham takes up the theme of Europeanization and pursues it further, analyzing the process of transnational party cooperation as a primary means of identifying the different party families that have emerged in central and eastern Europe. Its influence, he argues, has been uneven. It has tended to involve mainstream democratic parties and those of a broadly 'standard' nature rather than those that diverge from the established west European party spectrum. The process of Europeanization has, moreover, been distinctly one-sided in that it has involved the imprinting of political habits and attitudes from western Europe on the east rather than a process of mutual interaction and concerted integration, although this is hardly a tendency that should evoke much surprise. In the context of a broad movement to Europeanization in the more democratic countries of eastern Europe, nevertheless, this is a conclusion that demonstrates the differentiated nature of the process and the continuing importance of regionally specific factors in the overall process of party development.

As well as providing original and distinctive insights into party development and the democratization processes individual countries, then, the book directs attention to a number of general issues. The chapters that follow discuss the major themes of:

- the process and degree of institutional continuity in the course of regime change, and the impact of the issues involved on the construction of a democratic order (Oates, Miller and Grødeland, also Ishiyama);

- democratic consolidation and its links with processes of party development (Ishiyama, Markowski);

- questions of institutionalization and party system formation in the broader context of democratic change (Markowski, Pettai, Wightman);

- organizational development and the evolution of parties as structural entities (Szczerbiak, Krasovec, Pridham);

- the role of countervailing authoritarian pressures and obstacles to democratic change (Wightman, Korasteleva);

- the evolution of ideological families in the post-communist party context and the degree of their correspondence with western systems (Lok Chan, Pridham).

As well as being explored in particular contexts and from different perspectives in the following chapters, these themes will be further considered in the concluding chapter.

NOTES

1. See Bruce Parrott, 'Perspectives on Postcommunist Democratization', in Karen Dawisha and Bruce Parrott (eds.), *The Consolidation of Democracy in East-Central Europe* (Cambridge: Cambridge University Press, 1997), p.16; Gábor Tóka, 'Political Parties in East Central Europe', in L. Diamond *et al.* (eds.), *Consolidating the Third Wave Democracies: Themes and Perspectives* (Baltimore, MD: Johns Hopkins University Press, 1997), p.94; A. Ágh, Emerging Democracies in East Central Europe and the Balkans (Cheltenham: Edward Elgar, 1998), p.18; Paul G. Lewis, Political Parties in Post-Communist Eastern Europe (London: Routledge, 2000).
2. D.M. Olson, 'Political Parties and Party Systems in Regime Transformation: Inner Transition in the New Democracies of Central Europe', *The American Review of Politics*, Vol.14, No.4 (1993), p.632.
3. J. Bielasiak, 'Substance and Process in the Development of Party Systems in East Central Europe', *Communist and Post-Communist Studies*, Vol.30, No.1 (1997), p.28.
4. K. Jasiewicz, 'Elections and Voting Behaviour', in S. White, J. Batt and P. Lewis (eds.), *Developments in Central and East European Politics* (Macmillan: London, 1998), p.175.
5. Olson, pp.620, 623.
6. G. Wightman (ed.), *Party Formation in East-Central Europe* (Aldershot: Edward Elgar, 1995), p.241.
7. G. Evans and S. Whitefield, 'Economic Ideology and Political Success: Communist-Successor Parties in the Czech Republic, Slovakia and Hungary Compared', *Party Politics*, Vol.1, No.4 (1995), pp.565–78.
8. A. Mahr, and J. Nagle, 'Resurrection of the Successor Parties and Democratization in East-Central Europe', *Communist and Post-Communist*

Studies, Vol.28, No.4 (1995), pp.393–409.

9. J.T. Ishiyama, 'Communist Parties in Transition: Structures, Leaders, and Processes of Democratization in Eastern Europe', *Comparative Politics*, Vol.27, No.1 (1995), pp.147–66.

10. M. Waller, 'Adaptation of the Former Communist Parties of East-Central Europe: a Case of Social-Democratization ?', *Party Politics*, Vol.1, No.4 (1995), pp.473–90.

11. M. Orenstein, 'A Genealogy of Communist Successor Parties in East-Central Europe and the Determinants of their Success', *East European Politics and Societies*, Vol.12, No.3 (1998), pp.472–99.

12. See M. Cotta, 'Building Party Systems after the Dictatorship: the East European Cases in a Comparative Perspective', in G. Pridham and P.G. Lewis (eds.), Stabilising Fragile Democracies (London: Routledge, 1996), p.71; P. Mair, Party System Change: Approaches and Interpretations (Oxford: Clarendon Press, 1997), p.182; D. M. Olson, 'Party Formation and Party System Consolidation in the New Democracies of Central Europe', Political Studies Vol.46, No.3 (1998), p.460; R. Rose, N. Munro and T. Mackie, 'Elections in Central and Eastern Europe Since 1990', *Studies in Public Policy*, No.300 (University of Strathclyde, 1998), pp.118–19.

13. See Gábor Tóka, 'Parties and Electoral Choices in East-Central Europe', in Pridham and Lewis, *Stabilising Fragile Democracies*, pp.100–25; R. Markowski, 'Political Parties and Ideological Spaces in East Central Europe', *Communist and Post-Communist Studies*, Vol.30, No.3 (1997), pp.221–54; H. Kitschelt, Z. Mansfeldova, R. Markowski and G. Tóka, *Post-Communist Party Systems: Competition, Representation, and Inter-Party Cooperation* (Cambridge: Cambridge University Press, 1999).

14. S. Mainwaring, 'Party Systems in the Third Wave', *Journal of Democracy*, Vol.9, No.1 (1998), pp.67–81.

15. Paul G. Lewis, Party Structure and Organization in East-Central Europe (Cheltenham: Edward Elgar, 1996); Attila Ágh, *The Politics of Central Europe* (London: Sage, 1998), pp.103–9.

2

Towards a Soviet Past or Socialist Future? Understanding Why Voters Choose Communist Parties in Ukraine, Russia, Bulgaria, Slovakia and the Czech Republic

SARAH OATES, WILLIAM L. MILLER and
ÅSE GRØDELAND

Roughly a decade after jubilant crowds celebrated the collapse of the Berlin Wall and the subsequent fall of the Soviet Union, communist parties are winning votes and even dominating some parliaments of the former Eastern bloc. It is important to consider why voters have continued to support communist parties long after they rejected the communist system. This article will use election results and public opinion surveys to define and discuss communist electoral support in Russia, Ukraine, Bulgaria, Slovakia and the Czech Republic.[1] This study will first examine the ability of communist voters to identify and support various parties, as well as their commitment to voting itself. We will also search for cross-national trends among the communist constituencies in these five countries that might suggest the causes for the enduring presence of the far left party. What emerges from this research is that communist voters are, in general, better able to identify parties to support and are more committed to the act of voting than the general population. In addition, communist voters share similar socio-economic traits, although this is harder to trace in Bulgaria, the Czech Republic and Slovakia as communist parties are currently less successful there than in Russia or Ukraine. It also appears that communist voters share a strong dislike for a market economy and antipathy toward the EU and NATO. Overall, it would appear that communist voters in these five post-Soviet countries share important socio-economic characteristics, some attitudes and a heightened ability to translate their ideological preferences into actual votes.

The Comparative Context

The study of post-communist voting behaviour is much more dynamic than the exploration of the relatively static ties between voters and party in established democracies such as the United States and Great Britain. While the same concepts certainly could apply, they are thrown into the much more extreme conditions of fragile democracies, a sort of Big Bang of political effects. As Peter Mair suggests, we should see post-communist Europe as 'not a terminus but rather a departure point'.[2] Thus, if we look to the roots of cleavage formation in Lipset and Rokkan[3] or use other ideas of the formation of party identification,[4] we have a useful lens through which to view voter identification and party formation in new democracies. Meanwhile, a rapid sequence of elections, pressure to integrate with a world capitalist economy and quick formation of a new state and society force change at breakneck pace. As such, voter preferences and allegiances may be formed within years rather over the slower pace of decades as in other societies. As a result, these formative years can become immensely important for solidifying cleavages, consolidating party gains and fixing party identification within the minds of voters.

Evidence in this article suggests that communists – more so than other party groupings – have been successful in consolidating their support within a certain group in society. While many scholars have looked at the fluid and somewhat chaotic nature of voting behaviour and party organization in post-communist countries, it is equally important to consider where cleavages appear to have 'frozen' and party affiliation has been 'locked into' certain individuals. There has been great interest in this idea among scholars in new democracies. In Russia alone, much literature debating the nature of cleavages and other constituency formation has emerged.[5]

Richard Rose and William Mishler have examined conceptions of party identification though cross-national surveys in former communist countries.[6] Survey data from 1995 in Hungary, Poland, Romania and Slovenia found that 77 per cent of the respondents showed negative identification with particular parties while only 30 per cent had identified positively. Nonetheless, this study did help to legitimize the conception of party identification in post-Soviet states, although the scholars posited a greater movement toward scepticism than positive party identification. Rose examined the opinions of ex-Communist Party members on a range of issues and suggested that post-Soviet communists had to adjust to the times:

> they must produce platforms and promises that are in demand in the competitive marketplace dominated by voters. To survive in the new political system, ex-Communist politicians must do more than convince voters that they will defend social welfare programmes; they must also make clear that they have abandoned authoritarianism and all it conveys, such as censorship, armed border guards and the secret police.[7]

While this is true, communist parties also continue to enjoy an association with what many citizens would perceive as positive aspects of the former Soviet rule, such as political and economic stability, guaranteed minimum standards of living, free health care and global influence.

But is the presence of this far left of the political spectrum in post-communist states more an artefact of the former Soviet system or a movement that is allied with the socialist movement of a broader Europe? Communist parties, particularly in Russia, are fond of using the positive elements of the Soviet past – stable economy, more equitable distribution of wealth, military might – as political marketing tools. Are communist supporters looking backward to the glorious Soviet-dominated past or forward to a European socialist future? If there is a nostalgic element to the support for the Left, is that best considered as an aspect of party identification forged under Soviet rule or a legacy of authoritarian domination?

Communist Parties in Post-Communist Times

Russia has seen steady growth of support for communists since the collapse of the Soviet Union, through two parliamentary elections (1993 and 1995) as well in the 1996 presidential elections. In the 1995 Duma elections, the communists won 157 of the 450 seats in the lower house of the parliament. By the time of the 1996 presidential elections, communist candidate Gennadi Zyuganov was able to win 40 per cent of the vote despite losing to Boris Yeltsin in the run-off election. The communist party also has enjoyed significant popularity in Ukraine in post-Soviet elections. The number of seats the Communist Party of the Ukraine held in the Ukrainian parliament increased from 91 out of 450 from the 1994 elections to 122 in the 1998 elections, rising from 20 to 27 per cent of the total.[8]

In Eastern Europe, however, the pattern is different. It is difficult to say whether this is due to a difference in underlying vote preferences, party organization or to the nature of the overall political system itself. While Left voters have little realistic option but the communist parties in Russia and Ukraine, the choices are somewhat more complex in much of Eastern Europe where there are often viable socialist alternatives. In addition Russia and Ukraine have presidential systems in which the parliaments, although having substantial political influence, realistically find themselves with marginal power compared with the country's president. In consequence voters may be more willing to make radical choices in parliamentary voting, which would including voting for communists, as they are aware that in practice it makes relatively little political difference.

In Bulgaria, the former communist ruling party was able to transform itself into a successful socialist electoral movement called the Bulgarian

Socialist Party even before the collapse of the Soviet Union, and won a majority of the seats in the National Assembly in the 1990 parliamentary elections. In addition, there are several communist movements in the country, most notably the Bulgarian Communist Party.[9] But would those supporting the traditional ideals of communism, including state-owned property, a classless society and rejection of personal capital, pick the regime successor parties (Bulgarian Socialists) or opt for a more 'pure' communist choice (Bulgarian Communists)? This is not a question that arises in Russia or Ukraine, where there are no viable socialist alternatives for Left voters. There were also contrasts in voting patterns in other countries. In the 1996 parliamentary elections in the Czech Republic, the Communist Party of Bohemia and Moravia gained seats, winning 22 of the 200 seats in the lower house. There also is a Communist Party of Slovakia, but it received just three per cent of the vote in 1994.

Research Design

Most of the data used for this article comes from a set of surveys conducted in the Czech Republic, Slovakia, Bulgaria and Ukraine in a project carried out by Miller and Grødeland. In each country, a representative sample of the adult population was surveyed during the winter of 1997–98, with sample sizes ranging from 1,003 in the Czech Republic to 1,519 in Bulgaria. The Russian data are from a survey carried out by the All-Russian Centre for the Study of Public Opinion in Moscow on a nation-wide sample of 1,568 respondents carried out immediately after the December 1995 parliamentary elections. The question set is different and far less exhaustive for the Russian survey and, unlike with the surveys from the other four countries, none of the authors were involved in the survey design. While the four-country questionnaire included specific questions on party family preference, the Russian survey merely asks people to name the party for which they voted in the parliamentary elections. In addition, there were no general attitudinal questions asked on the Russian survey.

However, with some limitations, it is possible to make comparisons between Russians and the citizens from the other countries using the two databases.[10] While the overall findings put the market economy parties first in Ukraine, Bulgaria, Slovakia and the Czech Republic as a whole, cross-tabulations from the five countries find significant differences among them (see Figure 1: Support for Party Types Across Five Post-Communist Countries). The Czech Republic and Bulgaria both had strong support for market economy parties, at 30 per cent and 34 per cent respectively. However, while socialists enjoyed relative popularity in both countries as well (17 per cent in the Czech Republic and 14 per cent in Bulgaria), there also was relatively robust support (nine per cent) for communists in the Czech Republic. Communists, however, had almost no support in Bulgaria. In Slovakia, nationalist parties and the socialists had almost equal strength, with just five per cent support for the communists. The surveys show a far higher number of communist supporters in Ukraine and Russia. In Ukraine, the communists were the most popular party grouping at 14 per cent. That makes the communist selection more popular than any other party grouping in Ukraine. In addition, the communists dominate among Russian voters with 20 per cent of the Russian respondents picking a communist group as their party of choice, more than the support for any other party family.

FIGURE 1

SUPPORT FOR PARTY TYPES ACROSS FIVE POST-COMMUNIST COUNTRIES
(IN ROUNDED PERCENTAGES)

Party type	All 4 countries	Ukraine	Bulgaria	Czech Republic	Slovakia	Russia*
Communist	7	14	2	9	5	20
Socialist	13	5	14	17	18	0.2
Market Economy	22	9	34	30	12	17
Nationalist Minority	5	4	1	1	17	13
Nationalist*	3	0.6	4	0.1	7	0.2
Green	5	6	2	6	6	1
Other/None	19	27	20	14	14	20
Depends/Hard to say	8	5	10	7	8	1
Don't Know**	19	29	14	17	15	26
N	4,778	1,200	1,519	1,003	1,056	1568

* Calculated from responses to vote choice question rather than party family preference question (not included on Russian survey).

** In Russia, this response was 'didn't vote.'

The findings are affected to a fairly significant degree by the varying levels of commitment to any party type. For example, although the communists were the most popular party type of choice in the Ukraine, an unusually large number of respondents declined to pick any party type of all. In fact, 62 per cent of the respondents in Ukraine were unable to pick a specific party type to support. In contrast, only 43 per cent of the respondents were unable to select a party type in Bulgaria (the survey was held soon after elections in Bulgaria, which would have made people more aware of party choices) and just over a third of the respondents failed to give a specific party grouping in the Czech Republic or Slovakia (this data was not available for Russia).

Perhaps most significantly, communist supporters voters claim to translate their ideological preferences into voting. First, those who identify themselves as communist voters were far more likely to vote in general than either the population overall or those committing themselves to another party affiliation or (see Figure 2: Party Identification and Vote Intention). Among the communist identifiers in the four countries (333 out of 4,778 per cent) only four per cent either did not plan to vote or could not pick a specific party to support, compared with 18 per cent of the respondents overall who did not plan to vote and the 19 per cent who could not pick a specific party. One might argue that *any* party identification, ranging from pro-market to communist, would make a respondent more likely to pick a specific party or vote. However, 13 per cent of pro-market identifiers across the four countries said they either would not vote or could not pick a specific party. In addition, pro-market and nationalist party identifiers seem to have a harder time making up their minds not only with regard to any specific party but also in deciding whether to vote at all. As is clear from the figures on the chart, party identification of any type does have an impact on vote intention, for it is those that cannot pick a party type that are least likely to vote – 54 per cent compared with 18 per cent overall.

FIGURE 2
PARTY IDENTIFICATION AND VOTE INTENTION IN FOUR POST-COMMUNIST
COUNTRIES (IN ROUNDED PERCENTAGES)

Party type	Will pick independent candidate	Will not vote	Cannot pick a party
Communist	1	2	2
Socialist	2	3	3
Market Economy	6	5	8
Nationalist	4	5	5
Minority Nationalist*	3	1	6
Green	8	9	7
Other/None	10	54	12
Depends	17	18	31
Don't Know	8	20	58

In Ukraine, 94 per cent of those identifying themselves as communist supporters listed the Communist Party of Ukraine as their favourite party. In contrast, other party identifiers were far more lax in picking out a single party to reflect their ideological views. For example, those identifying themselves as most closely aligned with market economy parties in Ukraine chose 13 different parties for which they might vote. Perhaps most ominously for the pro-market cause, 26 per cent of the pro-market voters in

Ukraine said they did not plan to vote – and an additional 18 per cent said they either did not have a specific party preference or planned to vote for an independent candidate (it should be noted that Ukraine changed its electoral law between the 1994 and 1998 elections so that half of the parliamentary candidates were elected through parliamentary lists and half through single-member districts. This meant that voters could either choose a party or not vote at all on the party-list half of the ballot, which makes it difficult to interpret their answers). In addition, nationalist supporters were spread across eight parties, with six per cent claiming they could not pick a specific party or did not plan to vote. Meanwhile, the well-disciplined communist identifiers in Ukraine showed their clear intention of fulfilling their social responsibility to vote – only five per cent of the communist identifiers said they would not be participating.

Does this pattern hold in other countries, particularly as one moves from the former Soviet heartland of Ukraine into eastern Europe? Bulgaria had the smallest number of communist identifiers (only 26 out of the 1,519 respondents). Of the handful of communist identifiers, 57 per cent picked the Bulgarian Communist Party. Party coherence was far stronger, however, among the socialist identifiers. Among this group, 91 per cent picked the Bulgarian Socialist Party. This is interesting on two counts. Not only does it show that the socialist identifiers were successful at picking a single party, but it also suggests the Bulgarian Socialist Party has made a successful transition from its communist past into being accepted as a real socialist alternative. Also interesting is the question of whether, if the Bulgarian Socialist Party still had 'communist' in its name, these voters would consider themselves to be communist rather than socialist supporters? Pro-market supporters in Bulgaria, however, were more consolidated regarding party choice than their equivalents in Ukraine: 78 per cent of them chose the Union of Democratic Forces and only 12 per cent claimed that they either would prefer an independent candidate, did not plan to vote or could not pick a specific party. This suggests that a clear party alternative can make a great difference in consolidating pro-market supporters. Of course, the relatively consolidated support of the pro-market supporters could have been a reflection of greater party awareness due to the recent date of the campaign and the ballot in Bulgaria just prior to the survey. Nationalist supporters, on the other hand, were spread over five parties.

In the Czech Republic there were more socialist identifiers (17 per cent) than communist identifiers (nine per cent), but the latter group were more consolidated in their support for a single party. According to the survey, 97 per cent of the communist identifiers picked the Communist Party to support. In contrast, socialist identifiers were split among 11 parties, although 69 per cent of them chose the Social Democratic Party. While all of the communist identifiers were able to select a party to support – one picked the Social Democratic Party – the socialist identifiers were less sure-footed in their party choice. Of the socialist identifiers, eight per cent either could not pick a party, would choose an independent candidate or did not plan to vote. Again, pro-market supporters were distributed over a relatively wide number of parties (10), with about a third of them picking the Civic Democratic Party. As in other countries, though, the pro-market supporters were less inclined to either choose a specific party or vote – 19 per cent responded that they either could not pick a specific party or would choose an independent candidate, and five per cent did not plan to vote at all. There were so few nationalist party identifiers in the sample (14) that it is impossible to draw conclusions from their party preferences.

The 50 communist identifiers in Slovakia (five per cent of the sample of 1,056 people) mostly picked the Communist Party (58 per cent) while 26 per cent chose the Party of the Democratic Left (PDL), which suggests that there is not a clear choice for communist identifiers in Slovakia as there is in Russia, Ukraine, Bulgaria and the Czech Republic. The socialist identifiers were even less consolidated in their party choice: they were split among 15 parties, including 27 per cent for PDL, 14 per cent for the SDP and 12 per cent for the Movement for Democratic Slovakia. Other party identifiers in Slovakia showed the same type of uncertainty, including a spread of about 14 parties for the pro-market identifiers and 12 parties for nationalist identifiers. Apart from the communists, the only other pattern of party consolidation in terms of ideological interest can be found in the minority nationalist identifiers, with 51 per cent choosing the Hungarian CD and, among the Greens, 44 per cent picking the Green Party. Once again, communist identifiers showed a better ability both to pick a party and in terms of voting intention: only four per cent of the communist identifiers in Slovakia could not pick a party and only an additional four per cent did not plan to vote. In contrast, nine per cent of the socialist identifiers could not pick a party and two per cent did not plan to vote.

Even before considering socio-economic and attitude data, it is clear from the questions about party identification and voter choice that communist voters are special political animals. Most critically, they seem better able to translate their party identification into vote choice. The reasons for this remain slightly unclear and need to be examined at different levels. First, is there an individual level attachment to the communist party with its tangible presence for decades in each country that makes voters more loyal? In other words, is there a type of Left party identification in these five post-communist countries akin to that of the union member for the Labour Party in Britain or of feminists to the Democrats in the United States? If so, is this individual affiliation also linked to cleavages among the population, that is, do older people feel more attachment to the communists?

There are other interesting points to note in the Russian data for communist supporters. Like their communist counterparts in Ukraine, Bulgaria, the Czech Republic and Slovakia, they appeared to be committed party supporters. When asked why they had voted for a particular party, 43 per cent of the communist supporters gave the reason as 'this party expresses the interests of people such as myself', compared with 28 per cent of the 1,115 respondents who claimed to have voted overall (see Figure 3: Reasons for Vote Choice in Russia). In addition, nine per cent of the communist supporters claimed that they were 'accustomed to voting for this party' as opposed to three per cent of the non-communist voters.

FIGURE 3
REASONS FOR VOTE CHOICE IN RUSSIA

Survey question: What of the following things made the most impression on your party list decision? (Out of 1,161 respondents who claimed to have voted.)

Response	Communist Voters	Other Voters
This party expresses the interests of people such as myself.	43	25
I like the leader (leaders) of this party.	12	34
It has real strength and can change the situation in this country.	27	18
I'm accustomed to voting for this party.	9	1
Most of the people in my circle support this party.	12	7
I know more about this party than the others.	6	3
Maybe it's not a very good party, but the others are worse.	7	14
I voted this way as a protest against the situation in the country.	7	4
These people are not tainted by financial scandals or corruption.	2	7
It's a new, fresh political strength.	1	7
I liked their name.	...	2
N	314	847

Source: Survey by the All-Russian Centre for the Study of Public Opinion of 1,568 people across Russia from December 20 to December 26 1995. The percentages add up to more than 100 because people were allowed to select more than one response.

This individual-level attachment, however, can only be part of the picture. It is clear from the investigation of the data in the five countries that structures of the party system and proximity to elections both seem to make a difference in partisan affiliation identification and the ability to translate it into a vote for a specific party. The data from these five countries suggest that communist identifiers are particularly good at identifying specific parties to support. But in places in which there are no viable communist alternatives, such as in Bulgaria, a similar pattern emerges with the support of socialist identifiers for the dominant Bulgarian Socialist Party (the successor to the Soviet-era communists). Although it is beyond the scope of this chapter, it should be noted that there must be a link between clear choices in the electoral arena and support from the ideologically committed. For example, if there are several parties claiming to represent the far left cause, votes may be scattered. It is up to the parties to create and transmit the image of political platforms that clearly convey their underlying ideology in the context of the confusing and transitional society of post-communist Europe. The data suggest that the communist are doing a better job of providing ideological alternatives than the nationalist, pro-market parties or even socialist parties in most countries. This means that communist support is amplified at elections because of greater party consolidation, party identification and voting patterns. As a result, communists enjoy a greater degree of electoral success than their underlying support base in the population in these countries might suggest.

Socio-Economic Characteristics of Communist Supporters

Who are the communist supporters in these countries? In cross-tabulations measuring age, income, gender, urban residence and education, communist voters were mostly distinguished by their age (see Figure 4: Socio-Economic Characteristics of Communist Voters; Russian data not included here). While roughly 25 per cent of the respondents overall were under the age of 32, only 10 per cent of the communist supporters were that young. Conversely, 40 per cent of the communist supporters were 58 or older, compared with about a quarter of respondents overall. In addition, communist supporters felt the pinch of poverty more keenly than respondents in general: 84 per cent of them reported that their income is 'not enough' or 'just enough' compared with 76 per cent of the respondents overall. In addition, very few communist

FIGURE 4
SOCIO-ECONOMIC CHARACTERISTICS OF COMMUNIST VOTERS
IN FOUR POST-COMMUNIST COUNTRIES (IN PERCENTAGES)

Socio-economic characteristic	Overall	Communist supporters	Difference
Age up to 32	25	10	-15
58 years old and older	24	40	+16
'Not enough' income	33	39	+6
'Just enough' income	43	45	+2
'Good' income	4	4	—
Female	54	54	—
Lives in village	34	32	-2
Lives in big city	29	36	+7
Lives in capital	9	2	-7
No higher education	41	44	+3
Completed university education	6	2	-4

supporters were from the capital cities – a mere two per cent – and they were markedly less likely to have completed higher education (two per cent of the communist identifiers compared with six per cent overall among the respondents).

Are there distinct differences in communist supporters *among* the countries? Other evidence suggests that indeed the same patterns generally hold true *within* the four countries. Communist supporters are older, less well-educated and not from the capital cities. The findings for Bulgaria are slightly different, probably due to the very low number of communist supporters. There were some country variations, however, aside from Bulgaria. Communist supporters did not report less satisfaction with their incomes in Ukraine and fewer of them lived in villages. In fact, they seemed to be concentrated in large cities in Ukraine. Interestingly, more communist supporters reported their incomes as 'good' than the general respondent pool in Slovakia. For Russia, cross-tabulations of the data show that the communist supporters tended to be older, more likely to live in rural areas, to fall into lower income categories and have a lower level of education than the average respondent.

Attitudes and Communist Supporters

If one can identify communist supporters by membership of socio-economic groupings, how well defined are they through their opinions on important issues in post-communist society? This article looks at attitudes on five issues: whether to join NATO, whether to join the European Union, whether the respondent favours order over freedom, whether the respondent supports a market economy and whether the respondent believes 'a strong leader with a free hand would solve problems' (see Figure 5: Attitudes of Communist Supporters in Four Post-Communist Countries). Communist supporters are markedly less interested in joining the EU or NATO, slightly more authoritarian and much less enthusiastic about a market economy. All of these attitudes would be predicted from a far left standpoint, which suggests that there is some ideological coherence to this cleavage among voters in eastern Europe and the former Soviet Union.

Examined within each country under study (except Russia because of the different survey methods), these attitudes remain quite distinct. As with the socio-economic cross-tabulations, some of the attitudes are quite extreme in Bulgaria, probably due to the small number of communist respondents (26). It is interesting to note, however, that Czech communists seem quite dissimilar in their anti-West, anti-market attitudes from their fellow citizens while the Ukrainian communist supporters are closer to the attitudes of the general pool of respondents. That would suggest that there is a greater

FIGURE 5
ATTITUDES OF COMMUNIST SUPPORTERS IN FOUR POST-COMMUNIST COUNTRIES
(IN ROUNDED PERCENTAGES)

Attitude	All Four		Ukraine		Bulgaria		Czech Republic		Slovakia	
	All	Comms.	All	Comms.	All	Comms.	All	Comms.	All	Comms.
Country should join EU	74	55	75	63	74	31	68	38	77	68
Country should join NATO	48	25	38	28	49	4	57	18	50	38
We need order more than freedom	79	81	79	83	88	92	75	78	71	76
A strong leader with a free hand would solve problems	34	44	46	49	37	31	21	37	26	44
A market economy is right in principle	52	22	36	22	65	23	54	20	51	26
N	4445	333	1200	172	1519	26	1003	85	1056	50

ideological space between communist supporters and the general electorate in the Czech Republic than there is in Ukraine.

Predicting Communist Support Through Regression Analysis

Regression analysis can illuminate possible links between the socio-economic and attitudinal variables of communist support. This study uses several socio-economic variables (older age, higher income, female gender, higher education and more frequent urban residence) as well as the five attitudinal questions listed above (support for joining EU, support for joining NATO, seeking order over freedom, support for a market economy and a preference for a strong leader). In an OLS regression analysis across the four-country sample, older age is the only significant predictor of communist support among the socio-economic variables (see Figure 6: Predicting Communist Support Through Regression Analysis). However, three attitudes – anti-EU, anti-NATO and anti-market sentiments – are also significant predictors of communist support. Note surprisingly, dislike of a market economy is the strongest predictor in the model overall.

How much are these attitudes a function of the relatively large number of Ukrainian communist supporters, and are the post-Soviet communist supporters different from their east Europe counterparts? If one examines only the Ukrainian sample, the patterns are the same, except that urban residence is significantly correlated with communist support. This is not surprising, as the cross-tabulations reported above found that there was a

27

FIGURE 6
PREDICTING COMMUNIST SUPPORT THROUGH REGRESSION ANALYSIS

Dependent Variable = Supports communists

Independent variables	All Four Countries			Ukraine			Czech Republic, Slovakia and Bulgaria		
	Adjusted r-square = .055			Adjusted r-square = .066			Adjusted r-square = .052		
	Beta	t	Sig.	Beta	t	Sig.	Beta	t	Sig.
Constant		7.218	.000		1.453	.146		7.291	.000
Older age	.074	4.991*	.000	.165	5.605*	.000	.050	2.888*	.004
Better income	.009	.594	.552	.054	1.875	.061	.038	2.188*	.029
Female	-.018	-1.258	.209	-.025	-.877	.380	-.021	-1.261	.207
Higher education	.000	-.001	.999	.022	.788	.431	-.001	-.057	.954
Urbanicity	.020	1.424	.154	.083	2.919*	.004	-.032	-1.895	.058
Supports joining EU	-.043	-2.684*	.007	-.086	-2.926*	.003	-.048	-2.539*	.011
Supports joining NATO	-.090	-5.734*	.000	-.087	-3.008*	.003	-.084	-4.458*	.000
Supports order over freedom	-.014	-.970	.332	.031	1.053	.292	-.023	-1.373	.170
Supports strong leader	.0211	.428	.153	-.022	-.766	.444	.012	.723	.470
Supports market economy	-.150	-9.883*	.000	-.087	-2.962*	.003	-.144	-8.107*	.000

*Significant at the .01 level.

relatively high concentration of communist supporters in big cities (although not in Kyiv). In a regression model using the survey data from the Czech Republic, Slovakia and Bulgaria (where there were a total of 161 or five per cent communist supporters), the pattern is once again similar. However, in the east European sample there is a rather puzzling positive correlation between better income and communist support. This may be due to the fact that respondents were asked to rank their incomes subjectively as being enough to live on, enough for a fair standard of living, etc., rather than report them objectively. Thus, some of the poorer members of society may have reported that they had enough while those with greater ambitions (but more income in actual terms) may have reported dissatisfaction.

Conclusions

This research suggests that communist voters do constitute a distinct group, both within the former Soviet Union and in the three east European countries. Research using these two sets of public opinion survey suggest that communist voters are unusually assured of their ability to choose a party and in their plans to vote – even more so than people who support other well-defined party groupings, such as pro-market or nationalist party families. This trend, as shown in these surveys, has some important implications for parties and voting in post-communist states. Communist parties usually appear to enjoy the support of loyal voters. As a result, their success can be amplified during elections, as their supporters are better at both identifying particular parties (no doubt simplified by the fact that communist parties tend to use the word 'communist' in their party names) and at turning up at the polls.

Using the ideas of Lipset and Rokkan, there is a clear socio-economic cleavage along which to define communist voters. Communist voters are older and less well-educated than the general voting pool, although this varies from country to country. The surveys measured wealth only subjectively and the results are to this extent ambiguous, although evidence from other studies suggests that poorer people are more likely to support communist parties in the former Eastern bloc. Not only do these survey results support the concept of cleavage formation, they also suggest that communist parties have a large, readily identifiable group of potential voters. This makes it easier for the parties to focus their platforms, policies and campaigning more effectively.

The variations in terms of the number and behaviour of communist voters leads to some interesting insights into the sources of contemporary communist support in the Eastern bloc. For example, the percentage of communist supporters varied from about 20 per cent down to two per cent in the surveys. There are many factors that could cause this variation. First, there are vastly different experiences with Communist rule ranging from Russia to Ukraine. While Russia and the Ukraine (however reluctantly) were within the Soviet Union, the Czech Republic, Slovakia and Bulgaria were captured and placed under Soviet influence after the Second World War. There would be fewer – and far more historically shallow – ways for communist parties in the east European countries to hark back to the glories of the Soviet past in order to inspire modern voters. In addition, there would be at least some memory or experience of other party systems in eastern Europe. As noted above, the different electoral systems and the emphasis on presidential rule in Russia and Ukraine can also skew support for radical parties like the communists.

It should be noted again that the structure and political location of communist parties varies from country to country. In Russia and Ukraine, the primary communist parties carry the standard of the former Soviet regime. In Bulgaria, the Soviet-era communist party has been transformed into the powerful Bulgarian Socialist Party, technically leaving the tiny Bulgarian Communist Party as the representative of the far left. These and other variations within the Czech Republic and Slovakia will leave voters with very different party histories, organizations and even philosophies under the loose rubric of 'communism'. It is critical to consider the impact of party behaviour on communist support, hinted at in this chapter but not supported by any empirical evidence. For example, are those voting for the Bulgarian Socialist Party really supporting 'socialism' per se or rallying around a successor communist party? In order to answer this question, one needs far more information about the party and its marketing strategies. In addition, one needs to consider how the choices of voters are informed and/or constrained by their options. Can communists thrive when there is a more globalized socialist alternative? In addition, why have pro-market and nationalist parties, in general, failed to capitalize on their support within the population in the same way? Perhaps it is because they lack the communists' ability to refer back to positive feelings about the Soviet era, evoking a type of party identification for the communist voter that is far stronger than those for the newer nationalist, pro-market or even socialist parties.

At times, it is also difficult to say whether the voters are really supporting a traditional, Soviet-style communist movement, the former regime party with little reference to any particular ideological trappings, or a 'reformed' communist movement that more closely resembles west European socialism than Soviet communism. In fact, respondents who claim to support 'communist' parties in fact pick a variety of parties for which to vote in the surveys cited above. However, they are certainly more coherent in translating their party preference into specific votes – and usually pick a party closer to the ideals of the Soviet era than European socialism. While there is some variation, evidence suggests that these voters really do prefer Soviet-style communism within a multiparty system. It does seem that those supporting today's communists in the former Eastern bloc are looking backward to the glorious Soviet-dominated past rather than forward to a European Socialist future.

NOTES

1. The bulk of this research was funded by the Overseas Development Agency and the Economic and Social Research Council. The data from Ukraine, the Czech Republic, Slovakia and Bulgaria have been deposited with the ESRC archive at Essex University. The Russian survey results were purchased with funds from a Leverhulme Trust grant. The work was carried out by OPW (Opinion Window) in the Czech Republic, MVK in Slovakia, CSD (Centre for the Study of Democracy) in Bulgaria, USM (Ukrainian Surveys and Market Research) in Ukraine and VtSIOM (All-Russian Centre for the Study of Public Opinion) in Russia.
2. Peter Mair, *Party System Change: Approaches and Interpretations* (Oxford: Clarendon Press, 1997), p.180.
3. Seymour Martin Lipset and Stein Rokkan (eds.), *Party Systems and Voter Alignments: Crossnational Perspectives* (New York: Collier-Macmillan, 1967).
4. For example, Angus Campbell, Philip E. Converse, Warren E. Miller and Donald E. Stokes, *The American Voter* (New York: Wiley, 1960), Bruce Keith,

David Magleby, Candice J. Nelson, Elizabeth Orr, Mark C. Westlye and Raymond Wolfinger, *The Myth of the Independent Voter* (Berkeley, CA: University of California Press, 1992); Norman Nie, Sidney Verba and John Petrocik, *The Changing American Voter*, Second Edition (Cambridge: Harvard University Press, 1979).

5. This includes Geoffrey Evans and Stephen Whitefield, 'Cleavage Formation in Transition Societies: Russia, Ukraine and Estonia, 1993–95', paper presented at the American Political Science Association Annual Meeting, San Francisco, 1996; Stephen White, Matthew Wyman and Sarah Oates, 'Parties and Voters in the 1995 Russian Duma Elections', *Europe-Asia Studies*, Vol.49 (1997), pp.767–98; Matthew Wyman, Stephen White and Sarah Oates, *Elections and Voters in Post-Communist Russia* (Cheltenham: Edward Elgar 1998).

6. Richard Rose and William Mishler, 'Negative and Positive Party Identification in Post-Communist Countries', *Electoral Studies*, Vol.17, No.2 (1998), pp.217–34.

7. Richard Rose, 'Ex-Communists in Post-Communist Societies', *Political Quarterly*, Vol.67, No.1 (1996), p.24.

8. The 1994 figures are from B. Turner (ed.), The Statesman's Yearbook, 1998–1999, 135th edition (London: Macmillan, 1999), p.1399; 1998 figures are from Sarah Birch and Andrew Wilson, 'The Ukrainian Parliamentary Elections of 1998', *Electoral Studies*, Vol.18, No.2 (1999), pp.276–82.

9. A.S. Banks, A.J. Day, and T.C. Muller (eds.), *Political Handbook of the World 1997* (Binghampton, NY: CSA Publications, 1998), pp.112–16.

10. For more information on the surveys, please contact the principal author at the Politics Department, University of Glasgow, Glasgow G12 8RT, United Kingdom or via Email at s.oates@socsci.gla.ac.uk.

3

Sickles into Roses: The Successor Parties and Democratic Consolidation in Post-Communist Politics

JOHN ISHIYAMA

Introduction

In recent years much attention has been paid to the political resurgence of the former communist parties, as well as to their recent electoral declines. The attention paid to these communist successor parties, or those parties which *were formerly the governing party in the communist regime and which inherited the preponderance of the former ruling parties' resources and personnel,*[1] is not particularly surprising since, unlike 'new parties', the communist successor parties are not merely clubs of notables. They are distinct organizations, and, by any definition represent, 'real' political parties. Previous works, however, have tended to treat communist successor party electoral success as a *dependent* variable rather than as an *independent variable*, seeking to identify the factors that contributed to their success, and subsequently their decline.[2] Some scholars contend that the communist successor parties will play a vital role in consolidating democracy, largely because these parties serve to create channels of interest articulation for people who would be most alienated by economic and political transformation. Thus, the successor parties have the potential to act as agents of political integration in incipient democratic systems. In other words, the success of the communist successor parties can be seen as a positive factor in the consolidation of democracy.

Despite the theoretical appeal of this proposition, it remains a largely untested assertion. This article, however, proposes to investigate empirically how the communist successor parties have contributed to the process of democratic consolidation in new democracies (or not). In particular this article addresses three questions central to the process of democratic consolidation: (1) To what extent have the communist successor parties generally drawn their electorate, and especially the 'losers' of the transition, into the political process and the acceptance of the democratic rules of the game? (2) Are the supporters of more electorally successful communist successor parties more likely to embrace democracy than supporters of less successful successor parties since supporters of successful parties are more likely to perceive that they are empowered with 'voice'? (3) Does the level of support for democracy among supporters of the communist successor parties vary across different organizational types of parties?

To investigate these relationships, the analysis is divided into two major sections. The first briefly outlines the current literature on democratic consolidation and enumerates the ways in which parties in general and the communist successor parties in particular can potentially contribute to the process of democratic consolidation. From this section several hypotheses are derived. The second evaluates whether these parties have acted as agents of democratic consolidation empirically, in light of the political attitudes of supporters of the communist successor parties, particularly among those social strata most hurt by the political and economic transition from communist rule.

What is Democratic Consolidation?

Democratic consolidation is a notoriously slippery concept. Indeed, as Schedler has noted, there are so many different definitions of democratic consolidation that the concept has become expanded beyond all recognition. It has come to include such divergent items as: popular legitimation; the diffusion of democratic values; the neutralization of anti-system actors; civilian supremacy over the military, elimination of authoritarian enclaves; party building; the organization of functional interests; the stabilization of electoral rules; the routinization of politics; the decentralization of state power; the introduction of mechanisms of direct democracy; judicial reform; the alleviation of poverty; and economic stabilization.[3]

Further, as Power and Gasiorowski note, most of the literature on democratic consolidation 'is highly exploratory and tentative in nature.' Although the attempt to devise an ideal type of consolidated democracy is 'often of value, at its currently high level of abstraction the extant literature provides little guidance for *cross-national* (italics in the original) operationalization and measurement of the central concept'.[4]

None the less, there appears to be some consensus on at least one feature of democratic consolidation: the widespread acceptance of the general principle of democratic competition.[5] For instance, according to Parrott consolidation denotes the condition of a political system in which all major political actors and social groups expect that government leaders will be chosen through 'competitive elections and regard representative institutions and procedures as their main channel for pressing claims on the state.'[6] For Przeworski 'democracy is consolidated when it becomes self-enforcing ...

when compliance – acting within the institutional framework – constitutes the equilibrium of the decentralized strategies of all the relevant political forces'.[7] For Valenzuela consolidation is signified when there is a widespread assumption that free elections are the only recognized legitimate means for the constitution of government.[8] Laurence Whitehead contends that consolidation is the process by which the 'new regime becomes institutionalized, its framework of open and competitive political expression becomes internalized.'[9] For Gunther *et al.*, a democratic regime is consolidated when 'all politically significant groups regard its key political institutions as the only legitimate framework for political contestation, and adhere to democratic rules of the game'.[10]

Even more contentious than the conceptualization of democratic consolidation has been the debate over how to measure the concept empirically. Some have proposed indirect measures, such as those offered by Stepan and Skach, who operationally defined democratic consolidation as having occurred if a country received a scale score of 3 on the Coppedge-Reinicke Polyarchy scale for 1985 and no higher than a 2.5 averaged score on the Freedom House ratings for political rights and civil liberties for the period 1980–90.[11] Power and Gasiorowski suggest three operational measures for democratic consolidation. The first is whether a new regime survives through the holding of a second election for a national executive. The simplest sign that political elites have accepted the rules of the democratic game, or the notion that free elections be the only legitimate means of constituting government, is the onset of second elections.[12] The second measure involves whether an alternation in who controls executive power took place.[13] The third measure is longevity, where the yardstick for a consolidated democracy was 12 years since after this time 'the odds of democratic survival … at least appear to stabilize'.[14] Gunther *et al.*, however, specifically reject these indirect measures, especially the notion that the appearance of survivability and stability means that the regime must be consolidated. This argument is a kind of tautology – that the regime survived, therefore it must have been consolidated. They also reject the two-turnover test because they believe 'it reflects conceptual confusion, but also leads to some rather absurd applications to the real world (see Japan and Italy for instance). Further although they accept the notion that alternation in power between former rivals may constitute evidence that a regime has become consolidated, that test should not be confused with the concept of consolidation itself.[15]

Others have suggested more direct measures of popular support for democracy and existing political institutions. One approach has been to define consolidation in terms of mass acceptance of democracy, in particular the degree to which the population is satisfied with democracy. Many believe that satisfaction with the democratic experience promotes a greater commitment to democracy and hence signifies an important trend towards democratic consolidation.[16] Indeed even Gunther *et al.* acknowledge that widespread support and satisfaction with democracy may be an important and necessary condition, particularly insofar as it increases the chances that whatever new governmental system or regime may come into existence will be democratic. However by itself, widespread support for democracy 'undervalues or ignores the importance of the absence of fundamental disputes among politically significant groups over the acceptability of the basic framework for political contestation, and what this implies for democratic stability, predictability and ultimately sustainability'.[17] Therefore it is not a sufficient condition for the onset of democratic consolidation. None the less, although widespread support of democracy may not by itself be a sufficient condition for democratic consolidation, it certainly is recognized as a contributing factor.

The Role of Political Parties and Democratic Consolidation

What can parties do to promote consolidation? One area of particular interest to both academics and practitioners alike is the potential role of the post-communist political parties as integrative organizations which can contribute to democratic consolidation in the post-communist politics.[18] Indeed, the integrative function of political parties has long been noted by political scientists in the west.[19] Parties which are based on broad cross-cutting cleavages are seen as important institutions which both insulate incipient democracies from domestic challenges to stability and act as important channels of interest articulation. In particular, parties build the 'channels of communication ... between otherwise hostile or non-communicating groups, bringing them into sets of relationships on which the state is built'.[20] Lipset and Rokkan saw political parties as essentially 'agencies of mobilization and as such have helped to integrate local communities into the nation or the broader federation'.[21] The above suggests that political parties play a vital role in structuring participation and hence socializing followers into the acceptance of democracy.[22]

However, there has been considerable scepticism and reluctance thus far to view parties in post-communist politics as 'integrative organizations'. Part of the reason for this reluctance is due to the heretofore dominant belief that 'real' parties do not now exist in post-communist Eastern Europe, nor are they likely to emerge in the near future.[23] Some analysts have even termed post-communist politics 'non-party' politics.[24] The argument is grounded in the notion that transitions are 'different' from transitions elsewhere partly because of the legacy of the totalitarian past. As a result there is the 'well developed antipathy to the concept of party after 70 years in which it stood for political monopoly and sometimes repression' and a view that civil society remains only 'weakly developed with few of the autonomous business and labour associations that support parties in other countries.'[25]

Much of the literature discounting the applicability of theories of party organization to post-communist eastern Europe appears to be based on the assumption that the only 'real party' is the 'mass party', whose age 'appears over and parties in general appear obsolete as vehicles of popular mobilization regional and national identity, individual development, and ... even as instruments of power.'[26] Yet this conception of 'party' as 'mass party' runs counter to much of the party organizational literature which holds that there are multiple models of the party organization beyond the mass party.[27] For instance Lewis argues that 'it increasingly appears that arguments concerning the decline of the party *per se* were wrong and generally misconceived'. Indeed, much of the argument concerning the decline of the party in fact seemed to be concerned with the decline of the 'mass' party rather than the party in general.[28] If one only narrowly conceives of 'party' as the mass party then of course the concept is inapplicable to post-communist eastern Europe (or anywhere else for that matter). Indeed, Parrott suggests the pronouncements regarding the permanent irrelevance of parties in post-communist politics is in part based upon faulty comparisons with already established party systems. He notes that 'the rate at which post-communist parties crystallize into reasonably stable institutions might be closer to the rates of party-formation during the nineteenth century than to the rates in other new democracies near the end of the twentieth'.[29]

None the less the pattern of development of political parties in post-communist politics does differ from the pattern of west European party development. For instance, the sudden expansion of the scope of participation in post-communist politics contrasted with the step-by-step expansion of the franchise in most countries in the nineteenth century, a process which provided an incentive to create mass political parties that appealed to the interests of each newly enfranchised segment of the population. On the other hand, in post-communist politics 'the simultaneous admission of all social strata and economic groups into post-communist electoral systems has created an incentive to establish catch-all parties that appeal to many constituencies'.[30] Although this has led to relatively low levels of programmatic coherence in many post-communist parties this 'should not necessarily be equated with institutional weakness'.[31]

In fact, the pressure to pursue catch-all strategies (which is associated with low levels of party programmatic coherence) is most likely to lead to moderation in the demands made by parties, and presumably lead to the moderation of the party's followers. As Parrott notes, among some communist successor parties, like the Hungarian Socialist Party, the creation of widespread opportunities for personal political gain brought about by de-ideologization of the party has transformed the HSP into the champion of political and economic reform. Conversely, parties that have been less supportive of political and economic reform have also been characterized by an exodus of moderate and liberal members who had joined the party purely to advance their professional careers.[32] Thus the implication here is that parties which possess 'catch-all' characteristics are more likely to attract moderate supporters than are parties which are more mass-like. Further, this also suggests that as mass-like parties become catch-all parties, they may serve to moderate followers who are already in the party, particularly if that party represents the only viable option for political participation.

On the other hand, Kitschelt contends that parties which are more mass-like (or 'programmatic') are better equipped to promote the consolidation of democracy than are 'catch-all' parties. He identifies three 'ideal types' of parties which have emerged in post-communist politics: the *charismatic, clientelistic* and *programmatic.* The *charismatic party* is characterized by 'not much more than an unstructured mass of people rallying around a leader'.[33] Such parties are inherently unstable given that, in order to maintain allegiances of followers, leaders must sooner or later provide selective incentives to their constituencies and enter upon trajectories of organizational development that result in either clientelistic or programmatic parties. Clientelistic parties are characterized by an emphasis on personal patronage, and invest much into creating an organization which effectively disburses resources to followers. These parties, however, avoid the costs of co-ordinating the activities of followers since the role of the member is not to believe in a set of ideological goals, but to be personally loyal. Programmatic parties, on the other hand, are built to advertise ideals 'about a desirable society as the collective good they promise to produce and to attract activists and leaders ready to propagate and to implement these ideas'.[34] Programmatic parties are relatively harder to build than either of the other types, yet are 'more likely to reinforce the consolidation and stability of democratic regimes than the two alternative modes' of party organization.[35]

The above literature points to several factors that may affect the party's ability to act as an engine of democratic consolidation. These are summarized in the following hypotheses:

Hypothesis 1: Over time, the more the communist successor party participates in elections the more its followers will be satisfied with, and support, democracy.[36]

Hypothesis 2a: Parties which have organizational features that make them akin to 'catch-all' or 'cadre-like' parties are more apt to have supporters who will be satisfied with democracy and support democracy than parties that have organizational features which make them akin to 'mass-like' parties.

Hypothesis 2b: Parties which have organizational features that make them akin to 'mass-like' parties are more apt to have supporters who will be satisfied with, and support, democracy than parties which have organizational features which make them akin to 'catch-all' or 'cadre-like' parties.

Hypothesis 3: Parties which were electorally successful early on are more likely to have supporters who will be satisfied with, and support, democracy.

Variables

Satisfaction with Democracy

An important element in the development of consolidated democracy is the extent to which individuals are satisfied with the progress of democracy.[37] There are of course more direct measures of support for democracy, such as questions regarding approval of multi-party democracy, approval of free press and tolerance of 'deviant' groups. However, these questions have not been asked consistently over time (indeed they have been thus far restricted to the 1991 *Times-Mirror Study*) and hence cannot act as measures of democratic consolidation over time. Indeed Waldron-Moore notes the connection between levels of dissatisfaction and commitment and support for democratic processes when she argues that:

> In stable democracies, one would not expect short-term dissatisfaction to affect commitment to democratic processes. Citizens usually vent their dissatisfaction on those they hold accountable ... by 'throwing the rascals out'. However, in Eastern Europe, given their inexperience with government institutions that facilitate accountability, publics may be unable to do the same. Dissatisfaction alone may not change attitudes toward democracy but an inability to channel dissatisfaction might. It is therefore useful to ascertain empirically how likely individuals are to blame their dissatisfaction on the democratic process and the pace of democratization rather than on the vision of their governments to devise strategies for relieving economic burden.[38]

To measure satisfaction with democracy, Waldron-Moore employed four questions which appeared in the 1992 Central and Eastern Eurobarometer to construct a *satisfaction with democracy* scale. These were

(1) On the whole are you very satisfied, fairly satisfied, not very satisfied or not at all satisfied with the way that democracy is developing in our country?

(2) How much respect is there for human rights nowadays in (our country)? Do you feel that there is a lot of respect, some respect or not very much respect at all?[39]

(3) In general, do you feel that things in our country are going in the right or wrong direction?

(4) Taking everything into account, do you feel that things are better for you now under the present political system or do you think things were better for you under the previous political system?

A factor analysis of the four items demonstrated that they represented a uni-dimensional scale of satisfaction. Thus the four items were added together and divided by four to calculate an individual respondent's satisfaction with democracy score.

However, in years subsequent to 1992, the fourth question did not appear in the Central and Eastern Eurobarometer data, although the first three do. Thus a truncated version of Waldron-Moore's measure, which uses the first three items to calculate the satisfaction with democracy score for 1992–97, is employed here.

Party Organization

To differentiate between different types of party organizations I propose to use two simple measures derived from the classic literature on party organization: *organizational density* and *ideological coherence*. These dimensions have been cited as two of the most important characteristics of different kinds of political parties.[40] In the classic writings on political parties, most notably those by Duverger and Epstein, mass parties were characterized by *both* a reliance on mass membership *and* the valuing of ideological coherence. On the other hand cadre (and for Epstein, 'electoral') parties relied less on mass membership *and* placed less emphasis on ideological coherence and greater emphasis on ideological flexibility.[41]

To measure the various types of possible party organizational configurations, this study measures the degree to which parties are more 'mass-like' or 'cadre-like'.[42] The terms 'mass-like' and 'cadre-like' are preferred for two reasons. First, because comparativists working on party organization in Eastern Europe have already begun to use these terms as starting points in the analysis of post-communist parties, and it makes sense (if scholars are to be serious about bringing the investigation of developments in post-Soviet Russia fully into the field of comparative politics) to extend the use of these concepts as a starting point in the analysis of post-Soviet politics as well. Second, the terms 'cadre and mass' maintain conceptual continuity with the general literature on party organization when applied to the parties in post-communist politics. If we are to further the study of political parties in post-communist politics and reduce conceptual confusion, then it is absolutely imperative that we make every effort to become familiar and conversant with the rich existing theoretical literature on political parties, before going on to create a more area-specific terminology. Although there have been several ways in which to characterize the different organizational types of parties, they are simplified here to two features which characterize the 'more mass-like' party: (1) a relatively large membership which plays an important political role in the party; and (2) greater ideological and programmatic coherence. On the other hand, parties which are more cadre-like are characterized by a small, relatively unimportant membership and greater ideological and programmatic incoherence.

Party organization is measured here by the often-used basic indicator that reflects the *importance of the party's membership* or *organizational density.* It is defined as the proportion of estimated official party members *over* the number of votes a party receives. This measure was first developed by Duverger and subsequently adopted elsewhere as well: it measures the relative importance of the party's membership as a proportion of its electoral support.[43] Parties with more cadre-like or catch-all characteristics are likely to rely less heavily on membership for their support than are parties which are more mass-like. For the communist successor parties considered in this study, the latest estimated membership figures are used and divided by the average vote received by the party for the last two legislative elections.

There are many possible ways to conceptualize ideological coherence (such as consistency in the party's programme, or the level of homogeneity in policy preferences among groups associated with the party, such as voters activists and elected office holders, or the degree of party discipline exhibited by the party's office-holders). *Ideological* coherence is conceptualized here in a 'minimalist' way – *the degree to which the party displays discernable and consistent policy preferences that are readily perceptible as distinctly on one side of the ideological spectrum or the other.* Such an approach, although perhaps not ideal, none the less captures elements of each of the aforementioned alternatives. That is to say a party would be perceived as coherent if the party's programme appeared to be consistent, if there were no major ideological conflicts within the party, and there was a degree of party discipline.[44]

One such measure which would measure the degree to which the party displays in its public face discernable and consistent policy preferences, derives from the work of Huber and Inglehart.[45] An ideology score (ranging from 1 to most left and 7 to most right) was calculated by 'expert coding' for various parties in 42 countries, including the ten communist successor parties in this study. From, this, the standard deviation associated with the ideology score was calculated. This measure of variance indicated how much expert agreement there was on the ideological placement. The smaller the standard deviation, the greater the agreement among the coders (and presumably the more recognizable the ideological coherence of the parties). The larger the standard deviation, the less agreement among coders as to their placement (and hence the greater the *perceived incoherence* of that party).[46]

Party Success

The communist successor party's *electoral success* is defined here as the percentage of seats won in the lower house of the legislature in the second post-communist legislative election. Focusing on only the lower house is justified for two reasons: First, not all of the emerging constitutional orders of Eastern Europe and the former Soviet Union are identical – some have unicameral legislatures, as is the case in Albania, Bulgaria, Hungary, and the Baltic States; others, such as the Czech and Slovak Republics, Russia, Poland and Romania, have bicameral legislatures. Yet in all of the latter the more powerful house is the lower house. Therefore, for the sake of comparability, the lower houses of the legislatures have been chosen. Second, legislatures and not presidencies are the focus because, although in many of these post-communist political systems a relatively powerful and directly elected executive exists (such as in Russia, Poland, Serbia, Romania, Bulgaria, Belarus, Moldova and Ukraine), the executive throughout post-communist Eastern Europe has sought some accommodation with the lower house of parliament.[47]

Focusing on only second elections as a measure of success rather than the percentage of the vote received by the party is also justified for two reasons: (1) elections held immediately after the collapse of communist rule were often merely referenda on communist rule, rather than true expressions of political preferences; thus only the latest elections and or those held in or after 1992 are included in this analysis; (2) focusing on the second election, rather than the third election or beyond, allows for the examination of whether representation at the earliest stages of democratic consolidation affects the degree to which supporters of the communist successor parties are satisfied with democratic development.

Sample Composition

To assess the hypotheses listed above, data were compiled from the Central and Eastern Eurobarometer for 1991–92 and 1994–97 for the supporters of the communist successor parties who were most likely to be 'losers' in the political and economic transition.[48] Supporters of the communist successor parties were identified by the question: for which party did the respondent intend to vote in the next election? (for the 1991–92 data the variable VOTEINT and for the 1994–97 data item d4b). 'Losers' in the political and economic transition were identified as those occupational groups which were most likely to be hurt by the transition (and hence presumably least likely to be satisfied with the progress of democratic transition). These included state enterprise employees, pensioners and the unemployed (for the 1992 data OCCUP[49] and for the 1994–97 data item d5). These groups were also those who were originally attracted to the communist successor parties; hence if the successor parties have made any difference in terms of promoting the acceptance of democracy, it would be among these groups. The data-sets were 'cleaned' so that only the potential 'loser groups' remained. Further to minimize the possibility that satisfaction with democracy was a function of the economic condition of the respondent (rather than the affiliation with the successor party) only those who reported that their household financial situation had declined or not improved over the past year were included in the datasets.[50]

In terms of countries, three criteria were used to select the 14 national cases: (1) in each of the states selected all had at least one reasonably competitive election between 1992 and 1995, and all have continued, albeit at different speeds, along the paths of democratic transition and democratic consolidation (thus excluding the Central Asian and Caucasian states of the former Soviet Union, as well as Belarus); (2) none of the transitions in these states were interrupted by a prolonged civil war which significantly altered the political environment for the formerly dominant parties (thus excluding Serbia and Montenegro, Bosnia-Hercegovina and Moldova); (3) in all the states the communist successor parties faced new competitive conditions and a party system in the earliest stages of development (thus excluding the Party of Democratic Socialism in Germany). Using these criteria, data were collected on Albania, Bulgaria, the Czech Republic, Estonia, the former Yugoslav Republic of Macedonia (FYROM), Hungary, Latvia, Lithuania, Poland, Romania, the Russian Federation, Slovakia, Slovenia, and the Ukraine.[51] Croatia was excluded because Central and Eastern Eurobarometer data collection on Croatia commenced only beginning in 1995.

Analysis

In order to assess the above hypotheses, a simple set of descriptive statistics are presented in Table 1 and Figures 1–3. Two sets of comparisons are made – across time (in order to evaluate Hypothesis 1) and across party (to evaluate Hypotheses 2a, 2b and 3). Table 1 reports the satisfaction with democracy scores for supporters of the communist successor parties who came from the 'loser' population compared with the general 'loser' population scores for the 14 communist successor parties. 'Supporters' of the communist successor parties were identified by how the respondent answered the question: For which party did the respondent intend to vote in the next election? The 'loser' population was identified by the respondent's occupation. Respondents who identified themselves as pensioners, unemployed, or state enterprise employees (or manual workers for the 1991 and 1992 data) or those occupations most likely to have been negatively affected by the economic and political transition (and hence also most likely to view negatively the development of democracy) were assigned to the 'losers of the transition' or 'loser' category. Since we are interested in the extent to which the communist successor parties have promoted democratic consolidation, we would expect that parties which have acted as 'engines' of democratic consolidation would have supporters who are more satisfied with the development of democracy than the general 'loser' population. On the other hand, successor parties which have generally not acted as 'engines' of democratic consolidation would have supporters who are less satisfied with the development of democracy than the general 'loser' population.

To determine the extent to which communist successor party supporters compared with the general loser population, the satisfaction with democracy score for the supporters of the communist successor party was subtracted from the satisfaction score for the general loser population. If the score was positive, then successor party supporters tended to be relatively more satisfied with the development of democracy than the general loser population. On the other hand, if the score was negative, then the successor party supporters tended to be relatively less satisfied with the development of democracy than the general loser population. Finally, in order to assess overall trends, the last two columns of Table 1 report: (1) the average differences between successor party supporters and the general loser populations (as a composite score to assess the performance of each party in acting as engines of democratic consolidation); (2) the general trend of the successor party scores, with 'less' meaning the party's supporters were becoming less satisfied with the development of democracy and 'more' meaning the party's supporters were becoming more satisfied with the development of democracy (with 'same' indicating no change over time).

From Table 1, several observations can be made. First, three groups of parties can be identified (see Note to Table 1 for the full names of the parties and their acronyms): (1) parties whose supporters tend to be more satisfied

TABLE 1
SATISFACTION WITH DEMOCRACY OVER TIME: COMPARING SUCCESSOR PARTY SUPPORTERS AND 'LOSER' POPULATION

Country (Party)	1991 Successor Party Score; % of 'loser' sample supporting successor party; (Difference compared to 'loser' population score)*	1992	1994	1995	1996	1997	Average Differences in Scores	Trend Direction?
Albania (SPA)	1.95 48.6% (.02)	2.28 29.3% (-.20)	2.53 40.5% (-.27)	2.60 29.7% (-.48)	2.59 13.4% (-.78)		-.34	Less
Bulgaria (BSP)	2.16 10.3% (-.20)	2.67 25.5% (-.46)	2.78 29.1% (-.11)	2.55 37.5% (-.06)	2.70 20.4% (.02)	2.65 16.3% (-.29)	-.18	Same
Czech Republic (CPBM)		2.58 8.9% (-.40)	2.65 9.5% (-.47)	2.74 9.2% (-.57)	2.72 4.5% (-.42)	2.69 8.4% (-.31)	-.44	Same
Estonia (EDLP)		2.50 2.5% (-.13)	2.47 3.0% (-.28)	2.94 2.6% (-.84)			-.39	Less
Hungary (HSP)	2.14 25.5% (.08)	2.69 15.6% (-.28)	2.22 27.3% (.13)	2.04 26.9% (.39)	2.35 15.0% (.18)	2.09 17.2% (.22)	+.12	More
Latvia (Socialist Party)		2.65 7.1% (-.21)	2.74 3.0% (-.31)	2.76 3.0% (-.38)	2.73 3.0% (-.14)		-.26	Less
Lithuania (LDLP)		2.46 21.3% (-.20)	2.46 17.7% (.11)	2.41 10.5% (.29)	2.63 6.0% (-.05)	2.59 10.3% (-.17)	-.02	Less
Macedonia (SDUM)		1.97 15.1% (.23)	1.97 36.8% (.34)	1.78 29.9% (.38)	1.90 18.5% (.40)		+.28	More
Poland (SdRP)		2.70 6.3% (-.23)	2.59 15.8% (-.02)	2.07 23.8% (.13)	2.14 17.4% (.08)	2.08 19.0% (.02)	.00	More
Romania (PSDR)	1.84 38.0% (.25)	2.07 40.5% (.24)	1.97 11.7% (.56)	2.15 19.2% (.23)	2.16 13.3% (-.02)	2.46 9.5% (-.17)	+.17	Less
Russia (CPRF)			3.08 19.5% (-.16)	3.07 23.1% (-.19)	3.03 31.1% (-.16)		-.17	Same
Slovakia (PDL)		2.33 12.2% (-.14)	2.40 8.4% (-.06)	2.56 4.6% (-.17)	2.58 6.7% (-.08)	2.52 7.0% (-.07)	-.10	Same
Slovenia (PDR)		2.07 10.4% (-.02)	2.44 7.3% (-.09)	2.22 8.1% (-.03)			-.03)	Same
Ukraine (CPU)			3.00 15.3% (-.19)	3.09 12.2% (.20)	3.00 19.6% (-.19)		-.19	Same

Notes: *= 'Loser' population score minus successor party supporters' score; Parties: SPA (Socialist Party of Albania); BSP (Bulgarian Socialist Party); CPBM (Communist Party of Bohemia and Moravia); EDLP (Estonian Democratic Labor Party); HSP (Hungarian Socialist Party); LDLP (Lithuanian Democratic Labor Party); SDUM (Social Democratic Union of Macedonia); SdRP (Social Democracy of the Republic of Poland); PSDR (Party of Social Democracy of Romania); CPRF (Communist Party of the Russian Federation); PDL (Party of the Democratic Left); PDR (Party of Democratic Reform); CPU (Communist Party of the Ukraine).

More democratic over time

with the development of democracy than the general loser population (HSP, SDUM, and PSDR); (2) parties whose supporters tend to be as dissatisfied with democracy as the general loser population (SdRP, LDLP, PDR); (3) parties whose supporters are more dissatisfied with democracy than the general loser population (SPA, BSP, CPBM, EDLP, LSP, CPRF, PDL, CPU). Of the first three parties the HSP's supporters have become generally more satisfied with democracy over time (trend direction = more), with the SDUM's supporters consistently more satisfied with the development of democracy in Macedonia than the general loser population. For the PSDR's supporters, however, the trend has been in the direction of less satisfaction with democracy over time; so much so that, by 1996 (after the party's defeat at the hands of the opposition coalition) the PSDR's supporters had become less satisfied than the general loser population. For the second group, the SdRP has demonstrated a trend where its supporters have generally become more satisfied with democracy (even after the party's electoral defeat in the earlier part of 1997). Thus it appears that at least for the Polish party's followers, satisfaction with democracy is not merely a function of how well the party does at the polls. On the other hand, the LDLP's supporters have become less satisfied with democracy (particularly after their party's disastrous defeat in the polls in the fall of 1996), indicating that attitudes about democracy are still very fluid in Lithuania.

In the final group, none of the parties showed positive development in the direction of greater satisfaction with democracy amongst its supporters. In Albania and Estonia the supporters of the SPA and EDLP have become increasingly less satisfied with democracy, although this may have changed after the 1996 electoral victory of the SPA. The EDLP has, for all intents and purposes, disappeared. By and large, however, there has been little change among this third group of parties. Their followers remain generally (and resolutely) dissatisfied with the development of democracy.

Thus the evidence presented in Table 1 does not support the first hypothesis which held that over time, the more the communist successor party participates in elections the more its followers would exhibit greater degrees of satisfaction with democracy. Although for at least three parties this was the case (HSP, SdRP and SDUM), for the majority of the parties there was either no change or in the direction of greater dissatisfaction.

Turning to Hypotheses 2a and 2b, which linked the degree of supporter satisfaction with organizational features of parties, Figures 1 and 2 illustrate the relationships between organizational density and ideological coherence on the one hand, and supporter satisfaction on the other. Only ten parties were included in this phase of the analysis since both membership figures *and* the ideological coherence scores could only be found for these ten parties: the BSP, CPBM, EDLP, HSP, LDLP, SdRP, PSDR, CPRF, PDL and

FIGURE 1
AVERAGE DIFFERENCES IN SATISFACTION WITH DEMOCRACY SCORES BETWEEN
SUCCESSOR PARTY SUPPORTERS AND 'LOSER' POPULATION BY PARTY
ORGANIZATIONAL DENSITY

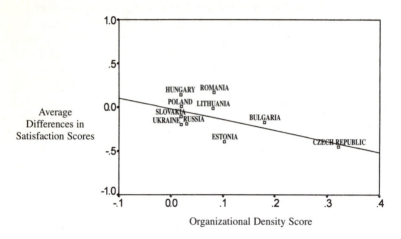

FIGURE 2
AVERAGE DIFFERENCES IN SATISFACTION WITH DEMOCRACY SCORES BETWEEN
SUCCESSOR PARTY SUPPORTERS AND 'LOSER' POPULATION BY IDEOLOGICAL
COHERENCE SCORE

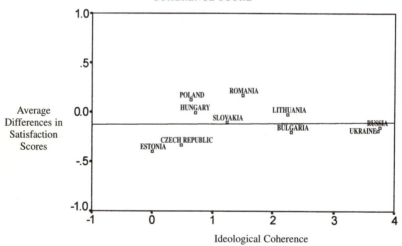

Pearson's R=-.03
Sources: Central and Eastern Eurobarometer 1990–97; Author's Compilation.

CPU. In order to test the proposition that the degree to which a communist successor party's supporters were more satisfied with democracy than the general loser population was a function of the organizational features of the party, Figure 1 plots the average differences between successor party supporters and the general loser population, by party organizational density scores. As indicated, there appears to be a fairly strong inverse relationship between the two variables ($r=.61$). Put another way, the more organizationally dense a party (a feature of a more mass party) the *less* satisfied are the communist successor party's supporters as compared to the general loser population.

This finding lends support to the claim made by Parrott that parties which are less mass-like are more likely to attract moderate supporters than are parties which are more mass-like (thus supporting Hypothesis 2a). On the other hand, this finding does not tend to support Kitschelt's claim that such parties are more likely to be associated with greater democratic consolidation (Hypothesis 2b).This is not an entirely surprising finding. Since the ideological forebears of the successor parties were the communist parties, whose programmes rejected both bourgeois democracy and liberal capitalism, it is not surprising that mass-like successor parties should be associated with supporters who are less satisfied with democracy. Yet this finding would suggest that parties which are 'looser' organizations than mass parties may be better at drawing in disaffected elements of the population (and hence better at promoting democratic consolidation) than is commonly claimed.

However, the results from Figure 2 are not consistent with those expressed in Figure 1. Indeed, no apparent relationship exists between the degree to which the parties appear to be ideologically coherent and the extent to which their supporters are relatively more satisfied with democracy. Thus although the evidence from Figure 1 tends to support Hypothesis 2a, the second feature of parties (the degree to which they are ideologically coherent) does not appear to be related to the dependent variable. Although this result may be due to the inadequacies of the measure of coherence (which might be better measured by the degree of legislative fraction voting cohesion for instance) the evidence on the relationship between party organizational characteristics and satisfaction with democracy appears to be mixed.

Finally, Figure 3 illustrates the relationship between early electoral success and supporter satisfaction with democracy. As indicated there appears to be a strong and consistent positive relationship between the extent to which the successor party was successful in the second legislative election and the extent to which the party's supporters were satisfied with democracy relative to the general loser population ($r=.48$). This result tends to support Hypothesis 3, or the contention that parties which were electorally successful early on were more likely to have supporters who would be more satisfied

47

FIGURE 3
AVERAGE DIFFERENCES IN SATISFACTION WITH DEMOCRACY SCORES BETWEEN
SUCCESSOR PARTY SUPPORTERS AND 'LOSER' POPULATION BY DEGREE OF
ELECTORAL SUCCESS IN SECOND LEGISLATIVE ELECTION

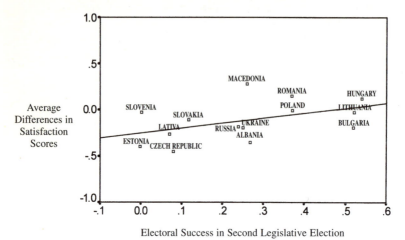

Electoral Success in Second Legislative Election

Pearson's R=-.48
Sources: Central and Eastern Eurobarometer 1990–97; Author's Compilation.

with democracy than parties which were less electorally successful. This
result supports the notion that parties which provide 'voice' to populations
which are most negatively affected by the political and economic transition
are better able to promote satisfaction with democracy among their followers
than are parties which are less politically successful.

Conclusions

The above article represents an initial attempt at investigating the posited
relationship between the communist successor parties and the process of
democratic consolidation in post-communist states. As indicated above, not
all of the communist successor parties have promoted democratic
consolidation, at least in terms of promoting the acceptance of democracy
among their supporters in occupational groups most hurt by the political and
economic transition. Indeed, the degree to which a communist successor
party appears to have a positive impact on democratic consolidation (at least
in terms of drawing those who lost out in the transition into acceptance of
democracy) depends on the kind of party it has become and whether that
party enjoyed some degree of success early on in the democratic transition.

In particular, the findings above suggested two things. First, communist successor parties which possess some (not all) of the characteristics of 'catch-all' or more 'cadre-like' parties such as lessened reliance on a mass membership for political support, appear better able to draw their supporters into the acceptance of democracy than 'mass-like' or programmatic parties. This finding tends to contradict much of the literature which insists that the only real party is the mass party and only the mass party can promote democratic consolidation. Second, parties which are able to score electoral success early on and those who have experienced real power (such as the HSP, the SdRP and SDUM) appear to be better able to draw their supporters into accepting democracy than are parties which remain marginalized or, worse, remain significant oppositions that have been almost completely excluded from real power (such as the CPRF).

This is not to say that parties like the CPRF, CPBM or CPU will never be able to act as agents promoting democratic consolidation. The fact that they have continually participated in elections, and have generally recognized the legitimacy of democratic competition is a testimony to their potential as actors promoting democratic consolidation. However, two factors will continue to impede their evolution from what are sometimes called *semi-loyal* opposition parties: (1) as long as these parties continue to cling to their pre-transition political identities and organizational practices (that is, Marxism-Leninism and mass party organization) it is unlikely that these parties will be able to resocialize their followers into the acceptance of democracy;[52] (2) this transformation is made even more unlikely with the continued demonization of the communist-successor parties in these states, and their continued exclusion from the centres of political power. Indeed continued exclusion is likely to reinforce anti-democratic sentiment in these parties, and lead to the growing alienation of the social and political groups they represent.

NOTES

1. John Ishiyama, 'Communist Parties in Transition: Structures, Leaders and Processes of Democratization in Eastern Europe', *Comparative Politics*, Vol.27 (1995), pp.146–77; John Ishiyama, 'The Sickle or the Rose? Previous Regime Types and the Evolution of the Ex-Communist Parties in Post-Communist Politics', *Comparative Political Studies*, Vol.30 (1997), pp.258–74; Andras Bozoki 'The Ideology of Modernization and the Policy of Materialism: The Day After for the Socialists', *Journal of Communist Studies and Transition Politics*, Vol.13 (1997), pp.56–102.
2. Herbert Kitschelt, 'Formation of Party Cleavages in Post-communist Democracies: Theoretical Propositions', *Party Politics*, Vol.1 (1995), pp.447–72; Attila Ágh, 'Partial Consolidation of the East-Central European

Parties: The Case of the Hungarian Socialist Party', *Party Politics*, Vol.1 (1995), pp.491–514; Ishiyama, 'The Sickle or the Rose?'; J. Ishiyama, 'Communist Parties in Transition'; Allison Mahr and John Nagle 'Resurrection of the Successor Parties and Democratization in East-Central Europe', *Communist and Post-Communist Studies*, Vol.28 (1995), pp.393–409.

3. Andreas Schedler, 'What is Democratic Consolidation?' *Journal of Democracy*, Vol.9 (1998), p.91.

4. Timothy Power and Mark J. Gasiorowski, 'Institutional Design and Democratic Consolidation in the Third World', *Comparative Political Studies*, Vol.30 (1997), p.131; See, for instance, Guillermo O'Donnell, 'Transitions, Continuities and Paradoxes', in Scott Mainwaring, Guillermo O'Donnell and Samuel Valenzuela (eds.), *Issues in Democratic Consolidation: The New South American Democracies in Comparative Perspective* (Notre Dame, IN: University of Notre Dame Press, 1992); M. Burton, Richard Gunther and J. Higley, 'Introduction: Elite Transformations and Democratic Regimes', in J. Higley and Richard Gunther (eds.), *Elites and Democratic Consolidation in Latin America and Southern Europe* (New York: Cambridge University Press, 1992); Phillipe Schmitter, 'The Consolidation of Democracy and the Representation of Social Groups', *American Behavioral Scientist*, Vol.35 (1992), pp.422–49; Samuel Valenzuela, 'Democratic Consolidation in Post-transitional Settings: Process, and Facilitating Conditions', in Mainwaring, O'Donnell and Valenzuela, op. cit.; Richard P. Gunther, Nikiforos Diamandouros and Hans-Jürgen Puhle, 'Introduction', in R. Gunther, N. Diamandouros and H. Puhle (eds.), *The Politics of Democratic Consolidation: Southern Europe in Comparative Perspective* (Baltimore, MD: Johns Hopkins University Press, 1996), pp.1–32. See also critical reviews by Scott Mainwaring, 'Transitions to Democracy: Theoretical and Comparative Issues', in Mainwaring, O'Donnell and Valenzuela, op. cit.; Philippe Schmitter, 'Transitology: The Science or the Art of Democratization', in J. Tulchin and B. Romero (eds.), *The Consolidation of Democracy in Latin America* (Boulder, CO: Lynne Rienner, 1995); Karen Dawisha, 'Democratization and Political Participation: Research Concepts and Methodologies', in Karen Dawisha and Bruce Parrot (eds.), *Democratic Changes and Authoritarian Reactions in Russia, Ukraine, Belarus and Moldova* (Cambridge: Cambridge University Press, 1997).

5. One notable exception is Schedler who advocates a return to the concept's original concern with democratic survival a restoration of 'its classical meaning which is securing achieved levels of democratic rule against authoritarian regression ... the term 'democratic consolidation' should describe a regime that relevant observers expect to last well into – the future – and nothing else.' Schedler 'What is Democratic Consolidation,' p.103.

6. Bruce Parrott, 'Perspectives on Postcommunist Democratization', in Karen Dawisha and Bruce Parrott (eds.), *Democratic Changes and Authoritarian Reactions in Russia, Ukraine, Belarus and Moldova*, p.6.

7. Adam Przeworski, *Democracy and the Market: Political and Economic Reforms in Europe and Latin America* (Cambridge: Cambridge University Press, 1991), p.26.

8. Valenzuela, 'Democratic Consolidation in Post-transitional Settings'.

9. Laurence Whitehead, 'The Consolidation of Fragile Democracies', in Robert A. Pastor (ed.), *Democracies in the Americas: Stopping the Pendulum* (New York: Holmes & Meier, 1989), p.79.
10. Gunther *et al.*, 'Introduction', p.7.
11. Alfred Stepan and Cynthia Skach, 'Constitutional Frameworks and Democratic Consolidation', *World Politics*, Vol.46 (1993), p.5, fn. 12.
12. See also Schedler, 'What is Democratic Consolidation?'. This measure is less stringent than the two-turnover test proposed by Samuel Huntington, *The Third Wave: Democratization in the Late Twentieth Century* (Norman, OK and London: University of Oklahoma Press, 1991).
13. Power and Gasiorowski, 'Institutional Design and Democratic Consolidation', p.133, fn. 16.
14. Ibid.
15. Gunther *et al.*, 'Introduction', p.13.
16. Geoffrey Evans and Stephen Whitefield, 'The Politics and Economics of Democratic Commitment: Support for Democracy in Transition Societies', *British Journal of Political Science*, Vol.25 (1995), pp.485–514; Dankwart Rustow, 'Transition to Democracy: Toward a Dynamic Model', *Comparative Politics*, Vol.2 (1970), pp.156–244; Pamela Waldron- Moore, 'Eastern Europe at the Crossroads of Democratic Transition: Evaluating Support for Democratic Institutions, Satisfaction with Democratic Government and Consolidation of Democratic Regimes', *Comparative Political Studies*, Vol.32 (1999), pp.32–62.
17. Gunther *et al.*, 'Introduction', p.15.
18. Ian McAllister and Stephen. White, 'Democracy, Political Parties and Party-Formation in Post-communist Russia', *Party Politics* Vol.1 (1995), pp.49–72; Richard Sakwa, 'Parties and the Multiparty System in Russia', *RFE/RL Research Report,* Vol.2, No.28 (1993), pp.7–15; Alexei M. Salmin, I.M. Bubnin, P.I. Kapelyushnikov and M. Yu. Urnov, *Partiinaya sistema v Rossii 1989-1993* (Moscow: Nachala Press, 1994); John Ishiyama, 'Red Phoenix? The Communist Party in Post-Soviet Russian Politics', *Party Politics*, Vol.2 (1996), pp.147–75.
19. Giovanni Sartori, *Parties and Party Systems: A Framework for Analysis* (Cambridge: Cambridge University Press, 1976); Samuel Huntington, *Political Order in Changing Societies* (New Haven, CT: Yale University Press, 1968).
20. David E. Apter, *The Politics of Modernization* (Chicago, IL: University of Chicago Press, 1965), p.188.
21. S.M. Lipset and Stein Rokkan, 'Cleavage Structures, Party Systems and Voter Alignments:An Introduction', in S.M.Lipset and Stein Rokkan (eds.), *Party Systems and Voter Alignments: Cross-National Perspectives* (New York: Free Press, 1967), p.4.
22. Huntington, 'Political Order', p.398; see also Joseph La Palombara and Myron Weiner, *Political Parties and Political Development* (Princeton, NJ: Princeton University Press, 1966), p.3.
23. Richard Sakwa, 'The Development of the Russian Party System: Did the Elections Change Anything?' in Peter Lentini (ed.), *Elections and the Political Order in Russia* (Budapest: Central European Press, 1995); Richard Sakwa, 'The Russian Elections of December 1993', *Europe–Asia Studies*, Vol.47 (1995), pp.195–227.
24. Sakwa, 'The Development of the Russian Party System'.

25. Stephen White, Matthew Wyman and Olga Kryshtanovskaya, 'Parties and Politics in Post-communist Russia', *Communist and Post-Communist* Studies, Vol.25 (1995), pp.199–200.
26. Sakwa, 'The Development of the Russian Party System', p.190.
27. See Maurice Duverger, *Political Parties* (London:Methuen, 1964); Leon Epstein, *Political Parties in Western Democracies* (New York: Praeger, 1967); Angelo Panebianco, *Political Parties: Organization and Power* (Cambridge: Cambridge University Press, 1988).
28. Paul G. Lewis, 'Introduction and Theoretical Overview', in Paul G. Lewis (ed.), *Party Structure and Organization in East Central Europe* (Cheltenham: Edward Elger, 1996), p.3; and see Peter Mair, 'Party Organization: from Civil Society to the State', in Richard S. Katz and Peter Mair (eds.), *How Parties Organize: Change and Adaptation in Party Organizations in Western Democracies* (London: Sage, 1994), and Richard S. Katz and Peter Mair, 'Changing Models of Party Organization and Party Democracy: the Emergence of the Cartel Party', *Party Politics*, Vol.1 (1995), pp.5–28.
29. Parrott, 'Perspectives on Postcommunist Democratization', p.17.
30. Ibid.
31. Ibid.
32. See also Ishiyama, 'Communist Parties in Transition'.
33. Kitschelt, 'Formation of Party Cleavages in Post-communist Democracies', p.449.
34. Ibid.
35. Ibid., p.450.
36. I acknowledge that this hypothesis may, on the surface, be somewhat problematic. The problem lies in the fact that the greater satisfaction with democracy of the party's followers may be due to *two* conceptually distinct factors. First, clearly followers of the successor party are not a static group (that is, the supporters of the party may change over time, especially as the party seeks to expand its appeal to other groups); thus greater satisfaction may be due to the inclusion of different kinds of supporters (and perhaps the exodus of more dogmatic hard-line communists). On the other hand, it may be due the changing attitudes of the original supporters of the party. However I defend the use of the satisfaction measure on two grounds: (1) the focus of the study is on 'loser groups' or pensioners, unemployed and those engaged in industries most injured by the transition (such as heavy industry) over all seven years of the study. In other words I am not examining supporters of the party who have done fairly well in the transition (and whom it is reasonable to assume will be more positively disposed toward the development of democracy). Thus if changes in attitudes occur, it is more likely to have resulted from the changing attitudes of the original 'loser' supporters of the party, rather than the influx of new supporters; (2) Currently, there is no other way in the Central and Eastern Eurobarometer data to discern who were new supporters of the successor party as opposed to original supporters of the party over time. Thus the indirect controls I introduce by focusing only on 'loser' groups is the best possible way to address the potential conceptual heterogeneity of this measure of 'satisfaction with democracy'.
37. Clearly satisfaction with democracy is not the only measure of consolidation (quite

the contrary) but given the level of analysis of this paper (individual/attitudinal) this aspect of consolidation appears to me the most appropriate.

38. Waldron-Moore, 'Eastern Europe at the Crossroads of Democratic Transition', p.53.
39. As Waldron-Moore notes in her justification for the use of this question, since respect for human rights is generally regarded as a fundamental feature of democracies, then a perception of new respect for human rights in formerly authoritarian societies is more than likely an indication of satisfaction with the democratic process. Waldron-Moore, 'Eastern Europe at the Crossroads of Democratic Transition', p.10, fn. 46.
40. Duverger, *Political Parties*; Katz and Mair, 'Changing Models of Party Organization'.
41. Duverger, Political Parties; Epstein, *Political Parties in Western Democracies*; John Ishiyama, 'The Communist Successor Parties and Party Organizational Development in Post-Communist Politics', *Political Research Quarterly*, Vol.52 (1999), pp.87–112.
42. It is important to note that the term 'cadre' party is not used here in the same sense as connoted by Leninist theory. Instead 'cadre' refers to the well-known concept in party organizational theory developed by Maurice Duverger.
43. Petr Kopecky, 'Developing Party Organizations in East-Central Europe: What Type of Party is Likely to Emerge?' *Party Politics*, Vol.1 (1995), pp.515–44.
44. For a discussion of the use of this measure see Ishiyama, 'The Communist Successor Parties and Party Organizational Development'.
45. John Huber and Ronald Inglehart, 'Expert Interpretations of Party Space and Party Location in 42 Societies', *Party Politics*, Vol.1 (1995), pp.73–111.
46. Granted this may still be an imperfect measure of ideological coherence. For instance, it might be the case that with an extremely 'incoherent party' that takes both positions on extreme left and right, judges might conclude that these positions balance one another out and hence the party is scored at the midpoint of four with a standard deviation of zero. Although that possibility must be recognised as a shortcoming (and is a problem which plagues all measures which rely on 'expert coding'), the measure used here represents a convenient substitute for a more rigorous measures of party coherence. One such measure is the degree of coherence in terms of party fraction votes in the Russian State Duma. Until such a measure is developed for all ten cases examined here, the data measure supplied by Huber and Inglehart is the most accessible measure to use at this point.
47. Indeed, even in the most 'Soviet-like' of the post-Soviet republics, Belarus, President Lukashenka has felt compelled to convene a legislature in order to govern.
48. The 1993 file did not list the party for which the respondent intended to vote for all countries.
49. For the 1992 data, a separate response category for state enterprise employee did not appear. However the categories 'skilled worker' and 'unskilled worker' appeared in the 1992 data which did not appear in the 1994–97 data. Thus for the 1992 data respondents who claimed to be skilled workers and unskilled workers were used along with pensioners and the unemployed.
50. Operationally this meant that the respondent completed the statement

'Compared to 12 months ago, do you think the financial situation of your household has ...' with either 'stayed the same' 'got a little worse' or 'got a lot worse'.

51. The following parties were thus identified as part of the sample: SPA (Socialist Party of Albania); BSP (Bulgarian Socialist Party); CPBM (Communist Party of Bohemia and Moravia); EDLP (Estonian Democratic Labor Party); HSP (Hungarian Socialist Party); LDLP (Lithuanian Democratic Labor Party); Social Democratic Union of Macedonia; SdRP (Social Democracy of the Republic of Poland); PSDR (Party of Social Democracy of Romania); CPRF (Communist Party of the Russian Federation); PDL (Party of the Democratic Left); PDR (Party of Democratic Reform); CPU (Communist Party of the Ukraine).

52. However, there is some evidence that these parties have already begun to move away from the mass party model – particularly the CPRF. See John Ishiyama, 'Red versus Expert: Candidate Recruitment and Communist Party Adaptation in Post Soviet Politics', *Party Politics*, Vol.4 (1998), pp.297–318.

4

Party System Institutionalization in New Democracies: Poland – A Trend-Setter with no Followers

RADOSLAW MARKOWSKI

Introduction

The paper consists of several broad sections. The first focuses on different aspects and indicators of party system institutionalization and dwells on its manifestations in Poland. In the second section issues of democratic consolidation are discussed together with its crucial sub-indicator – the diffuse political support phenomenon. By disentangling this notion, tracing its unblurred, clear manifestations in Poland we expect to shed light on the extent to which democratic consolidation has been achieved. The third section looks into the 'shape' of the party system – its polarization, issue structuring and the space of competition it delineates, as well as the meaning and salience of left–right semantics. Finally, in the concluding part I try to interpret the overall relationship between the phenomena discussed and its outcome.

The subtitle of the chapter is partly borrowed from a conference paper written by Paul Lewis.[1] Hardly anybody would disagree with the general assessment of Poland's pioneering role in the region or, equally, with the claim that the 'Polish status as a trend-setter of democratisation in the communist world did not make its own path any easier'.[2] The data presented in this chapter aim to show that the Polish route both to a market economy and consolidated democracy reveals idiosyncrasies considerably different from theoretical expectations and the experience of other countries of the region as regards the sequence and relation between the phenomena believed to be associated with party system institutionalization. The design of the chapter is comparative; testing certain hypotheses demands both diachronic and synchronic approaches. Comparisons are thus made both in time (for Poland 1991–97) and in space (mainly within the ECE region).

The Polish Party System – Institutionalization or Fragility?

Party System Institutionalization – its Manifestations and Indicators

Party development and associated processes of party system institutionalization are topics recently dealt with by many scholars.[3] As a starting point in conceptualizing party system institutionalization Mainwaring and Scully's proposal serves us well. They put forward four indicators as constitutive elements of an institutionalized party system: (i) stability in inter-party competition; (ii) the existence of parties with stable roots in society; (iii) the acceptance of those parties and of elections as the legitimate means by which the public determines who governs; (iv) the existence of party organizations with stable rules and structures. Finally, an important remark is made that 'institutionalizing a party system is important to the process of democratic consolidation'.[4] We shall often return to this point in the remainder of the paper.

There are other approaches to the analysis of party system institutionalization. Morlino prefers to talk of 'party system structuring' or of 'party system stabilization'.[5] He enumerates several broad indicators – electoral volatility, frequency of critical elections and stabilization of the political class, especially at the outset of democratization. This general proposal is divided into several detailed indicators: the fragmentation of the system, the effective number of parties, as well as measures of disproportionality. Levels of party identification and elite continuity are also believed to be crucial. Morlino includes – like Mainwaring and Scully – the institutionalization of particular parties as an indicator of party system institutionalization.

I definitely disagree with the latter proposal. In brief, I find unconvincing the claim of a direct link between the institutionalization of parties and that of the party system. The relationship between the two is far from being that simple and deterministic. In some instances the institutionalization of parties, their organizational stability and continuity might prove conducive to party system institutionalization but in other instances this does not necessarily occur, particularly in the case of young democracies. Here the needed flexibility and adaptability to a rapidly changing social context might prove more conducive to ultimate party system institutionalization and democratic consolidation than stable organizational structure. To conclude: when analyzing the institutionalization of a party system, one has to avoid relying on static parameters of the subsystem (i.e. parties) and should concentrate on the functions their outputs fulfil for the system as a whole. This proposal should not be treated as springing from pure functionalist dogma, it is aimed rather at securing heuristic and empirical utility.

There are many other ontological and theoretical problems connected with the operationalization of the institutionalization phenomenon. First, confusion stems from the entanglement of two analytically different phenomena: an institutionalized (static) and institutionalizing (dynamic) party system. The latter is a process of acquiring the quality of stability, and ought not be confused with the notion of *party system change*, which denotes a departure from a previous state of prolonged institutionalization.[6] Secondly, among the factors believed to be reliable indicators of institutionalization, categorically different ones seem to be intermixed – some are clear determinants, others are conducive correlates, yet others might be considered outcomes of institutionalization. Thirdly, the above mentioned problem of equating the phenomenon of party institutionalization with party system institutionalization calls for in-depth scrutiny. The crucial question here is which comes first and, if the starting point is lack of institutionalization of both: parties and party system, is it reasonable to expect that the institutionalization of one of the two can exist without the other? And if so, which one? I have discussed these issues in some detail elsewhere, so will not pursue them here.[7]

Voter Volatility in Poland

To begin with, several caveats. First, I find it plausible to distinguish between *general* aggregate volatility (which disregards parties going out of and into political business), and *citizens'* volatility (that is, volatility which accounts for the changing 'party system offer': mergers, dissolutions, etc.). Secondly, party mergers force us to consider some of them as direct continuities of previous political entities. On this basis the aggregate *general* volatility between 1991 and 1993 in Poland amounted to 34.9 per cent, the *citizens'* – 22.7 per cent. These figures were obtained under the following assumptions: (a) among 'other parties' contesting only one of the two elections are: ChD, BBWR, KdR, Samoobrona and numerous irrelevant, marginal parties; (b) WAK of '91 is treated as the political equivalent of KKW 'Ojczyzna' of '93, as is 'Solidarność Pracy' for UP.

Students of Polish volatility are faced with more acute problems when it comes to comparing 1993 and 1997 voting patterns, primarily because of the new political entity – AWS (Solidarity Election Action), which turned out to be the clear winner of the latter election with 33.8 per cent support. If we treat AWS as a direct heir of several rightist parties (the following parties of 1993 comprised the 1997 AWS: KKW 'Ojczyzna' — namely, ZChN, NSZZ 'S', PC, PK, SLCh and PL as well as the major parts of KPN and BBWR, plus some minor 'sofa' parties), the *general* aggregate volatility for the 1993/97 period goes down to 19.3 per cent and *citizens'* – to 15.2 per cent.[8] Other assumptions are that: (a) ROP is the political equivalent of KdR, (b)

UW — of UD and KLD, (c) among the most important 'other' parties are: KPEiR, BdB, KPEiR RP and a few marginal groupings.

In newly democratizing polities undergoing multi-dimensional change, such as those emerging from communism, there is good reason to look at the process of voter volatility through *party family* lenses. In order to avoid broad, artificial aggregations that would obscure rather than clarify the party system development, in the following calculations as many as ten party families are taken into account. The ten *families* are: (1) socialist, (2) social-democratic, (3) conservative, (4) Christian-Democratic, (5) nationalist, (6) religious, (7) ethnic, (8) liberal, (9) agrarian, (10) radical-populist. The rationale behind analysing all these – differently aggregated – data is manifold. First, at the beginning of the transformation, for the majority the numerous parties were hardly distinguishable. Second, small 'sofa' parties never (with few exceptions) contested an election alone and invariably formed part of a coalition.

In Table 1 below I present some of the important indicators of volatility:

(a) Total Volatility (TV), with a distinction being made between (i) the general and (ii) citizens' volatility;

(b) 'between-party family' Total Volatility (FTV), with the above distinction (i) and (ii);

(c) block volatility (BV);

(d) within-block volatility (WBV).

Two important points should be recognized: first, in the first two rows the TV and FTV account for the empirical reality of 1997 – namely the appearance of AWS and their ancestors; second, the computations of BV and WBV – presented in rows 3) and 4) – are thus based on 'party family' grouping (the left column of each row), as well as particular parties (right column).

If – as I am inclined to do – one follows tendencies in real politics and regards AWS as a direct follower of the parties that constituted it, then almost all (save WBV) volatility parameters have improved dramatically since 1991/3. The only increase in WBV, equaling 6.72 for 1993/97, is due to a reshuffle within the 'leftist' block.

In terms of implications for the *process* of party system institutionalization, we have to speculate a little as we lack any theoretical guidance as to which of the two main components of total volatility – BV or WBV – is more significant. Above all, I disagree with the expectation that newly emerging post-communist democracies can reasonably be expected to show signs of stability immediately after the *installation* phase. The point is that in order to arrive at both consolidated democracy and a viable market, during the initial phase of transformation considerable flexibility is needed.

TABLE 1
AGGREGATE VOTERS VOLATILITY IN POLAND 1991–97

		91/93		93/97	
TV	(general)	34.9		22.1	
	(citizens)	22.7		15.0	
FTV	(general)	18.52		12.49	
	(citizens)	16.01		12.16	
BV		FBV	PBV	FBV	PBV
		13.54	19.7	3.79	8.91
WBV		VWBV	PWBV	FWBV	PWBV
		0.93	9.59	6.72	2.87

The following acronyms stand for:
TV   – total volatility
FTV   – 'family' total volatility
BV   – block volatility
WBV   – within-block volatility
FBV   – 'family' block volatility
FWBV – 'family' within-block volatility
PBV   – party block volatility
PWBV – party within-block volatility

Notes: (1) The volatility figures are calculated following Pedersens (1979)* formula – that is half the sum of the absolute value of differences between the vote shares of each party in two consecutive elections. The data are thus aggregate, net volatility.

(2) In new democracies, where not only individual preferences fluctuate, but where parties often merge, dissolute and split, it is worth distinguishing between volatility that stems from both factors. In table 1, the overall volatility, labelled 'general', accounts for both sources of volatility. The one labelled 'personal-choice' volatility excludes the volatility that is determined by party system offer changes (some parties merging, other going out of business etc.); the latter one may call 'structural' volatility.

(3) In case of 'family' grouping the following party groups were distinguished: [1] socialist (UP, RDS, WUS, "S '80" in 1991; UP in 1993; UP and KPEiR in 1997); [2] social-democratic (SLD at all elections, plus SD in 1991); [3] conservative (UPR at all elections, plus BdP in 1997); [4] Christian-democratic (PC, NSZZ "S", ChD, PChD in 1991; PC, NSZZ "S", BBWR in 1993; AWS in 1997); [5] nationalist (KPN in 1991 and 1993; KdR in 1993 and ROP in 1997); [6] religious (ZChN in 1991 and 1993; none in 1997); [7] ethnic (German Minority - MN in 1991 through 1997, plus Belorussian Minority - MB in 1991 and 1993; [8] liberal (KLD, UD, PPPP in 1991 and 1993; UW in 1997); [9] agrarian (PSL at all elections; PL in 1991 and 1993 and SChL in 1991); [10] radical populist ("X" in 1991 and 1993; PWN-PSN at all elections; and "Samoobrona" in 1993 and 1997).

(4) Three 'blocks' have been distinguished: [A] LEFT ([1]+[2]+PSL from [9]); [B] RIGHT ([3]+[4]+[5]+[6] + PL from [9]) and [C] LIBERAL [8]

*Pedersen, M., 'The Dynamics of European Party Systems: Changing Patterns of   Electoral Volatility', *European Journal of Political Research*, vol. 7, no. 1, (1979).

This permits adaptive changes in the party system aimed at assuring a state of *equilibrium-seeking stability* for the whole socio-politico-economic system. One cannot have a 'frozen' party system while an enormous change in the social-structural sub-system takes place. If we agree with the above reasoning, the issue may be reworded thus – how long should this adjustment process of 'fruitful fluidity' between elites and masses, party system and society be treated as normal and conducive to the ultimate stability of the system? This question, if correct *per se*, can be answered only empirically, since the democratizations out of communism are new phenomena.

Bearing in mind the idiosyncrasies of transforming societies, and regarding the static (institutionalized party system) and the dynamic (institutionalizing party system) conditions as different phenomena, I submit that the patterned temporal sequencing indicative of party system institutionalization should appear as follows:

(a) after the initial phase of high volatility, as people become capable of choosing relevant political options, a decreasing tendency is expected;

(b) among the two major components of total volatility (TV), a temporary initial decline in 'block-volatility' (BV) should occur. What crystallizes first is a broad ideological orientation of individuals, say their personal preference for liberal, left or right packages perceived as appropriate to their (new) social position. This process takes a while, until individuals come to identify clear long-term interests derived from their labour-market position;

(c) Only then, after the longer time-span necessary for a deeper appreciation of individual interest and the influence of cultural factors (socialization, inherited political preferences), can a distinct identification, first with a party family and then with particular party, be reasonably expected.

Let us look again at Table 1 on this basis. As predicted, total voter volatility (TV) declined. So did volatility calculated via the 'party family' approach, as does block volatility (BV). In brief, the Polish party system between the early 1990s and 1997 did change in the direction of stability and institutionalization. This came about because in 1997 the average Polish voter was able to identify more clearly his or her interests with a particular ideological orientation. However institutionalization has not yet reached the level of clear party identification, as both 'within-block volatility' figures indicate an increase. Since we are inclined to interpret this result as indicative of the weak institutionalization of the last phase, the details of the vote flow should be borne in mind – the leftist block (SLD/PSL) retained almost the same support in 1997 as in 1993, although there was a dramatic shift in support for each of the two former coalition partners taken individually. The obvious paradox is that the shift, indicative of volatility and consequently of weak party system institutionalization occurred precisely because voters decided to abandon the non-democratic, irresponsible and destabilizing populist policies of the PSL. This seeming contradiction proves that the relationship between party system institutionalization and democratic consolidation is much more complex and indirect than some tend to believe.[9]

It is finally worth looking at Polish volatility from a global perspective. The mean Western European volatility has been calculated as 8.4 per cent for 1960–89, but if one concentrates on the more comparable figures for the new southern European democracies in their first ten years or so, these emerge as: 18.4 per cent for Greece 1974-85, and13.6 per cent for Spain 1977–87.[10] Lack of qualitative differences between Polish and some fragile Latin American democracies in the 1970s and 1980s are also visible; apart from stable Uruguay and Colombian figures (around nine per cent), Argentina, Chile, Venezuela and Costa Rica display levels of volatility similar to Poland – between 12.7 and 18.2 per cent, not to mention the astronomic figures for Peru, Brazil, Bolivia or Ecuador of 54.4, 40.9, 33.0 and 32.5 per cent, respectively.[11] Voter volatility figures for the neighbouring countries of East-Central Europe – Hungary, the Czech Republic and Slovakia are: 28.3, 25.8 and 23.5 per cent after the first round of elections and 33.6, 31.4, and 23.8 per cent, respectively, between the second and third elections. In the last Czech pair of elections 1996–98 volatility declined to about 19 per cent, although there was half the time between them and all other cases apart from Poland 1991–93.

Fragmentation and Deviation From Proportionality

All newly-established democratic party systems face a difficult institutional choice: the decision concerning electoral rules, and in consequence an option either for a more representative or a more accountable system. In reality they need not be treated as mutually exclusive alternatives, although hardly anybody would question the different merits of PR and plurality. Two categorically different factors – (a) high initial uncertainty and (b) huge, well-organized and mobilized masses – forced Polish constitutional engineers to opt for almost pure proportionality in the 1991 election. Very soon democratic political practice demanded changes in the rules of the game as there were several, all unsuccessful, attempts at creating stable governmental coalitions between 1991 and 1993. This was a demanding task given that – in practice – at least seven parties were needed for a government majority. Rae's index of fractionalization calculated for the Polish elections of 1991, 1993 and 1997 produces outcomes of (0.92), (0.90) and (0.78), respectively.[12]

The important message these figures suggest is that the new electoral rules of 1993, which introduced a standard threshold, did not work automatically. Numerous small parties, mainly of a rightist, religious-national or Christian-Democratic orientation and hardly renowned for their rationality, disregarded the unanimous message of public opinion surveys that their levels of support were so low that they had to consider crafting coalition pacts and decided to contest the election alone. The result was that almost 35 per cent of the vote was wasted. The index of deviation from proportionality jumped from 12.0 per cent in 1991 to an astronomical 37.3 per cent in 1993.[13] Nevertheless, the lesson of 1993 was digested accurately by both elites and masses. The numerous rightist parties contested the 1997 election under the umbrella logo of 'Solidarity'; the result – the Index went down to 18.5 per cent. Still high, but close to what a multiparty system with three important dimensions of competition can realistically arrive at.

Other indicators of party system fragmentation point to the same process: (a) the percentage of votes cast for parties obtaining less than five per cent support fluctuated in the three consecutive elections but tended to reduce, and totalled 23 per cent, 29 per cent and 13 per cent; (b) the number of 'effective parties' also went down rapidly to 4.6 per cent from 10.0 per cent in 1993 and 12.5 per cent in 1991. The 1997 figure for Polish 'party effectiveness' was – along with the Hungarian – the lowest in the ECE region. The Polish party system thus started off with rather unpromising legacies of transformation as far as institutionalization is concerned, as well as an unconducive institutional infrastructure, but amendments aimed at optimizing the party system's chances for crystallization and institutionalization were successfully implemented and largely achieved their intended effect.

Party Identification and Elite Continuity

In January 1991 only 17 per cent of Poles were able to name a party they could identify with.[14] It should be recalled that in January 1991 free parliamentary elections still lay ahead of the Poles, that there existed barely three real parties, and that the post-revolutionary public mood was strongly anti-partisan. After the 'wasted vote' of 1993 and the experience of gross disproportionality, parties became the major actors of Polish politics. Consequently, the party identification figures for December 1995 and October 1997 jumped to 43.5 per cent and 64.3 per cent respectively.

Elite continuity, conceived as the re-election ratio of 'incumbent' MP's, looks promising at first glance. The paradox is that the more frequently elections are called, the more likely one finds personal continuity for simple life-cycle reasons: what supposedly is expected to be an indicator of a stable institutionalized party system is dependent upon its structural instability. The two first terms of the Polish Parliament, one of which had not been elected under fully democratic laws, lasted two years each and only the third (1993–97) lasted a full term. The percentage of MPs who were first-comers to the parliament amounted to 91.7, 72.8 and 63.0 respectively for the 1989–91, 1991–93 and 1993-97 terms. If one believes these particular indicators to reflect the process, a clear trend towards of party system institutionalization is in place in Poland.

Social Roots of Party Affiliation

The conceivable ways of addressing questions of the social roots of party support are numerous, none of them uncontested. The topic deserves an in-depth longitudinal or panel-designed study of the transformations of social structure linked to changing political context, something we cannot offer here; for this reason the following presentation is a deliberately simple one. The issue addressed here is whether it is true, as many scholars tend to believe, that there is a very weak association of social class or/and social position with party preferences. It is hard to disagree with Mainwaring and Scully that normally (that is, in socially stable systems) it is plausible to expect clear and logical links (based on rational calculation) between party preference and social structure. Doubts as to the nature of this relationship in societies undergoing radical social change have already been expressed. In order to make the comparison more reliable huge social aggregates like classes have been disaggregated into several single-parametric groups based on social background traits. In some instances parameters denote groups which might in fact be considered a class (for example, farmers, workers), most of them however do not.

The data permit the following conclusions to be drawn:

a) No indication of stronger links between the social position of an individual and party preferences are found among stable Western polities as compared to ECE countries – in fact the opposite is generally true.

b) Among Western democracies only Germany and Britain's famous class cleavage comes close to the strength of association comparable to that in Polish during 1991.

c) Other class-related parameters indicate that Poland reveals strong rural/urban and also farmer/non-farmer divisions. Yet Poland is clearly exceptional in that all factors – whether ascribed, achieved or class – seem to be strongly associated with party preferences.

d) Change over time in Poland, however, shows the strength of the

TABLE 2

STRENGTH OF ASSOCIATION BETWEEN PARTY PREFERENCE AND SELECTED
SOCIAL BACKGROUND VARIABLES

Country	Residence	Education	Age	Church Attendance	White collar	Worker	Farmer
Poland 91	.07	.06	.02	.03	.04	.01	.04
Poland 93	.06	.06	.02	.03	.02	.02	.94
Poland 97	.04	.03	.01	.06	.01	.01	.04
Czech R.	.02	.02	.03	.o6	.01	.01	.02
Slovakia	.02	.03	.03	.08	.01	.01	.01
Hungary	.02	.03	.07	.05	.01	.00	.01
USA	.02	.02	.01	.01	.01	.01	.00
G. Britain	na	.02	.01	.02	.04	.04	na
Germany	.02.	.03	.02	.05	.00	.01	na
Italy	.02	.03	.02	.05	.00	.01	na

Explanation: (1) Table entries are 'uncertainty coefficients'.

(2 The 'na' data are due either to too small a sample or to coding problems which nullify the data.

(3) Data for Poland 93 and other East Central European countries are from longitudinal comparative project *The Development of Party Formation and Electoral Alignments in East Central Europe*, initiated and financed by Central European University. Data for Poland '97 – from the first edition of the Polish National Election Survey [PGSW].

(4) Data for Poland 91 and other East Central European countries come from comparative project entitled *Political Consequences of Dismantling Social Safety Net in East Central Europe* initiated and financed by Institute for East-West Security Studies (New York—Praha). The remaining data are from ISSP series on the *The Role of Government*. Distributor: Zentralarchive, Köln; adapted from Toka (1997).

association between the socio-demographic background variables and party preferences to be declining with just one exception – that of religion. This result fits very well with and confirms other data presented in this chapter, especially in the sections on polarization and dimensions of competition, which indeed indicates that in the Polish 1997 parliamentary election the politicization of the religious divide by elites had an extremely polarizing effect. Why should the effect of the religious factor continue to be so strong? One hypothesis grounded in empirical evidence is that the salience of the religious dimension derives from the ongoing blurring effects of the reshaping of the social structure. It is the least costly vehicle of direct communication between elites and masses, in a context of complex social repositioning and the inability of substantial portions of the populace to correctly identify the relevant representatives of their socio-economic interests. Religious labels simplify the world, even though religious issues have become less important for the Polish public.

To conclude: stabilization of the social roots of party support is unlikely so long as major changes in social structure are under way. The message for those currently disseminating misleading news about blurred socio-political relationships in east-central European polities is clear: such speculations have no empirical basis.

Changes in Satisfaction with Democracy and Diffuse Political Support

There is hardly any disagreement as to the importance of institutional factors for democratic consolidation. Yet as long as the majority of the public refrains from supporting whichever democratic design is installed, democracy still remains fragile. This concerns legitimacy, i.e. the belief that in spite of certain shortcomings the existing political system is better than any other that might conceivably be established. The literature is full of distinctions between the different objects of legitimacy: government, parties, parliament. The main distinction that is drawn concerns *'particular'* and *'diffuse'* political support, the latter being more persistent and of greater significance for overall system stability. The main question in the current context concerns how best to conceive satisfaction with democracy as a plausible indicator of democratic consolidation. It seems reasonable to assume that the higher the level of support, the more likely it is that democratic consolidation is under way. I submit here, however, that this is not enough to sustain the claim that democracy is consolidating. One needs to prove that diffuse political support emerges as an autonomous phenomenon, relatively independent from economic trends and particular political configurations.

This has been operationalized in the following way: the indicator of diffuse political support is the Eurobarometer's question about 'satisfaction with democracy'. The operational version of the idea I suggest has to do with sequencing and the development of a patterned relationship. In a nutshell, diffuse political support is in place if the following complex relationship develops: satisfaction with democracy becomes more positively correlated with: (a) political efficacy and (b) electoral participation, and either unrelated or more negatively related with both (c) the fortune of the economy and (d) support for winning or losing parties. To test the above hypothetical, complex relationship a dynamic comparison in time is needed. In this instance I assume that in a consolidated democracy the higher the satisfaction with democracy the less there is a direct impact from (c) economic factors and (d) political ones. In other words, diffuse political support is expected to be a phenomenon that is more autonomous and independent – from short-term economic and party configuration factors – in a consolidated setting than in a fluid one.

According to many public opinion surveys in the early 1990s satisfied Poles accounted for no more than 20–22 per cent of the adult population, while their number doubled between 1993 and 1996 to about 40+ per cent and finally reached 54 per cent in the aftermath of the 1997 parliamentary election. This almost trebled the number of those satisfied with democracy and permitted many to claim that democratic consolidation was in place. Problems of interpretation arose from the fact that in Poland this trend was accompanied by economic recovery and its socio-political consequences, booming consumer optimism, increasing household wealth and equivalent attitude changes. 1992 was the first year of positive change in GDP (up by almost three per cent), growing in subsequent years on average by five to six per cent, resulting in a cumulative growth by 1997 of about 130 per cent (if 1990 = 100). This was definitely the highest of all post-communist countries.

TABLE 3
PERCENTAGE MAGNITUDE OF APPROVAL OF SELECTED STATEMENTS

	SATDEM	SATGOV	A	J	B	L	K
92	19	72	70	92	91	90	18
93	22	58	74	91	93	91	15
94	24	40	73	92	91	91	19
95	35	57	82	90	85	81	26
97	54		73	83	80	77	32

SATDEM	– EUROBAROMETER question on 'satisfaction with democracy'
SATGOV	– satisfaction with incumbents
A	– 'In election in Poland voters have a real choice'
B	– 'Generally speaking, those we elect to Parliament lose touch with the people pretty quickly'
J	– 'People like me have no say in what government does'
K	– 'The way things are in Poland people like me and my family have a good chance of getting ahead in life'
L	– 'Parties are only interested in people's votes, not their opinions'

The New Democracies Barometer shows that the trend was accompanied by an increase both in disapproval rates of the communist regime (between 1991 and 1995, by nine per cent) and approval of the new political regime by 24 per cent. In both instances, this was the biggest change among the ten countries under scrutiny.[15] In Table 3 simple approval rates of selected attitudes from the CEU longitudinal series for Poland are shown. The almost trebling of 'satisfaction with democracy' responses is accompanied by decreasing 'particular' support in terms of satisfaction with incumbent governments. Poles revealed growing acceptance of democratic procedures whilst remaining critical of the government. Indicators of 'political efficacy' (A, B, J and L) and their change over time in terms of satisfaction with democracy show them to be the result of general diffuse political support rather than its cause. Subjective evaluation of the 'chances of getting ahead' improved some time after heightened satisfaction with democracy, and at a slower pace. This simple juxtaposition of the correlates of political support, as well as that of related phenomena, seems to hint at its autonomous status.

To substantiate this conclusion it is necessary to resort to the individual level and embark on a multivariate analysis which traces the direct effects of particular factors. The result of these efforts is presented in Tables 4A and 4A. Entries in part 'a' of the table show simple bivariate correlations between satisfaction with democracy and four other indices. The results confirm that, in comparison with 1993, Poland in 1997 was a polity in which indices of efficacy and participation had a significant impact on diffuse political support. And, clearly, the second part of the hypothesis is also confirmed: the link between individual economic success and satisfaction with democracy has become weaker, with similar tendencies occurring in the case of membership of the politically winning or losing party camp (the correlation of 0.04 is statistically insignificant).

TABLE 4A

CORRELATION BETWEEN SATISFACTION WITH THE FUNCTIONING OF
DEMOCRACY AND SELECTED VARIABLES

	POLEFF	WINLOS	PARTWINL	VOTER
SATDEM 93	0.19	0.38	-0.13	-0.04
SATDEM 97	0.23	0.33	0.04	-0.12

TABLE 4B

DETERMINANTS OF SATISFACTION WITH DEMOCRACY (REGRESSION ANALYSIS)

		Model 1	Model 2
1993	Exp. Variance:	16 %	4 %
		PARTWIN 0.09 (0.13)	POLEFF 0.20 (0.20)
		WINLOS 0.38 (0.39)	VOTER 0.04 (0.04)
1997	Exp. Variance:	11%	6%
		PARTWIN 0.03 (0.04)	POLEFF 0.21 (0.23)
		WINLOS0.33 (0.33)	VOTER 0.08 (0.12)

POLEFF   – political efficacy index (composite index of items A and J from table 3)
WINLOS   – index of winners / losers of the transformation (composite index based on six
                      variables indicative of both static status and its' dynamic change of an individual and
                      his/her prospects for the future)
PARTWIN – respondents party vote (1 = for winning parties; 0 = for losing parties)
VOTER   – participation in the last election (1 = participation; 0 = abstention)

Let us turn now to the direct net effects and explanatory power of independent variables on indicators of satisfaction with democracy. The empirical message is transparent and in line with the aggregated data analysis: as time passes democracy in Poland consolidates because diffuse political support is becoming less dependent on economic and political factors (model 1) and slightly more determined by participation and political efficacy (model 2). In short, diffuse political support, believed to be a strong component of democratic consolidation, has been demonstrated from four angles: (i) overall satisfaction with democracy has tripled; (ii) simple distributions of phenomena associated with it have changed in the same direction, although the pace has been slower; (iii) other factors believed by many to be troublesome correlates which blur 'pure' diffuse political support seem to be unrelated to the dynamics of satisfaction with democracy; (iv) both simple bivariate correlations and multi-variate regressions paint the same picture, that individual-level analysis confirms the proposed hypothesis – that in 1997 diffuse political support was less dependent on factors of economic and political well-being.

Party System Shape: Ideology, Polarization and Dimensions of Competition

Theoretical justification for focusing on party system shape, its constitutive dimensions and polarization, may be found in a 30-year-old observation of Samuel Huntington: while moderate fragmentation and cross-cutting cleavages seem to be conducive to democratic stability, in the initial phase of political system formation polarization might be a more desirable phenomenon as it helps establish a programmatically-based relationship between parties and masses.[16] This is due to it providing an unsophisticated electorate with a more clearly defined image of the policy goals pursued by parties and thus contributing to the belief that democratic rules matter for policy outcomes, a perception which ultimately stimulates participation.

Party system 'shapes' are described in many ways, and recently I have gone into this problematic elsewhere.[17] From a comparative east-central European perspective the Polish party system showed a ideological space defined by two major policy dimensions – the economic 'left–right' and a socio-cultural 'religious-secular' divide. A few terminological distinctions are due at this point. I distinguish between *ideological dimensions*, which are important bases for identifying party positions, and construct an issue-universe of the general public's perception of political reality in the form of coherent policy clusters – irrespective of whether politicians find them relevant to compete on or not. In depicting the party system's shape, ideological dimensions alone do not suffice. They exist independently of the elite's creative skills and active voter responses, which limit our analytic capacity since politics also ought to allow for the latter interaction. One thus needs a *'dimensions of competition'* concept and some idea of polarization semantics, which are created in the same issue universe but are differently constructed. First, they result from interactive games between elites and masses (in this presentation derived from *active voters'* perceptions of the issues/policies, not the whole population as in the case of 'ideological dimensions'). Secondly, the particular clustered issue composition of each dimension of competition is obtained by maximizing the differences between electorates.

The concept of *polarization* has also been conceived in various ways and takes into account factors like the number of parties in the polity, the respective share of votes obtained by particular parties, and their position on the left-right meta-dimension (as a difference between particular party positions compared to the mean left-right position of the whole system). In this chapter, I submit another proposal and ways of calculating the polarization index. It deviates from the above in three crucial respects: first, the clarity of party positions, technically measured by their standard deviation, is an important factor contributing to the overall polarization. One cannot seriously talk of polarization when party positions are blurred, that is, voters of the same party support clearly different policy stances. Substantial overlap by two or more parties of the same political space contributes to lower polarization than when overlap is absent or marginal. A second innovation is designed to allow for the magnitude of the party's support. It is obvious that parties are not equal entities and bigger ones, if located at the two polar end of a continuum, contribute to polarization much more than two small parties. The third amendment has to do with the very definition of the dimensions. Allowing for polarization on the left–right meta-dimension, I focus mainly on empirically created dimensions of competition as defined by the public. These are the religious–secular (RS) dimension and and the dimension of economic populism–economic liberalism (EC).

This leads us to another aspect of the discussed topic, namely that democratic consolidation is dependent on the ideological dimension according to which polarization takes place. It seems obvious that 'indivisible (non-distributive) goods' – first of all ethnic identities, but religious values as well – if politically polarized might impede democratic consolidation more considerably than comparable polarization concerning economic policies. The Polish system reveals two, sometimes three, clear ideological dimensions, none of them however is based on ethno-cultural divisions. On this basis a set of hypotheses is being tested which concern the relationship between democratic consolidation, party system institutionalization in terms of crystallization, and ideological as well as competitive dimensions.

In these terms, first, it is plausible to expect that as institutionalization develops the 'left–right' dimension semantics: (1.1) will be better explained by the content of empirically revealed ideological dimensions; (1.2) will become more strongly linked to the economic dimension (i.e. that the direct, net effect of economic issues increases with time). Secondly, if institutionalization succeeds (2.2) increases in polarization – as a means of clarifying party positions – should contribute to adjustments in the mutual positioning of elites and masses. Thirdly, in a two-dimensional political space (3.1) party system institutionalization increases if the two dimensions become less interdependent. Table 5 provides data that test some of these suppositions.

TABLE 5

POLISH PARTY SYSTEM: POLARIZATION, 'STRETCH', DIMENSIONS AND SALIENCE

Years	Polarization index	Universe/ ideological stretch	Competitive stretch	Ideological salience	Competitive salience
92	RS. 30	1.62	2.23	17.4	34.9
	EC. 31	.66	1.65	11.4	24.3
	LR. 36				
93	RS. 38	1.27	1.71	12.2	35.9
	EC. 38	1.43	2.07	25.4	23.8
	LR. 51				
95	RS. 44	1.70	2.31	16.8	50.6
	EC. 52	.80	1.93	11.1	18.5
	LR. 69				
97	RS. 62	1.54	1.57	17.7	54.3
	EC.41	1.17	2.23	8.4	24.8
	LR .91				

Note: In Table 5 (as well as 6 and 7) two (in Table 7 – three) political dimensions of competition appear as a result of factor analysis of many substantive-attitudinal items:

1 – RS – RELIGIOUS – SECULAR DIMENSION is composed (usually) of three major items: respondents' attitudes towards the role of the Church in public life, abortion law and religious criteria in public office recruitment.
2 – EC – ECONOMIC PROTECTIONISM vs. MARKET LIBERAL DIMENSION is composed usually of four items: attitudes towards privatisation, protectionist industrial policies, the role of the state in securing employment, the role of the government in reducing inequalities.
CN – COSMOPOLITAN-LIBERAL vs. NATIONALIST-AUTHORITARIAN DIMENSION is composed of items that directly depict nationalist attitudes (question whether nationalism is harmful to the development of a country), preferring patriots rather than experts among politicians and preference assigned to fighting crime and preserving morals rather than individual freedom and human rights issues.
L-R – LEFT–RIGHT (self-identification)

Before commenting on the validity of the above hypotheses note that:

(1) The polarization of the Polish party system increases on both salient dimensions, including the religious-secular (RS). Polarization on the 'left-right' ideological proxy is the highest and fastest (almost trebling).

(2) Analysis of the stretch of the system – the distance between any two parties located at polar positions – delivers two messages for the two conceptualizations of the political space. The *'ideological stretch'* (column 2) shows the following dynamics: (a) the RS dimension fluctuates though remaining almost constant if one compares the beginning and end of the period, whereas (b) the EC dimension, which fluctuates as well, goes up from .66 to 1.17. The *'competitive stretch'* (column 3) reveals that the RS dimension decreases dramatically from 2.23 to 1.57, whereas EC increases considerably. What is notable, however, is that the parliamentary election years (1993 and 1997) boost stretches of both EC dimensions, simultaneously reducing the stretch of RS dimensions. Generally, however, if one focuses on the one-dimensional simplification (data not shown), the message is: parties in Poland '97 competed within a much more "compressed" political space than before.

(3) The overall salience of these political dimensions (columns 4 and 5) indicates that the RS 'ideological' dimension remains almost the same throughout the years covered, whereas its 'competitive' dimension salience increases considerably. In the case of the EC dimension, the former decreases slightly and the latter remains almost constant.

Conclusion: the importance of the RS divide for Poles as a whole seems constant, it is the effective efforts of political elites that create competitiveness and growing religious–secular polarization. The polarizing potential of economic policies, on the other hand, seem to decline slightly, and even though this dimension's stretch grows considerably between 1995 and 1997 (see columns 2 and 3) its polarization decreases. Briefly, it seems that there are two rates of change at which the Polish party system institutionalizes. Thus in economic terms there seems to have been much more of a consensual agreement in 1997 than there was in 1993, when both the stretch of this dimension among the public as a whole was highest as well as its ideological salience. Quite the reverse story unveils on the religious – secular dimension: even though the stretch of this dimension is declining, the major actors of the political game find it desirable to launch antagonist appeals that advance polarization as well as competitive salience to a considerable extent.

TABLE 6
DIRECT EFFECTS ON, AND EXPLAINED VARIANCES OF, LEFT–RIGHT PLACEMENT
BY RELIGIOUS VS. SECULAR AND BY ECONOMIC PROTECTIONISM VS. MARKET
LIBERAL DIMENSIONS

Years:	92	93	95	97
R2	.08	.15	.25	.03
RS %	17.4	12.2	16.8	17.7
RSbeta (corr.)	.23 (.23)	.33 (.33)	.48 (.48)	.13 (.13)
EC %	11.4	25.4	11.1	8.4
ECbeta (corr.)	-.07 (-.08)	-.19 (-.19)	-.12 (-.14)	-.12 (-.12)

Entries are:
R2   – explained variance of the regression model
in row % – explained variance of a given dimension, a result of factor analysis
'beta'   – the magnitude of net, direct effect of the dimension on left-right self-placement

See note to Table 5.

TABLE 7
MEAN VOTERS-ELITE DISTANCES/PROXIMITIES IN TWO POINTS IN TIME ON
THREE IDEOLOGICAL DIMENSIONS AND THE LEFT–RIGHT IDEOLOGICAL PROXY
(FOUR RELEVANT PARTIES)

parties	DIMENSION RS		DIMENSION EC		DIMENSION CN		LR – identification 97/98
	93/94	97/98	93/94	97/98	93/94	97/98	
SLD	0.60	.24	0.20	0.54	0.46	0.04	0.18
PSL	0.12	0.02	0.70	0.37	0.37	0.70	0.01
UW	0.48	0.21	0.36	0.59	0.52	0.14	0.00
AWS	0.15	0.20	0.76	0.21	0.24	0.24	0.24
mean:	0.34	0.17	0.51	0.43	0.40	0.28	0.11

See note to Table 5.

The CN dimension is not discussed in the chapter, but it is included here to show that the
elite–mass proximity grows on all dimensions.

Further data presented in Table 6 permit us to test hypothesis 1.1. First,
the proposed hypothesis (1.1) turns out to be partially correct: with the
passing of the transformational period the explained variance of 'left–right'
identifications by joint economic and socio-cultural ideological dimension
grew considerably, tripling between 1992 and 1995. Then in 1997 a dramatic
decrease in their explanatory power occurred.

Second, the overall salience of these two dimensions is stable. Except for
1993, the religious-secular dimension is higher by about a half or more (see
Table 5). But the magnitude of the direct effects (standarized 'beta'
coefficients) and their relative weight differ considerably over time. The
religious–secular issue domain explains almost all of the variance in 'left–

right' self-identities in 1992 and 1995, although in the parliamentary election years both issue domains contribute to the left–right more considerably and in 1997 almost equally, though quite weakly. Thus the economic dimension becomes relatively more important (hypothesis 1.2).

Third, there is almost no overlap between the socio-cultural and economic dimensions (hypothesis 3.1) – at all points in time the standarized coefficients ('betas') are identical (save two minor exceptions) with bi-variate correlations. In other words, these two policy domains are autonomous and independent

The overall interpretation of these results from the party system institutionalization perspective is complicated because of developments in 1997. On the one hand in 1997 the direct effect of the two dimensions is for the first time equal, which encourages us to speak of a relatively decreasing influence of the socio-cultural factors in favor of economic ones as carriers of party competition. On the other hand, however, the impact of both on the 'left–right' self-identities becomes negligible, yet still independent. What is more certain is the latter point: the Polish party system space remains two-dimensional and is clearly structured by two independent policy domains.

In terms of hypothesis (2.1) presented above, the more polarized dimension should contribute to improvements in the elite–mass signalling game and consequently to their greater spatial proximity. This hypothesis in fact can be reworded into static and dynamic versions, the former indicating a one-point-in-time comparison, the latter comparing the temporal pace of changes in both phenomena. The overall means of voter–elite proximities in two around-election periods clearly confirm our prediction: voter–elite distances on the religious-secular dimension are both absolutely lower than on the economic dimension. The dynamics of change in this area is also more pronounced – the average proximity doubles in the four-year period (from 0.34 to 0.17), whereas on the economic dimension the change is rather marginal (from 0.54 to 0.41) and its absolute level quite different. Although we lack fully comparable data for 1993/94, the absolutely best voter–elite fit on this ideological proxy combined with the absolutely highest polarization potential and its rate of increase clearly support Huntington's prediction.

Conclusions

(1) Both the absolute and relative perspective on 'hard' as well as survey opinion data indicates that between 1991 and 1997 a considerable change in party system institutionalization took place in Poland; its major indicators coincide and cluster together logically.

(2) Systematic juxtaposition of the relevant data on party system institutionalization and democratic consolidation shows that there is a

remote, and far from deterministic relationship between the two. Thus the postulates claiming that party system institutionalization is important to the process of democratic consolidation remain – in my view – open to empirical inquiry.

(3) Evaluating party system institutionalization and democratic consolidation in Poland is troublesome for yet another reason: both phenomena are accompanied by impressive – by regional standards – economic success and a rise in public mood indicators. An effort at disentangling the phenomenon of satisfaction with democracy and concentrating on pure diffuse political support, allowing for the blurring influences of its economic and political correlates, proved rewarding. The result: as transformational time passes the diffuse political support becomes more autonomous and independent from economic and short-term political phenomena, simultaneously becoming more associated with political efficacy and participatory factors. In brief, the general socio-political context for party system institutionalization improves as the transition progresses, but clearly independently and ahead of the latter phenomenon.

(4) The detailed analysis of party system polarization, dimensions of competition and the relevance of 'left–right' semantics shows that the Polish party system has indeed become more polarized as time has passed, and this polarization seems clearly conducive to the increased transparency of the elite-mass signaling exchange. The 'left–right' meta-dimension with its superior – in comparison with the 'content' dimensions – polarizing potential, indicates that up to a certain point it had effectively incorporated both, economic and socio-cultural dimensions, and then in 1997 it became less related to the two. It did not, however, cease to polarize the party system space. And even though the religious-secular divide can 'substitute' for part of the abstract left-right positioning and discourse,[18] nevertheless a substantial part remains unexplained by it. This aspect of the picture seems to be partly incompatible with the remaining part of the story. The 'left–right' dimension has become more equally defined in terms of, and dependent upon, socio-cultural (religious) and economic dimensions. This contradicts the increased salience of residual, non-distributive religious-secular values in Polish politics. However, it is clear that growing salience of religious factors can be attributed to the elites' instrumental creativity effectiveness.

(5) Generally, one ought to stress the following – if we allow for temporal changes in particular indicators of party system institutionalization and democratic consolidation then little doubt remains that the causal link in

Poland runs from economic recovery and successive growth in consumption to satisfaction with democracy followed by an independent increase in diffuse political support, and only then to party system institutionalization. For individual Polish parties, the process of institutionalization is one that largely lies ahead of them. The two major entities which contested the elections of 1997 were formally coalitions of different organizations, only some of which were parties and most of which had unknown or very low levels of membership. Amongst the real parties, Unia Wolność applied to and became a member of the European People's Party – although no leader of UW could really explain why. Jaroslaw Kaczynski, leader of the PC which was an integral part of AWS in 1997, actually contested the election on the list of another party, the ROP. There were many more examples of such anomalies, all of which pointed to the weakness of party organization in Poland, even by prevailing east European standards.

Such features point to an especially low level of party system institutionalization in Poland. If this is so, on the basis of presented data, one important message for scholars interested in 'external influences' has to be emphasized. Poland is the only polity – for many reasons – to have launched a 'shock-therapy' mode of economic reconstruction and by the time populist/nationalist-friendly forces installed themselves as a governing coalition in 1992 the first macro-economic indicators of recovery were in place. And it is exactly at this point when tough IMF/WB stipulations proved decisive for the continuation of liberal economic polities, resulting in an average of about six per cent GDP growth in the 1993–97 period.

(6) No doubt, however, remains that the 'trend-setter' (in general terms of the drive towards democratization) reveals extreme idiosyncrasies that restrict others from following the same route. The seeds of this phenomenon lie in the transitional path taken. The combination of high initial uncertainty as to external reaction coupled with well-organized mass mobilization at a substantially higher level than elsewhere in the region all contributed to problems in the smooth passage from an over-turbulent civil society to a calm political society. This anti-formal mood coupled with a deep suspicion towards entities called parties has influenced the peculiarities of Poland as outlined.

(7) A clearly alternative path of development took place in Hungary: parties came first, relatively well organized and believed by many to be 'frozen too early'. They had certainly preceded the most dramatic economic change that occurred only in spring of 1995. Meanwhile no visible changes in satisfaction with democracy or in positive attitudes as regards

the old regime and economy, accompanied by criticism of the new ones, are visible till 1998 . As of 1997/98 comparison of the two genuine first-comers to the transformation does not show any – previously broadly alleged – superiority for the Hungarian party system in terms of its institutionalization as defined in this article. The same number of effective parties, almost the same below-five per cent vote share is accompanied by two differentiating factors: considerably higher voter volatility in Hungary 1994–98 than in Poland 1993–97 (34:19) and relatively higher electoral participation in Hungary (though lower between 1994 and 1998, by some 12 per cent).

What remains indisputable is the much better state of parties' internal organization and institutionalization as well as their parliamentary behavior in Hungary. Briefly put, the two routes to the ultimate goals of the market economy and consolidated democracy involve a different order of both the occurrence and importance of associated phenomena. In particular, the parties' and party system institutionalization seem to play a substantially different role. These two examples of recent successful transformation show that theoretical predictions concerning the relationship between party system institutionalization and democratic consolidation are far from borne out by empirical reality.

NOTES

1. Paul G. Lewis, 'Parties and Parliaments in East Central Europe: Poland as a Trend-Setter', paper presented at a conference, 'Ten Years After: Democratic Transition and Consolidation in East Central Europe' (Budapest, 17–20 June 1999).
2. Ibid., p.4.
3. For example Paul G. Lewis, 'Political Institutionalization and Party Development in Post-Communist Poland', *Europe-Asia Studies*, Vol.45, No.5 (1994), pp.779–99; Leonardo Morlino, 'Political Parties and Democratic Consolidation in Southern Europe', in R. Gunther, P. Nikiforos Diamandouros and H-J. Puhle (eds.), *The Politics of Democratic Consolidation. Southern Europe in Comparative Perspective* (Baltimore, MD and London: Johns Hopkins University Press, 1995); Scott Mainwaring and Timothy R. Scully, *Building Democratic Institutions: Party Systems in Latin America* (Stanford, CA: Stanford University Press, 1995); Gábor Tóka, 'Political Parties and Democratic Consolidation in East Central Europe', Studies in Public Policy, No. 279 (1997).
4. Ibid., p.4.
5. Op. cit., pp.316 ff.
6. Peter Mair, *Party System Change: Approaches and Interpretations* (Oxford: Clarendon Press, 1997).

7. Radoslaw Markowski, 'Polski system partyjny po wyborach 1997: instytucjonalizacja czy wichrowatość', *Studia Polityczne*, No.9 (1999); Radoslaw Markowski, 'Polish Party System: Institutionalization–Political Representation–Issue Structuring', paper presented at the ECPR Joint Sessions, Mannheim, 26–31 March 1999.
8. For details see Markowski, 'Polski system partyjny', 1999.
9. Along the same lines, see the persuasive argument of Tóka, 'Political Parties and Democratic Consolidation', 1997.
10. Mair, *Party System Change*, p.182.
11. Mainwaring and Scully, *Building Democratic Institutions*, pp.66–8.
12. On the basis of Douglas W. Rae, *The Political Consequences of Electoral Laws* (New Haven, CT: Yale University Press, 1967).
13. See Rein Taagepera and Matthew Shugart, *Seats and Votes* (New Haven, CT: Yale University Press, 1989).
14. Samuel H. Barnes, 'The Mobilization of Political Identity in New Democracies', in Samuel H. Barnes and Janos Simon (eds.), *The Post-Communist Citizen* (Budapest: Erasmus Foundation and Institute of Political Studies HAS, 1998).
15. Richard Rose and Christian Haerpfer, 'Change and Stability in the New Democracies Barometer: A Trend Analysis', *Studies in Public Policy*, No.270 (1996).
16. S. P. Huntington, *Political Order in Changing Societies* (New Haven, CT: Yale University Press,1968), pp.416 ff.
17. Radoslaw Markowski, 'Political Parties and Ideological Spaces in East Central Europe', *Communist and Post-Communist Studies*, Vol.30, No.3 (1997), pp.221–54; Herbert Kitschelt, Zdenka Mansfeldova, Radoslaw Markowski, and Tóka, Gábor, *Post-Communist Party Systems: Competition, Representation and Inter-Party Cooperation* (Cambridge: Cambridge University Press,1999).
18. For details see Markowski, 'Polski system partyjny', 1999.

5

The 'Professionalization' of Party Campaigning in Post-Communist Poland

ALEKS SZCZERBIAK

Bureaucrats and Professionals in Modern Party Development

The shift away from the traditional mass party and development of new models of party organization in Western democracies has had important implications for party campaigning and the character and disposition of party bureaucracies. The central role played by the bureaucracy attached to party headquarters (the 'party central office') was one of the defining characteristics of the mass party model. However, both Panebianco and Katz and Mair in their respective electoral-professional and cartel party models have posited a decrease in the importance of traditional party 'bureaucrats' – in the Weberian sense of full-time administrators dedicated the maintenance of the organisation – and a concomitant increase in the role of professionals and consultants with a much looser relationship with the party.[1] Indeed, according to Panebianco it is precisely this distinction between bureaucrats and professionals that is *the* key difference between his electoral-professional and the earlier 'mass-bureaucratic' model and the single most important aspect of the process of party change more generally.

According to Katz and Mair this process of 'professionalization' was rooted in a general shift towards a more capital-intensive, professional and centralized style of party campaigning.[2] The services provided by bureaucrats attached to the party headquarters may have been indispensable when party campaigning was labour-intensive, most party activities were directed towards the organization of a mass membership and greater emphasis was placed on the party's own independent channels of communication. However, as parties increasingly competed for access to non-partisan communication networks, many of the services required from the party central office bureaucrats could be secured through alternative sources, such as professional publicists and communication specialists. In other words, while the party bureaucracy may have remained useful as a means of organizing and coordinating the activities of the party membership (the 'party on the ground') it was no longer indispensable for campaigning purposes.

Indeed, while in Panebianco's electoral-professional model this shift from 'bureaucrats' to 'professionals' takes place *within* the party central office staffs. Katz and Mair are more explicit that the relationship between parties and professionals has become much looser and more contractual. Communication services, for example, can be bought on the open market 'perhaps at a higher price but without the added costs of subservience to a party organisation whose goal priorities may be quite different'.[3]

Most commentators who have made structured projections about the type of parties that are likely to emerge in post-communist Eastern Europe argue that they are more likely to conform to the recent electoral-professional and cartel parties than the traditional mass party model.[4] Consequently, we might expect to see the new East European parties developing with weak party central office bureaucracies and a much greater reliance upon external experts, public opinion specialists and communication advisers.

In order to examine whether or not we are seeing such a process of 'professionalization' of party campaigning in post-communist Eastern Europe, this paper considers the relationship between party 'bureaucrats' and external 'professionals' in the new parties that have emerged in post-communist Poland since the collapse of communism in 1989. It focuses on the six main parties and groupings that, as Table 1 shows, emerged as the most significant in the most recent parliamentary elections in September 1997 when most of the research for this chapter was undertaken.[5]

The two largest political groupings, Solidarity Electoral Action (Akcja Wyborcza Solidarność: AWS) and the Democratic Left Alliance (Sojusz

TABLE 1
SEPTEMBER 1997 POLISH PARLIAMENTARY ELECTION RESULTS

Above the threshold	*Votes cast 1997*	*% 1997*	*Seats won*
Solidarity Electoral Action (AWS)	4,427,373	33.83	201
Democratic Left Alliance (SLD)	3,551,224	27.13	164
Freedom Union (UW)	1,749,518	13.37	60
Polish Peasant Party (PSL)	956,184	7.31	27
Movement for Poland's Reconstruction (ROP)	727,072	5.56	6
Below the threshold			
Labour Union (UP)	620,611	4.74	
National Party of Retirees and Pensioners (KPEiR)	284,826	2.18	
Union of the Republic Right (UPR)	266,317	2.03	
National Agreement of Retirees and Pensioners (KPEiRRP)	212,826	1.63	
Christian Democratic-Bloc for Poland (ChD-BdP)	178,395	1.36	

Source: *Rzeczpospolita* 2 October 1997.

Lewicy Demokratycznej: SLD), were both political conglomerates comprising around 30 parties and other groupings. The SLD was dominated by Social Democracy of the Republic of Poland (Socjaldemokracja Rzeczpospolitej Polskiej: SdRP) which was, in turn, formed in January 1990 as the direct organisational successor to the communist Polish United Workers' Party (Polska Zjednoczona Partia Robotnicza: PZPR). It was the senior government coalition partner during the 1993-97 parliament and SLD leader Aleksander Kwaśniewski was elected President of the Poland in November 1995. The right-wing AWS conglomerate was formed in June 1996 and emerged as the largest parliamentary grouping and main government coalition partner after the September 1997 elections, although the hegemonic role within this grouping was played by a trade union, Solidarity, rather than a political party *sensu stricto*.

The Freedom Union (Unia Wolności: UW) was formed in April 1994 following a merger of two liberal, centrist parties that also emerged from within the Solidarity movement: the Democratic Union (Unia Demokratyczna: UD) and the Liberal Democratic Congress (Kongres Liberalno-Demokratyczne: KLD). Poland's first post-communist premier Tadeusz Mazowiecki originally led the party until he was replaced by former Finance Minister (and architect of Poland's post-communist economic reform programme Leszek Balcerowicz) in April 1995. The UW was the main opposition party during the 1993–97 parliament and went on to become AWS's junior coalition partner after the September 1997 parliamentary elections. The Polish Peasant Party (Polskie Stronnictwo Ludowe: PSL), on the other hand, was formed in May 1990 as the successor to the communist satellite United Peasant Party (Zjednoczone Stronnictwo Ludowe: ZSL), although it also attempted to draw on the historical traditions of the Polish agrarian movement which dated back to the end of the last century and provided the main political opposition to the communists during the late 1940s. The PSL had been the SLD's junior coalition partner in the 1993–97 parliament, although both its share of the vote and parliamentary representation were slashed following the September 1997 election and it was reduced to being only the fourth largest parliamentary grouping.

The Labour Union (Unia Pracy: UP), which was formed in 1992 by a number of smaller social democratic groupings emerging from within Solidarity and reformed ex-communists who chose not to join SdRP, was the fourth largest formation in the 1993–97 parliament but narrowly failed to cross the five per cent parliamentary threshold in September 1997. Finally, the Movement for Poland's Reconstruction (Ruch Odbudowy Polski: ROP) was a right-wing party formed in November 1995 by the supporters of former Solidarity premier Jan Olszewski in an attempt to capitalise on his relatively good showing in that year's presidential elections. Although ROP won just enough support in September 1997 to secure parliamentary representation this only translated into a tiny number of seats.

Weak Party Bureaucracies

As Table 2 shows, all of the parties surveyed were characterized by weak party bureaucracies with only a tiny number of paid staff attached to the various party headquarters. The analysis in this section focuses on the five political parties *sensu stricto* and does not include the SLD and AWS electoral committees. Although large numbers of individuals worked in the campaign headquarters of these committees they are not included in this discussion as the focus here is on permanent administrative staff dedicated to continuously maintaining a bureaucratic machine rather than organizational structures that only exist for the duration of an election campaign and are wound up immediately afterwards.

TABLE 2
NUMBER OF STAFF EMPLOYED IN PARTY HEADQUARTERS, JUNE 1997

Party	Number of staff
Polish Peasant Party (PSL)	20
Freedom Union (UW)10	
Social Democracy of the Polish Republic (SdRP)	4
Movement for Poland's Reconstruction (ROP)	3
Labour Union (UP)	1.5

Source: Information supplied by party headquarters, June 1997.

Of the five parties surveyed only the PSL had anything which might with any degree of accuracy be termed a 'party bureaucracy' with the full-time equivalent of twenty employees working at its party headquarters. Significantly, it was also the only party with paid central office staff specifically responsible for policy and programmatic development. However, it is worth noting that about one third of these employees were purely administrative or clerical rather than so-called 'meritocratic', staff.[6] As the party's programmatic director Jan Wypych put it, 'our office is not some kind of decision-making organ but an executive organ which runs the technical-service side for the party's governing bodies ... It is not a large outpost or cell, it is modest ... It is (run) at the basic level so that the party's main organizational tasks ... can be fulfilled.'

This relative organizational robustness was, perhaps, predictable given that a number of commentators have hypothesized that 'successor' formations such as the PSL are likely to be the beneficiaries of a material and financial legacy from the communist period. As such they are likely to display more of the characteristics of the mass party model – including a relatively strong party bureaucracy – than the completely 'new' parties that were formed since the collapse of communism in 1989.[7] The PSL certainly retained many of the former ZSL's assets including its large headquarters building.[8]

More surprising, given this hypothesized organizational legacy, was the fact that, as Table 2 also shows, SdRP only employed the equivalent of four full-time staff working in its party headquarters. In fact, SdRP was able to hang on to much fewer of its predecessor's assets and, although much controversy surrounded their fate, the party was legally required to divest itself of them.[9] While its party headquarters was located in a large office block at least three quarters of the floor space was rented out to various companies and organizations and, as one Polish commentator put it, 'entering the (SdRP) party headquarters you get the impression that it is abandoned. Politics take place somewhere else'.[10]

It is worth noting that in addition to *stricte* party employees there were also 14 staff attached to 11 'local' SdRP parliamentary offices located in the party headquarters building, together with an (unspecified) number of staff who worked there voluntarily but on a full-time basis. The latter included all members of the party executive (most of whom were parliamentarians) and both the party's national spokesman and head of party organization. None the less, given that these staff were either voluntary or formally linked to the parliamentary party rather than the party central office, SdRP still appeared to conform more to the electoral-professional and cartel than the mass party models. Indeed, perhaps more than any other party surveyed, SdRP resembled a 'sleeping army' with a modest party central office bureaucracy that could transform itself into the organizational backbone for professionally organized and well-financed election campaigns.

With the full-time equivalent of ten paid staff, the UW had the second largest party headquarters 'bureaucracy' and the largest of any of the 'new' parties examined (it was, for example, the only party other than PSL to employ full-time press officers), although still extremely modest for what was then the main parliamentary opposition party. The main reason why the UW developed such a comparatively large party headquarters staff was the fact that Balcerowicz was not (unlike his predecessor) a parliamentarian at the time of his election as leader and, consequently, increased the party's staff compliment from three to ten in order to provide him with a separate extra-parliamentary support service.[11]

Meanwhile, the UP and ROP both had tiny party central office staffs that barely warranted the title 'bureaucracies'. Although it was then the fourth largest parliamentary party with more than 30 deputies, the UP's headquarters consisted of literally a couple of rooms and employed the full-time equivalent of only one-and-a-half administrative staff. The ROP central office was located in equally modest accommodation and employed only three full-time staff, although a loosely organized group of around 20 part-time volunteers drifted in and out of the office and assisted them with various organizational tasks.

Evidence of Professionalization

In most cases, therefore, the concept of a party 'bureaucracy' was virtually meaningless. Moreover, not only were all the new Polish parties characterized by the weak party central office posited in the electoral-professional and cartel party models, there were also some indications that party campaigning was becoming 'professionalized' in a number of significant ways.

First, there was some evidence of party leaders increasingly drawing on the services of external policy advisers and programmatic experts. For example, the then SdRP party leader Józef Oleksy was assisted by a group of party members and sympathisers from the academic community and regularly organized meetings with supporters working in the Polish Academy of Sciences to discuss policy development. Similarly, according to PSL programmatic director Jan Wypych his party had 'a wide range of contacts and specialists in various areas and intellectual milieu ... organised in 17 ... Supreme Executive Committee commissions which are comprised ... of specific specialists in the appropriate subject.' The party also had a separate 30-strong experts group chaired by an academic economist Professor Władysław Szymański and, if it did not have policy specialists in a given field, then it ordered a specially prepared expert report from a non-party member.[12]

With its origins in two parties that enjoyed strong support in the academic and intellectual communities, the UW also drew upon a large number of policy specialists among both party members and sympathisers. These were organized in 20 'National Secretariats' responsible for developing the party's detailed policies on the economy, foreign affairs, health, social policy, the environment, rural affairs, national security and education. Moreover, two academic research institutes were also closely aligned with the party: the Gdańsk-based Institute for the Research of the Market Economy established by two former KLD members (Jan Szomburg and the UW economy spokesman Janusz Lewandowski) and the prestigious Institute of Public Affairs whose governing body included the then UW parliamentary fraction leader and foreign affairs spokesman Bronisław Geremek. Similarly, AWS formed 13 policy groups involving more than 300 experts to draw up the grouping's 1997 election programme.[13] Both the UP and ROP also recognized the importance of utilizing external policy specialists, although they encountered much greater difficulties in developing such networks among sympathetic intellectuals.

Secondly, all the parties and groupings surveyed paid a great deal of attention to analysing polling data; both generally-available, published opinion polls and their own, specially-commissioned sociological research. A defining moment here, and in Polish party campaigning more generally, was Aleksander Kwaśniewski's November 1995 presidential election campaign. As two Polish commentators put it, Kwaśniewski's campaign staff, which included the sociologist and director of the Polish branch of the Gallup Institute polling company Sławomir Wiatr, 'analysed public opinion research scrupulously and ordered it systematically'.[14] More generally, according to SdRP party executive member Krzysztof Janik, the party carried out its own polling and occasionally paid for market research companies to attach 'one or two questions' to their general surveys – although, according to some commentators, the Gallup Institute's polling for the SLD in the run up to the 1997 election was actually much more systematic than this.[15]

The UW also used sympathetic commercial polling organizations such as the Gdańsk-based Social Research Workshop which was closely associated with the KLD milieu and academic sociologists[16] and, for example, undertook detailed opinion research before determining how much exposure to give Balcerowicz during the September 1997 election campaign. AWS established a special Electoral Analysis Group headed by academic sociologist Professor Tomasz Żukowski to analyse polling data and design surveys to be conducted specifically for this grouping.[17] Even the cash-strapped UP found the resources to fund polling research into its bases of support and target electorates in the run up to the 1997 election. The PSL, on the other hand, felt that the main commercial polling organizations took insufficient account of its predominantly rural electorate and established its own Peasant Institute for Public Opinion Research, comprising sympathetic sociologists and polling specialists, specifically for election campaigns. The ROP, which shared the PSL's mistrust of mainstream polling companies (although for ideological rather than methodological reasons) also set up an unofficial polling workshop in the run up to the 1997 parliamentary elections, the Centre for Public Opinion Research.

Thirdly, there was also evidence that some Polish parties – particularly the SdRP/SLD, UW and AWS – were becoming increasingly interested in using specialist media and communications consultants – although this was still very much at an experimental stage. Once again, Kwaśniewski's 1995 presidential campaign was the watershed. According to Polish advertising specialists, Kwaśniewski's was 'the first really, modern election campaign in

Poland' where the candidate subordinated himself to media advisers that included the French Socialist Party and François Mitterrand's campaign consultant Jacques Seguella.[18] Media specialists and consultants (including, according to some accounts, the French socialists) were also involved in the SLD's 1997 parliamentary campaign – although to a much lesser extent.[19] As SdRP's head of organisation and 1995 and 1997 election campaign organiser Maciej Poręba put it, 'the time of voluntary activity is ending ... There are now several dozen various types of marketing firms in Poland who do this as professionals taking advantage of the very great expertise that is available in the West ... If we can find people among these who want to work with us, then we will.'

Similarly, according to the party's National Press Spokesman Andrzej Potocki, the UW 'always uses paid professional media experts and communications consultants'. Both of its progenitor parties used media advisers in their election campaigns, as did the UW itself in the 1995 presidential elections when it employed the Polish–Belgian firm Corporate Profiles and utilized a number of television specialists who offered their services voluntarily.[20] During the 1997 parliamentary campaign the party also employed a Polish–American media relations company to act as strategic campaign advisers. Similarly, AWS's September 1997 election broadcasts were produced by a group of young, and highly professional, right-wing current affairs journalists and production staff who had been closely associated with the AWS media adviser Wiesław Walendziak during his spell as head of Polish television between 1993–96.

Professional media and communications specialists were also used, to a lesser extent, by the PSL, UP and ROP. During the 1993 parliamentary campaign, for example, the PSL hired a Polish advertising agency (Józef Węgrzyn) to produce their television election broadcasts and in 1997 the party used both television specialists and a well-known graphic artist (Waldemar Świeży) to design their posters. Similarly, the UP hired the Polish-Swedish advertising agency Marketpoint to design their posters and leaflets in 1997, while, according to ROP election organiser Wojciech Włodarczyk, his party also employed media specialists to prepare 'specific segments' of their election campaign such as their TV and radio slots, and drew upon the expertise of a group of sympathetic journalists who voluntarily analysed the impact of the party's media campaign.

The Limits of Professionalization

Other evidence, however, suggests that there are clear limits to the extent to which such outside professionals are being utilized in Polish party campaigning.

First, it is questionable to what extent most of this activity could really be described as 'professionalization' given that much of it was motivated by political (if not personal) sympathies and supplied on a voluntary rather than a contractual basis. For example, according to SdRP's head of organization Maciej Poręba, 'if we ask for (professional polling or media) help from outside then they are aware that they are working voluntarily ... We operate on the basis of sympathizers who take responsibility for these matters ... but not on the basis of payment.' Similarly, PSL executive office director Marian Zalewski pointed out that, although there were some media specialists 'with whom we work on the usual (commercial) basis', generally such advice was provided by 'journalists who are party members and help us in view of the fact that they are party members.' UP national spokesman Tomasz Nałęcz also drew attention to the fact that even the paid work undertaken by the party's professional communications specialists in the 1997 campaign was 'to some extent, voluntary' with 'the payments of a kind that will involve a certain degree of sympathy from people ... It will not be ... an occasion for these people to make the large amounts of money that they would if they worked for industry or in some other non-political role.' Similarly, ROP national spokesman Jacek Kurski felt that 'unpaid people will offer themselves' to help the party with specialist media and communications advice during the 1997 parliamentary campaign.

An interesting example of how Polish parties drew upon unpaid external advisers and specialists was the support provided to them by their Western 'sister' party organizations or foundations, as well as from the American Democrat and Republican parties. In addition to the aforementioned assistance which the SdRP/SLD and Kwaśniewski received from the French Socialist Party, UP national spokesman Tomasz Nałęcz also acknowledged that his party benefited from training schools organized by 'the British Labour Party and the foundations connected with the European social democratic parties.' Indeed, according to the UP's 1997 election organizer Piotr Marciniak, Swedish social democrat campaign specialists helped the party to analyse polling data and 'to a large extent, we formulated the concept of our election campaign in contact with them'. The Polish office of the International Republican Institute, provided unpaid advice to AWS and training schools for ROP and UW activists, while the National Democratic Institute's Polish branch adopted an even more catholic approach and organized training for representatives of the UW, UP, ROP and SdRP youth sections and a number of AWS affiliates, on subjects such as organizing local party structures and targeting women voters in election campaigns.[21]

Secondly, the use of paid external consultants and advisers was generally (and, in the case of opinion polling and communications specialists, almost exclusively) confined to the periods running up to national elections. For example, speaking six months prior to the 1997 parliamentary election UW general secretary Mirosław Czech pointed that while the 'kind of consultants who relate to everyday matters – experts, professionals, sociologists – we are using them all the time ... Only now will we be hiring paid consultants who will be working with us on the question of determining an election strategy.' Similarly, UP vice-chairman for organizational affairs Wojciech Borowik drew attention to the fact that 'we are trying to get together the resources so that in the last six months in the run-up to the election campaign we can have professional groups supporting us'. In one sense, of course, this conformed to the notion of parties as primarily election-orientated organizations posited in the electoral-professional and cartel models. On the other hand, it also made it difficult to see these parties as somehow 'contracting out' large portions of their central office organizational and campaigning functions, with 'professional' consultants directly replacing and *substituting* for weak party bureaucracies.

By far the greatest impediment towards the more systematic use of professional advisers was the sheer cost of hiring them, particularly given that the best marketing, advertising and communications consultants were generally American or West European firms and, therefore, very expensive. According to PSL programmatic director Jan Wypych, for example, while the party had been approached by a number of companies involved in media and communications strategy during the 1997 campaign, 'the costs involved were of a different level to that which we could put into the campaign ... This was the main reason, they were too expensive.' ROP's head of information Andrzej Kieryło also argued that, 'if someone agrees to work with us for nothing then we will happily utilise their advice' but the party 'simply cannot afford ... to hire foreign specialists'.[22] Moreover, as UP national spokesman Tomasz Nałęcz pointed out,

> there is no sense in hiring experts in order to get their ideas on the specific means for implementing a campaign and not take advantage of these ideas on grounds of poverty ... So in order to hire consultants you have to have certain material capabilities to implement their plans, at least in some meaningful way if not in full.

Ironically, the parties which could draw on the largest pool of sympathizers with professional campaigning skills to assist them voluntarily were generally those with the strongest financial bases, while those with the smallest networks of sympathetic specialists were (like the UP) also those who could least afford to hire paid advisers.

A secondary factor constraining the 'professionalization' of Polish party campaigning was a residual suspicion about the real value of using external experts and advisers, particularly advertising agencies and marketing firms.

An extremely important element here was the disastrous experience of the UW's progenitor, the KLD, during the 1993 parliamentary elections. The KLD ran the first truly 'Western' Polish election campaign under the supervision of the British advertising agency Saatchi and Saatchi and, in spite of the large sums of money invested, achieved a derisory result well below the five per cent threshold. Although this mistrust was, to some extent, evident across the political spectrum, it was particularly striking in the PSL and right-wing parties such as the ROP. PSL programmatic director Jan Wypych, for example, argued that the

> supporters of more traditional methods of mobilising the rural electorate ... are not just reactionaries and have a point that there is a large element of the PSL electorate that would be put off by too slick a campaign ... Indeed, the evidence of the KLD's 1993 campaign suggests that such a campaign can easily backfire and not just among the rural electorate.

Moreover, the greatest hostility tended to be directed at 'Western' media and communications advisers both on the grounds that they did not properly understand Polish political culture and, more generally, because there was considerable cynicism about the 'exportability' of Western campaigning techniques. Predictably, the PSL and ROP expressed the greatest unease on this score. For example, although generally a supporter of his party adopting more modern campaigning techniques, PSL national spokesman Aleksander Bentkowski also expressed anxieties about the KLD experience which he saw as, 'an example of taking advantage of a means of campaigning which is transferred to our conditions from the West without due regard' for Polish conditions. Similarly, ROP national spokesman Jacek Kurski said that his party was 'not convinced about...these experts ... from Western firms who are paid large sums of money and have already led one Polish political party to the grave ... because here in Poland you have to have your own original scenario.'

Such anxieties could also be found in parties which were generally more sympathetic towards the use of professional media and communications advisers. SdRP national spokesman Dariusz Klimaszewski, for example, argued that while, 'there are certain ... experiences ... that you can take advantage of' he was 'fairly sceptical about hiring an American PR firm ... because you have to know the Polish reality, the methods of getting to people and I know that a couple of political parties lost out as a result of doing this ... organised their activities in an American style and simply transplanted them here.' UP national spokesman Tomasz Nałęcz also expressed a preference for using Polish specialists on the grounds that, 'there aren't always good results from consulting experts used to operating in countries with a different experience from that in Poland'. Nałęcz cited the 1993 KLD campaign which 'ended in catastrophe precisely through trying to transfer certain Western models' as an example of the dangers of non-Polish campaign specialists and argued that 'every idea transferred from a different country, different culture or different cultures should be modified in a natural way'.

Similarly, AWS only hired Polish companies during its 1997 campaign because, according to its election organiser Andrzej Anusz, 'the Polish specific is different to the American or British and (Polish) specialists know best with which words to reach the citizens of their own country'. Even UW national spokesman Andrzej Potocki – representing a party overtly committed to using professional Western campaign specialists and techniques that hired a Polish-American firm of advisers in the run up to the 1997 election – admitted that there were both 'advantages and disadvantages' to 'dealing with people who are new to the Polish scene'. While their lack of direct involvement in Polish politics allowed it to provide more objective assessments, 'the danger, of course, is that it is possible that they won't know a lot of things about Poland that are worth knowing'.

The greatest anxieties were related to fears of losing political control to 'strategic' campaign advisers rather than hiring individual specialists or specific organisations with particular skills such as TV and radio production, artistic design and copy writing. According to AWS's 1997 election campaign organizer Andrzej Anusz, for example, 'the most important political and strategic decisions were taken by the (Election) Staffs. There were obviously advertising agencies and people from advertising agencies who advised us ... but the policy decisions were taken by us.' SdRP national spokesman Dariusz Klimaszewski also pointed out that the SLD's use of media specialists in the 1997 election campaign, 'did not have an institutional rank, it was more a case of cooperation with specific people'. Similarly, according to programmatic director Jan Wypych, the PSL 'didn't go in the direction of hiring one firm' but rather turned to 'experts, directors, artists...hired on an individual basis ... whether it was for photos, film, radio, posters or graphics.' ROP national secretary and election campaign organiser Wojciech Włodarczyk also pointed out that, 'there wasn't a firm which determined the whole of our campaign ... We didn't turn to advertising firms...apart from those who prepared specific segments...according to the principles that we laid down for them.'

Even the UW, the only party that actually hired a firm of strategic campaign advisers in 1997, expressed anxieties about the possible consequences of losing political control. According to the party's election organizer Paweł Piskorski (who was also involved in the 1993 KLD campaign), 'it wasn't a case of handing over our campaign to one firm and it "ran" the campaign for us ... We didn't depend on any one firm or expert...We had experience of such models from earlier years ... and it did not turn out as we had expected.' Rather, according to Piskorski, 'this time ... we decided the whole strategy, the method of implementation must be in the hands of politicians ... it was the Election Staffs that decided on all important matters and we used consultants for help and experts for specific elements – TV, graphics, etc. – they were the "under-executives" of tasks determined by the Staffs.'

Indeed, it is worth noting that there was even some evidence of a slow but steady decline in hostility towards the idea of using professional (and even Western) media and communication advisers even in those parties that were most uneasy about modern political marketing techniques. At one stage in 1997, for example, even the PSL had toyed with the idea of hiring the campaign advisers to Jose Maria Aznar's Popular Party (although nothing, ultimately, came of this). Right-wing parties were also becoming increasingly aware of the need to run more sophisticated and professional campaigns, exemplified by the September 1997 AWS campaign which, as noted above, drew on the expertise of experienced broadcasting professionals, and stood in marked contrast to previous efforts by the Polish right. Even the ROP's head of information Andrzej Kieryło acknowledged that his party took 'seriously the indicators provided to us by the (American) International Republican Institute'.

Finally, a third factor holding back the 'professionalization' of Polish party campaigning was the fact that most media and communications consultants were, themselves, reluctant to become too closely involved or identified with either a particular party or politics in general.[23] First, such an assignment generally involved working for a 'client' with both an unrealistically high set of expectations and such a small potential campaign budget that success could not be guaranteed (which, thereby, also rebounded on the firm's reputation). Secondly, most Polish advertising and marketing companies were afraid of the potential damage to their longer term commercial interests which could follow from becoming too closely identified with a particular party. Thirdly, parties were a particularly difficult 'product' for a (still nascent) Polish advertising and marketing industry to promote given the fact that many Polish politicians retained lingering suspicions of the medium and did not, therefore, always willingly accept advice from political marketing consultants. A classic example of this was former President Lech Wałęsa, who refused to accept his consultants' advice on how he should project himself during the 1995 presidential campaign.

Conclusion

As hypothesized, then, most of the parties and groupings surveyed employed a tiny number of staff in their party headquarters and, in this respect, conformed more to the recent electoral-professional and cartel party models. Only the PSL bore a greater resemblance to the traditional mass party model and had something that could be described with any degree of accuracy as a party central office 'bureaucracy'. However, evidence was much more limited when it came to the other key feature of the electoral-professional and cartel party models: the replacement of salaried party bureaucrats by external advisers and consultants with a looser contractual relationship with the parties.

This was partly due to a lingering suspicion of, and a residual hostility to, (particularly Western) professional communication advisers, largely based on one party's extremely bad experience; together with a reluctance on the part of advertising and marketing firms themselves to become too closely associated with political parties. The main obstacle to the greater 'professionalization' of Polish party campaigning was, however, the sheer cost of hiring consultants on anything other than a very occasional basis, together with the general lack of resources and extremely modest financial bases of most Polish parties. On the basis of the Polish experience, therefore, there appears to be little realistic prospect that the new parties in post-communist eastern Europe will utilise external 'professionals' in such a way that they could act as a substitute for their weak party central office bureaucracies, as envisaged in the electoral-professional and cartel models.

NOTES

1. A. Panebianco, *Political Parties: Organization and Power* (Cambridge: Cambridge University Press, 1988), p.264; R.S. Katz and P. Mair, 'The Evolution of Party Organizations in Europe: The Three Faces of Party Organization', *The American Review of Politics*, Vol.14 (1993), pp.615–16; P. Mair, 'Party Organizations: From Civil Society to the State' in R.S. Katz and P. Mair (eds.), *How Parties Organize: Change and Adaptation in Party Organizations in Western Democracies* (Sage Publications: London, 1994), p.13.
2. R.S. Katz, and P. Mair, 'Changing Models of Party Organization and Party Democracy: The Emergence of the Cartel Party', *Party Politics*, Vol.1, No.1 (1995), p.20.
3. Katz and Mair, 'The Evolution of Party Organizations', p.615. Panebianco in fact also acknowledged that some of the latter are recruited on short-term contracts.
4. P. Kopecky, 'Developing Party Organisations in East-Central Europe: What Type of Party is Likely to Emerge?' *Party Politics*, Vol.1, No.4 (1995),

pp.515–34. P.G. Lewis (ed.), *Party Structure and Organization in East-Central Europe* (Cheltenham: Edward Elgar, 1996).

5. The information on which this chapter is based comes primarily from interviews with party officials responsible for organizational and electoral strategy (together with other information supplied to the author by party headquarters) conducted between February–November 1997. Unless otherwise stated, all citations are taken from these sources.
6. J. Paradowska and M. Janicki, 'Pływanie w mętnej wodzie', *Polityka*, 3 Dec. 1994.
7. Kopecky, 'Developing Party Organizations', pp.529–30; and Lewis, Party Structure and Organization, pp.6–7.
8. S. Gebethner, 'Problemy finansowania partii politycznych a system wyborczy w polsce w latach 90', in F. Ryszka *et al.* (ed.), *Historia, Idee, Polityka* (Warsaw: Wydawnictwo Naukowe Scholar, 1995), p.429. Although much of this building was rented out to the Bank of Foodstuff Trading and, as one Polish commentator put it, the conditions in which the PSL's staff operated were 'far from luxurious' (J. Paradowska, 'Oswajanie ludowców', *Polityka*, 5 March 1994).
9. Gebethner, 'Problemy finansowania partii politycznych', p.429; P.G. Lewis, 'Party Funding in Post-Communist East-Central Europe', in P. Burnell and A. Ware (eds.), *Funding Democratization* (Manchester: Manchester University Press, 1998), p.151–3.
10. E. Nalewajko, *Protopartie i protosystem: szkic do obrazu polskiej wieolpartyności* (Warsaw: Instytut Nauk Politycznych Polskiej Akademii Nauk, 1997), p.184.
11. Paradowska and Janicki, 'Pływanie',1994. Balcerowicz was subsequently elected to parliament in September 1997.
12. *Rzeczpospolita*, 17 July 1996.
13. *Rzeczpospolita*, 10 Feb. 1997.
14. M. Janicki and M. Pęczak, 'Wojna na miny: czyli polityk jako towar', *Polityka*, 14 Oct. 1995.
15. R. Wróbel, 'Zasada ograniczonego zaufania', *Rzeczpospolita*, 25 April 1997; J.S. Mac and Z. Strachura, 'Kampania reklamowa', *Wprost*, 15 June 1997.
16. Mac and Strachura, 'Kampania reklamowa', 1997; Janicki and Pęczak, 'Wojna na miny',1995.
17. Wróbel, 'Zasada ograniczonego zaufania', 1997.
18. J. Paradowska, 'A kolor jego jest niebieski', *Polityka*, 9 Dec. 1995; A. Nivat, 'Convincing Voters that Kwaśniewski is 'the Choice of the Future', *Transition*, Vol.2, No.8 (1996), pp.32–5.
19. K. Olszewski, 'Kampania doradców', *Rzeczpospolita*, 1 July 1997.
20. Janicki and Pęczak, 'Wojna na miny', 1995.
21. Olszewski, 'Kampania doradców', 1997.
22. ibid.
23. Janicki and Pśczak, 'Wojna i miny', 1995; Mac and Strachura, 'Kampania reklamowa', 1997.

6

Party and State in Democratic Slovenia

ALENKA KRAŠOVEC

Introduction

The democratization of political life in Slovenia got under way with the first free elections of the post-war period in 1990. The League of Communists agreed to renounce their 45-year political monopoly after the formation of new political parties and the transformation of former socio-political organisations (League of Communists: LC, Socialist League of Working People: SLWP, League of Socialist Youth of Slovenia: LSYS) into new bodies at the end of the 80s. Under the previous constitution, until 1989, socio-political organisations had a privileged role (with the LC dominating) in organizing and managing all political interest and activities. Political pluralism was formally permitted from October 1989 when constitutional amendments were passed (they were codified in more detail but still quite loosely worded in the Law on Political Association adopted in December 1989), although in practice many different political associations were formed before December 1989 within the legal framework of LSYS and the then SLWP. The democratization of LC, its tolerance of new associations and its decision to defend Slovenian interests in Belgrade (even if this meant conflict with the Federal LC), was rewarded at the 1990 elections when it received the highest percentage of votes (17 per cent) in the Socio-political Chamber and its former leader Milan Kučan was elected President of Slovenia.

In December 1989 the Democratic Opposition of Slovenia (DEMOS) was formed. It was the product of three newly established associations which later became parties: the Slovenian Democratic Alliance, Slovenian Christian Democrats and Social Democratic Alliance of Slovenia. DEMOS was a loose coalition of political associations with weak organization and a political programme based mainly on the 'sovereign state of the Slovenian people, parliamentary democracy, human rights and liberties, and a social and political system which is able to provide its citizens all their human rights' (Article 4 of DEMOS's Founding Agreement). The origins of the programme lay in the May Declaration of 1989 (similar to one promulgating emancipation from Austria in 1917, but within the existing Yugoslav state)

The author would like to thank Professor Danica Fink-Hafner (University of Ljubljana, Slovenia) and Dr Paul G. Lewis (Open University, UK) for their helpful comments.

signed by members of the opposition.[1] Among other newly established parties was the Slovenian Farmers' Association (later Slovenian People's Party), which had many characteristics of an interest group at the outset but later became a political party. The newly established parties initially represented a form of mass protest (with many sympathizers but a small number of members) against the existing political system and claiming a more sovereign status for Slovenia within the Yugoslav Federation. In the beginning there was little ideological differentiation between them, but major differences soon developed between the newly established parties in this respect. At this stage they shared a common aim for which the parties were prepared to put aside their ideological divisions and which allowed them to emerge at this stage as 'movement' parties.[2]

The new parties mainly appeared from a stronger civil society, under the 'legal umbrella' of the two socio-political organizations. This meant that at the beginning of their development they were mainly societal actors without structural links with society and were faced by a lack of various resources (human, organizational and mainly financial). There were also major problems of organization. After the 1990 parliamentary elections some newly established parties entered parliament and began to receive both funding from the state budget and the support of parliamentary and governmental administration, which helped them develop their organizational structure throughout Slovenia.[3] The development of Slovenia's new parties was therefore greatly dependent on their being in parliament.

The development of the transformed parties was somewhat different. This concerned the Liberal Democracy of Slovenia (constituted from March 1994 by the Liberal Democratic Party – the former LSYS, the Socialist Party of Slovenia – the former SLWP, and fractions of the Greens and the Democrats of Slovenia), and the United List of Social Democrats, which from May 1993 was constituted by the Party of Democratic Renewal (the former LC), the Social Democratic Union and Workers' Party. From the beginning of their transformation they played the role of both societal actors and institutional actors as defined by Katz and Mair.[4] Parties which evolved from the old socio-political organizations had far fewer problems with resources and developing their organizational network.[5] They mostly preserved their organizational network as well as some human and some financial resources, buildings and equipment.[6]

Party Funding in Slovenia

The Law on Political Association was passed in December 1989 and legitimated three basic forms of party funding: public subsidies, membership fees and donations from individuals and enterprises. Parties which were members of Socio-Political Chambers at national or local levels were entitled to receive public subsidies, which privileged transformed parties because they already had representatives there. This privilege lasted until the first free and democratic elections were held in 1990, although new non-parliamentary parties were entitled to some temporary public subsidies at a very low level. This law remained in force until October 1994, when it was replaced by a Law on Political Parties, under which only parliamentary parties can receive public subsidies.

The 1989 law did not expressly prohibit party funding from abroad. The situation in Slovenia was probably similar to other CEECs where 'it was certainly the case that western foundations and foreign agencies played a significant role' in the survival of new parties during their initial phase, 'although the precise extent of their contribution remains uncertain'.[7] Low membership levels meant that this was not an important financial source. For these reasons the development of parties, especially new ones, has been highly dependent on entry into parliament.

There is another reason why becoming a parliamentary party was so important. In December 1989 a Law on Elections in Assemblies was passed which regulated the issue of election campaign financing. Election campaigns could now be financed by donations from individuals and enterprises. Each person could donate up to the level of an average salary to one candidate or party, while enterprises could donate ten average salaries. But there was no expenditure limit for election campaigns. In 1990 candidates and parties were obliged to submit reports on money received and spent in election campaigns, although only two parties (the former LSYS and LC) and the two representatives of minorities did so.[8] Only candidates or parties which succeeded in entering parliament were entitled to reimbursement on the basis of the number of votes received.

From September 1992 to October 1994 election campaign financing was not legally regulated. In September 1992 a Law on Elections in the National Assembly was passed which replaced the previous Law on Elections in Assemblies but did not regulate campaign financing. This meant that during the parliamentary and presidential elections of 1992 candidates and parties could receive and spend money for their campaigns almost without any formal control.

The Law on Political Parties of October 1994 now regulates the area of party funding. Parties can receive financial resources from membership fees, donations from individuals and enterprises, property revenue, gifts, public subsidies and surpluses of revenues from enterprises. The latter refers only to enterprises in a party's ownership involved in publishing or culture (although the idea of ownership itself remains ambiguous). The share of this last type of funding source must not exceed 20 per cent of a party's total annual income. Total donations from an individual or enterprise in a given year should not exceed ten average monthly salaries. If donations are higher than three average monthly salaries parties must list the donors in their annual reports. Parties must submit annual reports on their financial activity which are reviewed and appraised by the Court of Auditors, although it does not have any legal basis for revision. For this reason the anticipated sanctions for breaking the law have not been implemented, and it is hardly possible in Slovenia to talk in terms of the transparency of party funding (although there is some control of this dimension at enterprise level).

Some forms of party funding, which includes resources from abroad, government bodies, public enterprises and institutions, municipal bodies, humanitarian and religious organisations. and enterprises in which the state holds more than 50 per cent of the capital are not allowed. Parties represented in the National Assembly receive monthly public subsidies which depend on the number of votes received at elections, as well as public subsidies at local level (for votes received at municipal council or mayoral elections). Municipalities (of which Slovenia has 192) are responsible for this expenditure.

TABLE 1

MONTHLY PUBLIC SUBSIDIARIES TO PARLIAMENTARY PARTIES
(AMOUNT IN JANUARY 1999)

Political party	% of votes at 1996 elections	No. of seats	Amount in DEM
Liberal Democracy of Slovenia (LDS) *Liberalna demokracija Slovenije (LDS)*	27	25	119,492
Slovenian People's Party (SPP) *Slovenska ljudska stranka (SDS)*	19	19	85,729
Social Democratic Party of Slovenia (SDP) Socialdemokratska stranka Slovenije (SDS)	16	16	71,364
Slovenian Christian Democrats (SCD) Slovenski Krščanski demokrati (SKD)	9	10(-1*)	42,558
United List of Social Democrats (ULSD) Združena lista socialnih demokratov (ZLSD)	9	9	39,969
Democratic Party of Retired People of Slovenia (DPRPS) *Demokratična stranka upokojencev Slovenije (DeSUS)*	4	5	19,096
Slovenian National Party (SNP) Slovenska nacionalna stranka (SNS)	3	4	14,243

One seat is reserved for the representative of the Italian, and one for the Hungaria, minorities.
* The SCD obtained 10 seats, but soon after the elections one MP left both the party and the parliamentary group and is now an independent MP.
Source: Data obtained from the National Assembly.
Parties printed in italics were members of government coalition.
1 DEM is 99.57 SIT (as at 1999, Bank of Slovenia). All calculations are made on that basis. To aid better understanding, in May 1999 the average monthly salary stood at 1,070 DEM.

TABLE 2

PARTY FUNDING IN 1996, 1997 AND 1998 (IN DEM)

	funds transferred from previous years	all incomes	percentage of public subsidies*	funds transferred from previous years	all imcomes	percentage of public subsidies*	funds transferred from previous years	all incomes	percentage of public subsidies*
LDS	207,711	3,007,380	83	-	2,730,995	85	-	2,915,258	82
SPP	412,193	2,092,196	81	276,530	2,251,248	88	-	2,315,776	78
SDP	324,360	2,378,780	53	96,517	2,552,354	64	73,722	2,942,060	60
SCD	646,479	2,475,278	80	323,668	2,058,734	80	507,435	2,346,278	79
ULSD	-	3,577,777	39	85,236	3,053,669	43	155,044	3,110,219	44
DPRPS	170,197	558,880	67	128,506	698,398	84	170,473	758,143	76
SNP	180,803	786,622	96	59,303	385,160	99	68,147	401,322	99

* *Source:* Party financial reports, 1996, 1997 and 1998. Percentage of public subsidies is calculated with regard to all incomes in 1996, 1997 and 1998. From those amounts, we subtracted the income representing funds transferred from the previous year. On the basis of financial reports it was impossible to ascertain whether these transferred funds were public subsidies and what their percentage was. Given the fact that public subsidies for the parties identified (the ULSD is an exception because) already represented the largest part of financial resources in 1995 we can assume that also in 1996 and 1997 public subsidies constituted the lion's share of funds transferred. See A. Krašovec, 'Financiranje političnih strank v Sloveniji', *Teorija in praksa*, No. 34 (1997), pp. 210—27.

To picture the financial resources available to Slovenian political parties we have analysed annual financial reports from 1996, 1997 and 1998. It was not possible to define the percentage of the three most important funding sources (membership fees, donations from individuals and enterprises, public subsidies), and we can only present the total of publicly declared annual party incomes and the percentage of public subsidies within them. We must stress that the data contained in financial reports were not subject to any external review.

We can see that in 1996 Slovenian political parties were mainly funded from public subsidies. Only two social democratic parties were not publicly financed to such a great extent, although the SDP had DEM 425,186 of transfers from local organisations. That is a relatively high amount and we assume that this amount also includes public subsidies from local levels, but as there is no clear evidence supporting our assumption they are not presented as public subsidies. In the case of the ULSD, it is interesting that the party received DEM 379,228 from property revenues. This funding category also includes rents (DEM 222,109). As the legal successor to the Party of Democratic Renewal (the PDR being in turn the successor to the LC) the ULSD inherited some of the former ruling party's real estate, which meant that the party was able to rent out its holdings to earn additional financial resources. In 1996 two parties also reported debts: the LDS with DEM 465,145 and the SPP with DEM 498,191.

The level of public subsidy changed after the November 1996 parliamentary elections. In 1996 the LDS, SPP and SDP increased their share of the vote and received greater public subsidy. The SCD, ULSD and SNP lost votes compared to 1992, while the DPRPS only began receiving public subsidies at national level in November 1996 when it became a parliamentary party. Transfers from local organizations to the SDP once again revealed a relatively high amount of financial resources (DEM 357,020). The ULSD received DEM 216,587 in property revenues, with rents representing DEM 114,630. The largest two parties again showed debts: the LDS with DEM 201,915 and the SPP with DEM 257,021. Two smaller parties also made public the (very low) level of their debt: DEM 1,300 in the case of the SCD and DEM 100 for the SNP.

The financial picture from previous years continued into 1998. The two social democratic parties were exceptions with their relatively low share of public subsidies. The ULSD continued to receive significant revenues from property. In 1998, it received DEM 196,393 from that source of which DEM 98,843 was revenue from rents. Such funds were an exception for other parties or represented a very marginal source. In 1998 three parties reported debts. LDS debt was DEM 1,036,822, while the SPP owed rather less (DEM 725,823). For the second time the SCD reported a very small debt of DEM

630. If the disclosure of the level of LDS debt was something of a surprise, that of the SPP was less so. Over the past three years the SPP has been involved in strange financial arrangements which have cast a shadow on the party's publicly proclaimed honesty. These arrangements were disclosed by the mass media (mostly by the weekly political magazine *Mladina*), and none have been denied very convincingly. Related cases are now before the court, as the SPP is suing Mladina.

It would be enlightening to obtain data on the share of membership fees in parties' total income. But that is impossible because in the obligatory financial reports membership fees are included with donations. Only the SDP and ULSD presented membership fees separately in their reports. In 1996, the SDP received from this source DEM 163,410 and the ULSD DEM 487,554. A year later, the SDP received DEM 130,333 and the ULSD DEM 509,037, while in 1998 only the ULSD reported such data (DEM 500,566). Once again, such large amounts were an exception.

Slovenian political parties like to claim that their membership is extensive. Reported numbers are the following:[9]

LDS	5,342
SPP approximately	40,000
SCD	36,576
SDP approximately	20,000
ULSD approximately	23,000
DPRPS	26,000
SNP	5,783

This suggests that the membership of parliamentary parties represents 10.3 per cent of the electorate (this is calculated on the basis of number of voters – 1,522,475 – registered for the 1998 local elections). Parties outside parliament have far fewer members. The overall percentages should not, therefore, be significantly different if members of these parties are included.

On the above basis, we might expect that membership fees would be a relatively important funding source. But the numbers set out in financial reports do not support our assumption. Even if we suppose that the financial category of membership fees and donations does represent money collected by membership fees, we can conclude that parliamentary parties do not receive much from membership fees. Further, according to the figures available (number of party members, membership fees, and category of membership fees and donations) the amount received under this heading is not as high as it should be.

On the basis of information about membership fees, we need to ask two questions: first, are Slovenian parties particularly ineffective in collecting fees from their members and, secondly, are the numbers of party members not so high as the parties claim? Slovenian public opinion polls indeed showed that in 1995 only 4.7 per cent of respondents declared they were party members. Further, according to previous (1995) party data on party membership, we can hardly identify any significant increase in membership (the SDP being an exception here).

Election Campaigns

In September 1994 the Election Campaign Law was passed. According to its provisions, parties are reimbursed for their campaign expenses following the directives of the Law on Political Parties. Parties are obliged to collect and spend money for campaigns from a separate account and submit a report on campaign expenditures to the National Assembly within 30 days of the election. The Law sets a limit on expenditures for election campaign. The cap in the 1996 elections was set at SIT 30 (approximately DEM 0.30) per voter. In 1996, there were 1,542,218 voters and, as a consequence, the highest amount that could be spent on the parliamentary election campaign in 1996 was DEM 462,665. Only the SPP overstepped this total but has so far not been prosecuted for breaking the law.

TABLE 3
EXPENDITURES ON ELECTION CAMPAIGNS BY PARLIAMENTARY PARTIES IN 1996
(DEM)

LDS	SPP	SDP	SCD	ULSD	DPRPS	SNP
450,703	531,275	403,441	456,289	417,670	270,879	262,612

When we analysed the reports on incomes and expenditures on election campaigns it was discovered that, first, the biggest share of parties' campaign incomes were financial transfers from their 'normal' accounts, where public subsidies represented the largest contribution to party funding. In the LDS and SNP such transfers represented 97 per cent of all incomes for their election campaign, in the DPRPS 96 per cent, in the SPP and SDP 90 per cent, but in the ULSD only 53 per cent (the SCD did not submit the compulsory data on income). We may conclude that the election campaigns of parliamentary parties were mainly publicly funded. Second, another striking feature of election campaign data is the accuracy of Slovenian parties; four parties (LDS, SPP, SDP and DPRPS) spent exactly the same amount of money they had collected for this purpose. The SNP had a surplus of DEM 239 and the ULSD a deficit of DEM 2,872 (while the SCD failed to submit income data).

Parties or candidates who have entered parliament, or received at least two per cent of all votes at the national level, or six per cent within one electoral unit (of which Slovenia has eight, each with 11 electoral constituencies: altogether 88 constituencies), have been entitled to a reimbursement of their expenditure on election campaigns. In 1996 one political party, the Democrats of Slovenia, was entitled to reimbursement of campaign expenditures under the latter provision. The party was in parliament until the 1996 elections but then lost representation while receiving more than two per cent of votes at the national level, so they were entitled to reimbursement. The actual amount of reimbursement depends on the number of votes received. Total levels of reimbursement must not exceed actual party expenditure.

Parliamentary parties passed a modification to the Election Campaign Law just one month before the elections in 1996. This confirmed the expectation that election campaigns are becoming more and more expensive. Pursuant to this law, parties increased the limit on election campaign expenditure from SIT 30 to SIT 60 per voter. The Law also regulated the level reimbursed from SIT 30 to 60 per vote received. However, the increase only involved parliamentary parties, and non-parliamentary parties still received only SIT 30. The Court of Auditors was given the role of reviser. Now it legally reviews the financial reports on the campaigns of all parties claiming reimbursement. Sanctions for breaking the law are also more strict than under the previous regime, although current practice suggests that they are unlikely to be applied.

Parties were very keen to accelerate the law-making process as they wanted it (especially the regulations capping expenditures) to come into operation before the 1996 elections. This would have meant the parties could have upped their expenditures just a few days before the elections. However, the plan did not work out as the National Council issued a veto suspending passage of the law. The suspensive veto meant that the National Assembly had to repeat its vote. The veto was overridden in February 1997.

During an election campaign parties also have the possibility of access to the mass media – of which TV is the most important. The Law on the Radio and Television of Slovenia says that candidates and parties have the right to present themselves. Hence, payment-free access to national television is provided for all candidates and parties contesting a parliamentary seat. In 1996 all independent candidates and parties were allocated two minutes for their own presentations under the same conditions and in the same (prime) time slots. Second, there were so-called 'confrontations' between independent candidates and party representatives, led by journalists. In this case, and according to the law, non-parliamentary parties and independent candidates who are not members of the National Assembly have the right to one-third (the law does not specify whether this is the minimum or maximum amount of time) of the total time allocated to such 'free' election programmes. In practice, therefore, the parliamentary parties were specially privileged in 1996.

Three commercial television stations (POPtv, Kanal A and TV 3) also gave the parties free access for making media presentations. Of these three commercial television stations, POPtv is the most popular. POPtv gave more free and open access to parliamentary than to non-parliamentary parties. There was further discrimination within the group of parliamentary parties, whereas national television had to give all parliamentary parties an equal amount of time. The larger and, for the media, more interesting parties had more free time on POPtv (this was an advantage restricted to the five largest parliamentary parties). The station also conducted public opinion polls on party characteristics and invited those parties identified by the poll results as more interesting for its audience for more frequent 'confrontations'.

Other Forms of Public Subsidy

The system of monthly public subsidies, reimbursement of expenditures for election campaigns, and access to television are only three forms of public subsidy where the parliamentary parties are in a privileged position. In addition, only these parties are entitled to receive SIT 33,000 (approximately DEM 330) per month for each MP. This amount is considered to be support for MPs' offices in electoral constituencies. Parliamentary parties also receive certain amounts (every month) for so-called additional professional help (one-third of a consultant's salary of the National Assembly for each MP).

Another indirect public subsidy flows to parliamentary parties in the form of those secretaries, experts and administrative staff who work in parliamentary groups and are paid for by the state. Members of parliament can also use the expertise of civil servants who work in parliament offices, like department experts and the parliamentary research section. There are also less visible forms of public subsidy for parliamentary parties (use of state buildings, aeroplanes, phones, cars, and so on. for meetings and international activity), which often border the fine line of legality or cross over it.[10]

Public Funding and Voting Behaviour

In order to identify the voting behaviour of individual MPs when passing laws concerning party access to public subsidies, we analysed four selected examples. They concerned voting behaviour on: the Law on Political Parties (1994), the Election Campaign Law (1994) and the Law on Modification and Amendments to the Law on Election Campaign (1996 and 1997). It was found that in the cases of the Law on Political Parties and the Law on Election Campaign MPs voted quite uniformly. A large majority of all MPs, no matter whether their parties had governmental or opposition status, voted for the laws (an exception was the SDP whose MPs were not present at the time of voting and the SPP, some of whose MPs voted against the Law on Political Parties and whose MPs did not vote on the Election Campaign Law).

Careful tactics were used during the passage of the Law on Modification and Amendments to the Law on Election Campaign one month before the 1996 elections. The law contained one regulation with negative implications for the public, which allowed an increase in the limit on election campaign expenditures. On one hand, MPs were interested in passing the law but, on the other hand, they did not want to lose their public credibility just before elections. The result was that individual MPs from several different parties voted against it or abstained. However, the majority of MPs from almost all parties voted for the law. Once again, members of the SPP and SDP did not vote. After the suspensive veto of the National Council, the second round of voting on the law in February 1997 was quite different (the content of the law was nevertheless identical to that of October 1996). MPs from government parties (LDS, SPP, DPRPS) voted for the law, while MPs from opposition parties (SDP and SCD) voted against. The majority of the ULSD opposition party voted for it. The voting behaviour of some MPs was very interesting in that a few voted against, only to vote in favour of the same law some months later.

Analysis of voting behaviour shows, however, that in three cases where the privileged position of parties with respect to the receipt of public subsidies was at stake, different parties acted as a relatively homogeneous bloc. Only in the last case (of repeated voting) was there a more pronounced difference between government and opposition parties.

Conclusion

Successful political activity and the maintenance of an effective political presence nowadays requires the harnessing of considerable financial, human and media resources. We must be very careful when drawing a correlation between the level of those resources and success at elections and in daily politics, but we can certainly say that at least some level of such resources is necessary. With regard to maintaining the flow of such resources, Slovenian parliamentary parties are almost completely dependent on the state. Only parliamentary parties receive continuous direct and indirect financial and human resources from the state, and only the parties in receipt of such funds can employ and pay the necessary staff to work in parties. In April 1999, the Constitutional Court decided that the monthly public subsidies paid only to parliamentary parties were not in accordance with the Constitution. The National Assembly had to change the Law on Political Parties and remove the unconstitutional article within six months. The Court will, however, allow the National Assembly to apply certain conditions, for example concerning the number of votes received, when determining who receives the monthly public subsidies. It remains to be seen if the National Assembly fulfils the court's decision and changes the law; on some previous occasions the National Assembly has simply ignored the court's decisions, or respected them after a significant delay.[11]

When compared with non-parliamentary parties, parliamentary parties have also had a privileged position with respect to free access to the mass media – especially important in this area is national television. In the case of commercial television the privileged position of the parliamentary parties is even more obvious. Their advantaged position with respect to financial and human resources is almost completely the result of relatively homogeneous voting in the National Assembly. There is as yet no clear evidence that public subsidies have had a significant effect on political and parties' development in CEECs, and so far the question as to whether state funding solely of parliamentary parties prevents new entrants appearing is still open.[12] But at least some tendency in this direction is already evident in Slovenia.

Slovenian non-parliamentary parties have difficulties acquiring the resources that could enable them to enter the National Assembly. Since they do not have many members, they cannot expect significant amounts from membership fees. Large donations from individuals and enterprises are legally proscribed. As non-parliamentary parties, they are not entitled to the various forms of public subsidy (they are only entitled to reimbursement of expenditures on election campaigns if they receive at least two per cent of the vote at national level or six per cent within one electoral district), and with regard to television access they are in an equally disadvantaged position.

The consequence of the absence of public subsidies for non-parliamentary parties is also seen in the National Assembly. Since the first elections in 1990 only two new non-parliamentary parties have amassed enough votes to become parliamentary parties (the threshold for the National Assembly is three mandates or approximately 3.25 per cent). The two parties are the SNP in 1992 and the DPRPS in 1996, whose success was largely attributable to skilful election strategies. In the first case, the SNP succeeded in accurately reflecting national sentiments following the creation of the Slovenian nation-state (after the dissolution of the Yugoslav Federation). There were many populist statements in its election campaign, wholly dominated by its leader, one of the most outstanding being: 'Make this country Slovenian once again' (a direct reflection of Hitler's injunction in 1941 with regard to Slovenian Maribor).

In the second case, the DPRPS had expressed its willingness to protect the existing social rights of retired people during a period when the Slovenian government announced its readiness to begin comprehensive and radical reform of the pension system (although the announced reform refers only to the future retired population rather than to the currently retired). Retired people indeed represent quite a large part of the Slovenian electorate (there were 442,105 retired people out of 1,542,218 voters in total in 1996, or some 28.6 per cent of the electorate).

We may therefore conclude that Slovenian parties share the same patterns of development as those from other CEECs with regard to their dependence on the state. In most such countries public subsidies soon became the main support of party activity with, for example, membership fees representing only a small proportion of party funding. In some ways this trend seems to follow empirical trends recently seen in western democracies, as well as reflecting models of contemporary party development such as the cartel party.[13] But there is one important difference here between Western Europe and Slovenian parties, as well as those in other CEECs. In terms of resources, these parties have actually never been anything other than cartel parties, features of their development that are likely to be associated with some of their other characteristics like the low level of trust they attract from the electorate.

NOTES

1. Key references here and other sources in the text identified as:
   – Agreement on formation of DEMOS, 1989,
   – Data obtained from PRO PLUS (POPtv),
   – Data obtained from National Assembly,
   – Decision of the Constitutional Court on Article 23 of the Law on Political Parties, Gazette, 24/99,
   – Law on Election in Assemblies, Gazette, 42/89,
   – Law on Election Campaigns, Gazette, 62/94,
   – Law on Elections in the National Assembly, Gazette, 44/92,
   – Law on Modification and Amendments to the Law on Election Campaign, Gazette, 7/97,
   – Law on Political Association, Gazette, 42/89,
   – Law on Political Parties, Gazette, 62/94,
   – Law on Radio and Television of Slovenia, Gazette, 18/94,
   – Party Financial Reports from 1996, 1997 and 1998,
   – Slovenian Public Opinion Polls 1995, 1998 (led by Prof. Niko Toä, Faculty of Social Sciences, Ljubljana),
   – Statute of Radio and Television of Slovenia for Election Campaigns for parliamentary elections in the National Assembly 1996.
2. A. Ágh, 'Development of East Central European Party Systems: From

"Movements" to "Cartels"', paper presented to Conference on Political Representation: parties and parliamentary democracy (Budapest, 1995).
3. D. Fink-Hafner, 'Development of a Party System', in D. Fink-Hafner and J.R. Robbins (eds.), *Making a New Nation: The Formation of Slovenia* (Aldershot: Dartmouth, 1997), p.142.
4. R.S. Katz and P. Mair, 'Changing Models of Party Organisation and Party Democracy: The Emergence of the Cartel Party', *Party Politics*, Vol.1, 1 (1995), pp.5–27.
5. Fink-Hafner, 'Development of a Party System', p.142.
6. U. Vehovar, 'Socialdemokracija, sindikati, korporativizem? Druìboslovne razprave', Vol.10 (1994), pp.50–63.
7. P.G. Lewis, 'Party Funding in Post-Communist East-Central Europe', in P. Burnell and A. Ware (eds.), *Funding Democratization* (Manchester: Manchester University Press, 1998), p.140.
8. S. Kranjc, 'Financiranje političnih strank', in I. Lukšič (ed.), *Stranke in strankarstvo* (Ljubljana: Slovensko politološko društvo, 1994), pp.81–96.
9. M. Pašek, 'Zaradi kariere, veselja do politiziranja in druženja', *Delo*, 27 Feb. 1999; R. Praprotnik, 'Stranke in njihovo zaledje', Delo, 26 March 1998.
10. A. Bebler, 'Večna nevarnost kleptokracije', *Delo*, 7 Aug. 1999.
11. M. Krivic, 'Parlament proti ustavnemu sodišču: greh ali ne ?', Delo, 31 July 1999.
12. Lewis, 'Party Funding', 1998.
13. Ibid., p.140.

7

Institutions and Party Development in the Baltic States

VELLO PETTAI and MARCUS KREUZER

A number of sociological, institutional and behavioral perspectives prevail In the study of parties and party systems.[1] Each has something to offer to our understanding of how parties are linked to society, ideologies, democratic representation, and effective governance. In the domain of party formation and democratization, the debate is particularly acute, as scholars argue the preconditions for these processes to take root in previously authoritarian or totalitarian societies. In the post-communist context, our focus on institutions results from two observations.

First, public commentators and the general population in these countries (along with many Western scholars) all too frequently attribute weak parties to a low level of political culture or to communist-era legacies. According to this view a country's party formation is largely predetermined by its totalitarian past. Such explanations, while seeming plausible at first, ultimately have a defeatist quality and contradict the historical experience of various Western democracies. Germany after 1945 and France after 1958, for example, successfully strengthened their political parties by changing the institutional incentives under which they operate. Second, extensive research on parties in United States and Western European has demonstrated that cultural or historical factors generally account for little cross-national variance in the organization of parties. This research has instead identified electoral systems, parliamentary procedures and executive-legislative relations as having a far more significant effect on the organizational cohesion of parties.[2]

Our project evaluates therefore the general hypothesis that political institutions contribute to strong and effective parties by creating incentives for individual politicians to act as team-players pursuing collective, long-term policy goals and discouraging them from behaving as individual entrepreneurs seeking short-term, particularistic benefits. Political institutions create such organizational incentives by affecting political career patterns, resource mobilization and electioneering practices. Electoral and legislative procedures determine the extent to which the recruitment and promotion of politicians is left to individual actors or is collectively controlled by parties. Similarly, political institutions profoundly affect whether campaigning practices and fund-raising are carried out by individual politicians or by parties.

Empirically, we concentrate our attention on the Baltic states because of their special degree of comparability. On the one hand, when the three Soviet republics restored their independence in 1991, they shared a very similar socio-political heritage and post-communist condition. The three states had been under Soviet occupation for 50 years, but had also (in contrast to the other Soviet republics) experienced a period of independent statehood during the inter-war years. This gave them on the whole a more developed political and social consciousness. At the same time, during the immediate post-independence years (1992–93), the three countries went on to adopt vastly different electoral and other political institutions. As a result, one can say that a near-laboratory situation exists, in which we are able to observe the effects of political institutions on the formation of parties while holding socio-economic factors constant.

The full project (for which this chapter is a theoretical beginning) will involve three clusters of institutions: electoral law, party law, and parliamentary rules. This chapter (as well as an article previously published in *East European Politics and Societies*)[3] presents some findings from our initial research and allows us to begin to think about the possible effects that institutions can have on the formation of post-communist parties. In the fall of 1999, we will begin a second stage of the project, which will involve a survey of political elites to find out how they respond to incentives created by their representative institutions.

Constitutional Background

A striking aspect of politics in the Baltic states concerns the wide-ranging diversity of their electoral institutions. The spectrum runs from a fairly simple PR-list system in Latvia to a personalized PR system in Estonia to a dual PR and majoritarian system in Lithuania. In Table 1 below, we lay out the main features of each state's electoral system. However, before describing these mechanisms in detail, a brief constitutional overview of the three states is in order.

When in August 1991 the three Baltic countries leapt to freedom from the Soviet Union, all three insisted that they were in fact *restoring* their statehood after 50 years of Soviet occupation and that they were not successor states to the Soviet Union. As a result, the issue of legal restorationism has been an important one for all three nations (for instance, with regard to citizenship for Soviet-era immigrants in Estonia and Latvia, but also concerning property restitution in all three Baltic states).

Constitutionally, however, only Latvia ended up actually reinstating its constitution from the pre-war period, namely its constitution from 1922. Although short by modern standards, the pre-war constitution was generally viewed as good enough for the initial term, while any necessary alterations were put off until later. The constitution itself is strongly parliamentary in nature, with only a ceremonial presidency, elected by parliament and vested with limited veto powers.

In Estonia, a similarly quick constitutional decision was taken, but here it was in the direction of drafting an entirely new basic law. A Constitutional Assembly was convened immediately after independence, which worked for seven months before proposing a parliamentary regime similar to Latvia's. – Estonia's system, too, would feature a president elected by the legislature with only suspensive veto prerogatives. In June 1992, the draft constitution was ratified by the Estonian people. In Lithuania, constitutional consensus was delayed as supporters of the popular nationalist leader Vytautas Landsbergis first sought to make the country's existing Soviet constitution more presidential. This attempt failed after a referendum on such a change in May 1992 did not receive the necessary two-thirds majority. Still, the strong support expressed for presidentialism served as a benchmark for a non-partisan commission formed later to draft a new constitution. This commission subsequently drew up a semi-presidential system in which a popularly-elected president and a parliament-based prime minister would share executive power. The new basic law was ratified by a referendum in October 1992.

Electoral Law

Electoral laws were also adopted in the Baltic states during the course of 1992. Here Estonia was the first to begin planning new elections by adopting its law on 6 April 1992. Having opted overall for a strongly parliamentary system, the country was also inclined toward proportional representation. However, strict voting on the basis of party lists was shunned, since many politicians (especially leaders of the former *nomenklatura* parties) wanted to retain an element of personality voting, which would favour them and their revamped political images. Thus, the law that was finally adopted was a compromise, creating an overall PR system, which was based, however, on direct voting for candidates in 11 electoral districts and a triple-tier vote-counting system.[4] In this sense it represents a hybrid of the German and Finnish electoral systems.[5] Voters are obliged to vote for individual candidates, who at the same time, however, represent particular party lists. Independent candidates are also allowed to run.

Thus at the first level of mandate distribution, individual candidates can be directly elected if they surpass the vote quota for the district (based on the

TABLE 1
ELECTORAL SYSTEMS IN THE BALTIC STATES

	Estonia	Latvia	Lithuania
1. Basic system	List – PR with triple-tier districting; voting for individual candidates	List – PR with single-tier districting; voting for party lists with preferential marking of candidates possible	Dual PR – Majoritarian – 70 seats elected in one nationwide district based on party lists with preferential marking possible. – 71 seats elected in single-member districts and two-rounds of voting
2. Electoral formulas	Lower tier: seats allocated directly to candidates by Hare quota (Q=V/M); Middle tier: seats allocated to district party list by Hare quota; Upper tier: Compensatory seats allocated by modified d'Hondt formula (distribution series I, 20.9, 30.9, 40.9,...)	Seats allocated within districts based on Saint-Lague formula	PR seats allocated based on altered Hare quota (Q=votes for threshold parties only/70) and largest remainders: Majoritarian seats elected based on first-round absolute majority or second-round plurality among two highest vote-getters.
3. District magnitude	1992: 5-13 1995: 8-11 1999: 7-13	1993: 14-26 1995: 14-27 1998: 14-28	1992: 70 and 1 1996: 70 and 1
4. Thresholds	1992: 5% 1995: 5% 1999: 5%	1993: 4% 1995: 5% 1998: 5%	1992: 4% (except minority parties: 1/70 of national vote total) 1996: 5% for parties 7% for coalition

Hare formula of number of votes cast in the district divided by the number of available mandates). These are known as 'personal mandates'. At the second tier of vote counting, the total number of votes cast for an individual party list (via its candidates) in the district is tabulated and a further number of mandates is allocated based on whether this new total surpasses the district's Hare quota. If a local list in its entirety surpasses the Hare quota, this entitles its top vote-getter to a seat. At this tier, however, only parties surpassing a nationwide threshold of five per cent are eligible for such seats. Finally, all remaining mandates gathered together from across the country are allocated based on each party list's national vote total (again using the five per cent threshold); however, here the allocation proceeds based on a modified d'Hondt formula with the sequence of divisors (1, 2, 3, 4, etc.) raised to the power of 0.9. As will become evident below, the system was clearly tailored with the politicians' interests in mind, for candidates are able both to reap the benefits of individual popularity through direct election, as well as to control the composition of national party lists for the allocation of remainder mandates. Voters, meanwhile, are often frustrated by the mandate distribution process, since quite frequently a popular candidate will receive thousands of votes, but will not be elected due to low placement on the national list, while unheard-of candidates get into parliament thanks to their prominent list position.[6]

Latvia in October 1992 also opted for a PR system, but with five high-magnitude districts and a single-tier proportional allocation system based on the Sainte-Lague formula. Indeed, the law represented another re-adoption of a pre-war system, this time the country's first electoral law adopted in 1922.[7] The districts are based on the republic's historical division into four regions (Kurzeme, Zemgale, Vidzeme, and Latgale) along with the capital city of Riga as its own district. In 1998, the magnitudes were respectively 14, 15, 25, 18, and 28, making for a total of 100 seats. In line with the 1922 system, voters are also allowed to express preferences votes within the party lists. Thus the ballot structure is not entirely categorical nor ordinal, but intermediate (see more below). To avoid, however, a repeat of the interwar experience of 27 parties being represented in parliament, a four per cent national threshold (later raised to five per cent) also now applies. Thus, the entire system is fairly straightforward, allowing for a significant degree of proportionality and representativeness.

In Lithuania, the combination of the failed presidential referendum in May 1992, an ensuing government crisis, and the move toward a brand-new constitution all eventually pushed the parliament into scheduling new elections for October 1992. The electoral law, which was adopted in July, reflected (as in Estonia) a struggle between those who wanted party-list voting and those who preferred a first-past-the-post system. However, in the end the compromise was a literal one in that 70 of the *Seimas*'s 141 members would be elected based on party lists within a single nationwide 70-mandate district and a threshold of four per cent (later raised to five per cent), and the remaining 71 seats would be contested based on 71 single-member districts using two rounds of voting. In the party-list voting, seats are allocated using a modified Hare quota and largest remainders (under this system, the number of votes used as the numerator in the equation is the number of votes cast *only* for the threshold-level parties, and not the total of votes cast for all the parties).

As of 1996, voters are also allowed (as in Latvia) an approval vote among the candidates on a particular party list, although this has much less bearing on final mandate distribution since the parties are also allowed to rank their candidates. Within the single-member districts, voting is similar to French presidential elections. A candidate who wins 50 per cent +1 votes in the first round is directly elected; barring that, the two highest vote-getters in each district proceed to a run-off, where a plurality is sufficient. All in all, this combination of PR and majoritarian systems is fairly unique in the world, followed only by Hungary and Russia in Eastern Europe; indeed, little research has been done on such hybrids and their ultimate political effects are largely unknown.[8]

Theoretical Considerations

Our more conceptual examination of Baltic electoral law concentrates on six particular electoral institutions: electoral coalitions (or *apparentements*), the division of power and election timing, ballot structure, multiple candidacies, physical district size, and candidate recruitment. We examine each of these institutions in turn.

Apparentements

During their first two post-independence elections, the three Baltic states belonged to a small group of countries (such as Switzerland, Israel and the Netherlands), whose electoral law allows parties to form joint electoral lists or *apparentements* (other countries like Sweden in 1948, Norway in 1945 and 1985 have sporadically used *apparentements*. In 1951 and 1956, France employed *apparentements* in conjunction with a majoritarian bonus).[9] In 1998, such *apparentements* were formally banned in Estonia and Latvia, but in a concealed way they continue to exist, since many parties now simply run together under only one party's name, whereas before they used some special coalition name.

The essential thing about *apparentements*, however, is that they permit small parties to pool their votes and hence overcome the gate-keeping effect created by district magnitude and legal thresholds. Drawing on a sample of established democracies, Lijphart found that *apparentements* increased the effective number of parties by only 0.17 parties in countries with the same district magnitude as the Baltics.[10] Lijphart's low figure almost certainly underestimates the permissive effect of *apparentements* in the Baltics. In our analysis, we suggest ways in which *apparentements* create disincentives for strategic voting and resource allocation.

First, *apparentements* increase the uncertainty of interest groups and voters about party labels and thus complicate the assessment of a candidate's or a list's viability. In the Baltic states, parties which have formed *apparentements* have frequently run under a new collective label and have been physically listed by the electoral commission on the same ballot. In Latvia, for example, the ballot has included the names of the individual *apparentement* parties, while in Estonia and Lithuania the list has contained only the *apparentement* label. The ballot format of Baltic *apparentements* thus creates a far stronger disincentive for strategic voting than in Western Europe where parties are listed on separate ballots with only limited reference made to other *apparentement* members.

Second, *apparentements* impede retrospective assessment of parties' electoral viability. They are often formed shortly before elections and involve an extra-electoral bargaining process. Such bargaining obscures the electoral history of parties, from which voters and interest groups might infer the viability of parties. *Apparentements* facilitate strategic coordination among politicians in order to evade strategic voting by voters and strategic resource allocation by donors. It thus enfeebles the reductive effect of district magnitudes and legal thresholds.

In the Baltic cases, it is difficult to precisely estimate the permissive effect of *apparentements*. We try, however, to infer their importance from the level of *apparentement* activity. As Table 2 shows, Baltic parties have made extensive use of *apparentements*. During the first two post-independence elections, an average of 44.7 per cent of all parties participated in some kind of *apparentement*. In turn, these parties won 34 per cent of all the parliamentary seats. *Apparentements* thus clearly contributed to the continued existence of a plethora of political parties. However, Table 2 also shows important cross-national differences. *Apparentements* seem to be more permissive in Estonia than in Latvia or Lithuania (even during the second election). These cross-Baltic differences reflect the incentives other electoral mechanisms create for small parties to form electoral alliances. In Lithuania, for example, the dramatic drop-off in *apparentement* activity in 1996 is directly related to the introduction of a special seven per cent electoral threshold for electoral coalitions. This threshold had the effect of requiring larger and more heterogeneous coalitions between parties that would be less appealing to voters. The higher threshold thus lowers the advantage of forming an *apparentement* as compared to a go-it-alone strategy. Latvia's rise in *apparentement* activity between 1992 and 1995 in turn reflects the increase in the legal threshold from four per cent to five per cent. Estonia's high level of *apparentement* activity can only partly be explained by its five per cent threshold. Overall, Estonia's high number also seems to be a by-product of the country's simply large number parties.

Apparentements thus clearly impede strategic voting and resource allocation and hence have a permissive effect on the number of parties.

TABLE 2
LEVEL OF *APPARENTEMENT* ACTIVITY

	Estonia			Latvia			Lithuania	
	1992	1995	1999	1993	1995	1998	1992	1996
1. Number of *apparentements* in each election	8	7	3	3	5	3	4	1
2. Number of parties participating in *apparentements* as a proportion of all parties running in each election	29/38	21/30	7/16	7/28	12/26	9/27	10/23	2/25
3. % of seats won by *apparentements*	89%	60%	30%	6%	16%	30%	31%	2%

However, in our analysis we also find that in the Baltics *apparentements* have somewhat unexpectedly contributed to the consolidation of parties by facilitating coordination among political elites. Row 1 in Table 3 shows that of the 25 *apparentements* winning seats, 14 (56 per cent) ended up either as permanent coalitions or party mergers. Row 3, in turn, illustrates that electoral defeat did little to prompt unsuccessful *apparentements* into forming permanent political formations. Row 2 indicates the significance of the consolidation process induced by *apparentements*. Increasingly, winning *apparentements* have either merged into one party or remained as permanent coalitions. By contrast, among unsuccessful electoral alliances (Row 4) the consolidating effect of *apparentements* has been weaker. The only permanent *apparentement* in this category (row 4b, Latvia 1995) subsumed just three parties.

Still, overall we would characterize the consolidation effect of *apparentements* as far weaker than their permissive effect. Moreover, we would argue that such a consolidation effect is only made possible by the particular conditions of democratic transition and is less liable to occur in consolidated democracies. In established democracies, *apparentements* are unlikely to lead to new, permanent organizations because they bring together parties with a good sense of their electoral strength and well-institutionalized organizations. Parties which know their smallness, but are electorally protected by *apparentements* are unlikely to agree to a complicated organizational merger which halves the number of party-internal career opportunities. This problem is less pronounced in transitional democracies where parties are more uncertain about their viability, are less institutionalized, and are much more numerous. As a result, there is more of a need to cooperate and less of an obstacle to merge. In such an environment, *apparentement* functions both as a match-maker that facilitates elite coordination, as well as a permissive mechanism that allows parties to linger on if they want to.

TABLE 3
APPARENTEMENTS AND PARTY CONSOLIDATION

	Estonia			Latvia			Lithuania	
	1992	1995	1999	1993	1995	1998	1992	1996
1. Of *apparentements* winning seats, number that were:								
a) temporary coalitions[1]):	5	2	0	1	0	0	3	0
b) permanent coalitions[2]):	1	0	3	0	2	2	0	1
c) party mergers[3]):	1	2	0	1	0	0	1	0
Total:	7	4	3	2	2	2	4	1
2. Number of elective parties in *apparentements* winning seats that								
a) were in temp. *apparentements*	19	7	0	2	0	0	8	0
b) were subsumed under party merger or permanent coalition	4	4	7	3	5	6	2	2
3. Of *apparentements* not winning seats, number that were:								
a) temporary coalitions:	1	3	0	1	2	1	0	0
b) permanent coalitions:	0	0	0	0	1	0	0	0
c) party mergers	0	0	0	0	0	0	0	0
Total:	1	3	0	1	3	1	0	0
4. Number of elective parties in *apparentements* not winning seats that								
a) were in temp. *apparentements*	6	10	0	2	4	3	0	0
b) were subsumed under party merger or permanent coalition	0	0	0	0	3	0	0	0

Notes: [1]) Defined as coalitions that broke up into separate parties (or parliamentary factions) or disintegrated into independent deputies after the election

[2]) Defined as coalitions that formed a unified faction in the parliament or maintained cooperation as individual deputies

[3]) Defined as parties that merged and ceased to exist as separate juridical entities.

Division of Power and Election Timing

A number of theorists have pointed out that presidential elections increase strategic voting in parliamentary systems.[11] In particular, these authors argue that a popularly elected presidency, being the single biggest political prize, will frequently induce voters, interest groups and parties into concentrating their respective resources on front-runners. Since presidential contests often exert a coat-tail effect, such strategic behavior can spill over into parliamentary elections, especially when they are timed together.

In the Baltic context, Lithuania's popularly elected and powerful presidency has the potential for inducing strategic voting during parliamentary elections, much more than in Estonia and Latvia, where presidents are elected by parliament. Again, it is difficult to estimate precisely this reductive effect, since it is contingent on the presidential electoral system, the parliamentary electoral system, as well as the proximity of presidential and parliamentary elections. We can, however, make some qualitative inferences from presidential systems that share Lithuania's institutional characteristics.

France's semi-presidential system comes closest to Lithuania's form of presidentialism. The French system's reductive effect, according to Shugart and Carey, is moderate compared to other presidential systems. France and Lithuania both elect their president through a majoritarian run-off formula, which induces less strategic voting and withdrawals than a straight plurality formula would. Moreover, France (and even more so Lithuania) hold presidential and parliamentary elections non-concurrently which weakens the coat-tail effect of the former.[12] Given the majoritarian run-off formula and non-concurrent timing, Lithuania's presidential elections have a weak reductive effect as presidential systems go, but they must still be considered as a relevant factor in accounting for why the country has fewer parliamentary parties than Estonia and Latvia.

Ballot Structure

We have so far confined our analysis of strategic voting to the choice of candidates belonging to different parties. Yet, certain electoral ballots also permit voters to express preferences for the ranking of candidates within the same party in addition to voting for different parties. Such ordinal ballots differ from categoric ballots which require voters to make a single choice for a fixed, multi-member list. A number of other mechanisms (for example, run-off elections, dual ballots, single-nontransferable votes) also are classified as having ordinal-like qualities even though they do not permit ordinal ranking of preferences.

The central effect of ordinal ballots is to personalize the basis on which voters cast their ballots. The voters' possibility to rank candidates and thereby affect their electoral prospects induces candidates to establish their own electoral machine and solicit a personal vote.[13] In different countries ordinal ballots vary as to the scope of preference voting they permit and consequently the incentive they create for a personal vote. The more ordinal a ballot is, the more it will impede strategic voting, since it is more difficult for voters to coordinate local, personalized voting than voting based on national, collective appeals. Ordinal ballots, in other words, dilute the process of strategic voting by giving voters the possibility to cast a sincere (i.e. non-strategic) preference vote. They also increase the incentive candidates have for seeking a personal vote which might damage party cohesion.

In terms of the Baltic states, the ordinal ballots in use are arguably even more permissive than those in established Western democracies, mainly for two reasons. First, Estonia, Latvia and to a lesser extent Lithuania use ballots (discussed below) that give voters a wider scope for preference voting than most Western ones (in fact, Baltic ordinal ballots share many more characteristics with the highly ordinal single-transferable vote systems used in Ireland and Australia than the ordinal or ordinal-like ballots used in Italy, Austria, Luxembourg, Germany and Switzerland). Former communist notables were the strongest advocates of these highly personalized ballots because they hoped to capitalize on their name recognition and oftentimes continued control over local authorities.

Unfortunately, ordinal ballots in established democracies are rarely analysed and, if they are, important differences among them are overlooked (Lijphart, for example, overlooks differences between ordinal ballots and treats ballot structures as a strictly dichotomous variable. Katz, however, represents a detailed analysis of ordinal ballots).[14] As a result, it is not possible to systematically compare their permissive effect with Baltic ordinal ballots. Anecdotal evidence, however, suggests that countries with a weakly ordinal ballot see little personalized voting and thus face fewer obstacles to strategic coordination and vice versa. Secondly, we would argue that ordinal ballots in the Baltic states weaken party consolidation to the extent that they hinder the establishment of collective political identities as well as organizations which might facilitate strategic coordination (the presence of well-organized parties and interest groups in established democracies might help to explain why Lijphart found no significant effect of ordinal ballots on the number of parties.[15]

TABLE 4
INDICATORS CONCERNING THE EFFECT OF BALLOT STRUCTURE

	Estonia			Latvia			Lithuania	
1. Type of indicator	%of seats allocated at each electoral tier			% of possible preference votes cast			% of possible preference votes cast SF-ratio	
2. Data	1992	1995	1999	1993	1995	1995	1992	1996
	I: 17%	I:15%	I: 11%	Data as			No pre-	-2%
	II: 24%	II: 34%	II:44%	yet un-	12%	12%	ference	0.74
	III: 59%	III: 51%	III: 45%	available			voting	
							0.51	

Estonia has the most ordinal ballot in the Baltics. Normally, ordinal ballots give voters a separate list vote and separate candidate vote. Estonia, however, uses what Cox calls a 'pooling vote'.[16] In this system, a voter gets to cast a single vote which is then counted at each of the three levels of seat allocation, first as a preference vote and then as a list vote. The important thing to note is that a candidate's individual votes directly affect his or her electoral prospects at the first two tiers, thus creating a very strong incentive for a personal vote.

The hypothesis here would therefore be: the more parliamentary seats are allocated at the first and second levels of vote counting (where candidates can be elected based on their personal vote totals), the more one can say the ballot system induces personalized voting, which in turn can have a party-weakening effect. Indeed, during Estonia's three post-independence elections (1992, 1995, and 1999), an average of 47.8 per cent of the seats were allocated via the first two tiers of vote pooling (see Table 4). This means that nearly half of the deputies in parliament owed their seats to some degree of personal name-recognition or personal vote-getting as distinct from a clear party vote. Although one can see that during the three elections the share of first-tier seats (where candidates won purely on their individual vote totals) has declined, the share of seats allocated at the second tier has steadily increased, meaning that more and more candidates in total have been elected based on some form of personal vote.

Latvia's ballot structure is not quite as ordinal as Estonia's. Rather, it resembles a more standard type of ordinal ballot. Under the Latvian system, voters choose a party list, in favour of which they directly cast a list vote. However, within that party list, a voter can express a 'positive opinion' for one or more candidate(s) by marking an '+' behind their names and a 'negative opinion' by crossing out one or several names. It is left to the voter's discretion as to how many such preferences, if any at all, he or she desires to express.

This preference voting device permits the grouping of candidates (that is, preferred, neutral, opposed), but no ordinal ranking. Seats are allocated to each party according to its vote share and within each party list according to a candidate's number of preference votes. Still, Latvia's ordinal ballot differs from most others, since it ranks candidates based only on their preference vote totals and gives no weight to the original list ranking. This makes the system more ordinal in that a candidate at the top of the list has no advantage over candidates at the bottom of the list (other than marginally higher visibility). The system puts voters in charge of ranking candidates and thus gives candidates a very strong incentive to seek a personal vote.

In our own analysis, we try to approximate the importance of such personal votes by calculating preference votes cast as a percentage of the total number of possible preference votes (example: a list with ten candidates and 1,000 votes permits 10,000 possible preference votes since each voter can cast either ten negative or ten positive preference votes. We compare this to the actual number of preference votes cast, since each voter can also choose to express either none or only some of her ten possible preference votes).

In the 1995 election, for example, Latvian voters cast just 12 per cent of all possible preferences votes; in 1998, this figure remained at 11.9 per cent As a result, we can say that Latvia's ordinal ballot does less to encourage sincere voting than Estonia's personalized PR system. Latvian voters rely more on parties' collective appeals than on their candidates' personal popularity to make their choice. They consequently were more likely to make strategic voting decisions (still, some candidates have been very eager seekers of personal votes. For instance, during the 1993 elections, a German-born candidate Joachim Siegerists (running on the nationalist LNNK ticket) organized a special bus campaign to transport voters from Riga to his electoral district in Jelgava. This effort clearly helped to boost the party's showing in the town, while it also added to Siegerists's own preference vote total and subsequent election to parliament.

The ballot structures of Lithuania's two-part electoral system each have only a moderately ordinal quality. In the single-district voting, the two-round voting procedure yields an ordinal-like ballot because it provides voters with the possibility to 're-vote' or 're-orient' their choices between the two rounds. It particularly encourages sincere voting on the first ballot and therefore has a permissive effect in terms of parties. It also discourages strategic withdrawals before the election, as candidates will be encouraged to try at least for second place in the first round or use a strong showing to extract side-payments for supporting one of the two run-off candidates.[17]

One way to measure this degree of sincere voting induced by a double ballot is to calculate the ratio of the second to the first loser's vote total. Cox was the first to use this measure and termed it simply the SF ratio. It indicates how extensively voters have strategically concentrated their votes behind the second candidate and abandoned a trailing third candidate. A near-perfect two-party system would yield an SF ratio of 0 and reflect a high degree of strategic voting while an SF ratio close to 1 would demonstrate sincere voting for a large number of candidates.[18] During the 1996 parliamentary elections, the SF ratio for Lithuania was 0.74, which indicates a fairly high degree of sincere voting and thus a potential barrier to party consolidation. Indeed, this figure was an increase over the 1992 ratio of just 0.51.

At the same time, in Lithuania's multi-member districts, strategic voting seems more in line, since even though Lithuania also has a system of preference voting as in Latvia, a candidate's final score is calculated based on both his or her number of preference votes as well as his or her party ranking (in 1996, Lithuania's electoral law also introduced an opt out clause that permits parties to bar preference voting within their list as long as they notify voters and authorities before each election). This weakens a candidate's incentive to seek a personal vote and instead facilitates strategic coordination by party elites. For example, in 1996 Lithuanian voters cast only 2.05 per cent of all possible preference votes, meaning that most people voted straight for the party. Moreover, in no instance did a candidate seriously buck the party's list-ranking through an unusual amount of preference votes. Thus, Lithuania's dual electoral system yields some conflicting institutional incentives for candidates, especially if a candidate is only running in one of the two systems.

Multiple Candidacies

Multiple candidacies can be significant in cases where candidates can use such options to choose where they want to be elected, thereby distorting the voters' true preferences. In the Baltic countries, this possibility exists to varying degrees. In Estonia, it is worst, since although candidates are permitted to run in only one district, they are also always included on a national list, from which they may subsequently be elected regardless of their district showing. Thus, one candidate in 1995 received as few as 37 votes in her local district, but was elected to parliament off the national list, while another candidate with over 3,000 votes was denied a seat because he did not make his district quota and was also placed too low on the national list. Moreover, the three-tiered system of seat allocation has led to significant regional discrepancies, whereby many more candidates from Tallinn and Tartu have been elected than the official distribution of mandates would have it. As a result, many rural areas of Estonia have been short-changed (for example, during 1997–98 the southern electoral district of Valga-, Võru-, and Põlvamaa had only six MPs, who had originally campaigned in that district, as opposed to the 11 mandates it was ostensibly allocated by law).

In Latvia, multiple candidacies are possible to the extent that parties can nominate an identical list of candidates in as many of the five electoral districts as they want. This allows parties to boost their appeal by placing their star candidates on each district list. Voters, however, have no guarantee that these candidates will actually be elected from their district until after the counting of preference votes is complete. In the 1995 election, Latvian parties nominated their candidates to run in an average of 2.05 districts, although this figure ranged widely from 1.01 within the Latvian Farmers' Union/Christian Democratic Party coalition to 4.62 within the Russian Citizens Party. In 1998, this figure rose slightly to 2.2, however, among parliamentary parties the figure was just 1.5.

Lithuanian candidates, finally, can run simultaneously in both a single-member district as well as on their party's national list. This clearly provides protection for party notables, who can be re-elected via the national list if their district support is weak (indeed, in 1996, 12 of the 22 incumbents from single-seat constituencies who were returned to parliament owed their re-election to their high placement on the national list after suffering defeats in their local districts). If the candidate is elected in the district, however, he or she is struck from the national list. At the same time, this dual system raises an interesting hypothesis of whether deputies elected via a single-seat district act differently in parliament as opposed to deputies elected via the party list. In theory, one can imagine that the former will continue to behave with an eye to maintaining personal connections and support groups within his or her district, while party-list deputies will be more subservient to party elites. However, more research has to be done into this question.

Physical District Size

The physical district size (P) is calculated as the average number of registered voters per district. Although little studied in the electoral systems literature (the one exception being Katz, 1980), it is clear that different physical district sizes impose different organizational and informational exigencies on parties. The larger the physical district size, the more resources on average a party must acquire to wage an effective campaign. In the three Baltic countries, the physical district size varies significantly. In 1995/1996, Estonia's P was 69,693, Latvia's was 264,168, and Lithuania's was 36,588 for the single-seat constituencies and 2,597,714 for the nation-wide district. In this case, one might expect Latvian and Lithuanian parties to develop more centralized campaign and party structures, while in Estonia the smaller physical district size will prompt parties and candidates to work more autonomously on the local level.

Candidate Recruitment

Until now, we have treated parties as single unitary actors. We have paid no attention to internal party cohesiveness and the possibility of breakaway candidates forming new parties. Investigating this possibility requires a two-step analysis. First, we have to look at how much authority party elites have to coordinate the recruitment of candidates and avoid the desertion of ambitious candidates. Second, we need to account for what sort of incentives breakaway candidates have to form their own parties or join other existing ones.

Recruitment itself involves three discreet phases: (1) the *nomination* of candidates after an initial screening and short-listing; (2) the *selection* from these nominees of an official candidate or candidates, and (3) in the case of multiple candidates, their *ranking* on a party list. The capacity of party elites to coordinate candidate recruitment is shaped by the ballot structure and district magnitude. We have already discussed how ordinal ballots lessen the control of party leaders over the ranking stage of the recruitment process. The district magnitude in turn influences the coordination of candidate recruitment for two reasons.

121

First, large district magnitudes reduce the number of recruitment sites. The number of seats is inversely related to the number of districts available for selecting candidates. Large district magnitudes thus centralize the nomination process and enhance the control of party leaders. Second, large district magnitudes also create longer electoral lists with more safe list-positions. They make recruitment more hierarchical and facilitate the coordination of nominations.[19] The ballot structure and district magnitude have a particularly important effect on candidate recruitment when it is not regulated by special statutes (for example, US primaries, German party law) or when parties are weakly organized and lack effective statutes.

Table 5 looks at three behavioral indicators to make inferences about the organizational state of Baltic parties. Roughly speaking, these indicators look at different aspects of the candidate recruitment process as proxy measures for how institutionalized and disciplined the internal governance of Baltic parties has become. In Table 5, rows 1 and 2 bring out the percentage of candidates who ran for a second time in each country's second election (as well as in 1998/1999 for Latvia and Estonia). Row 1 provides an aggregate indicator for the turnover rate of all electoral candidates, while Row 2 singles out the turnover rate of 'established' parties, or parties which fielded candidates in both elections. The significance of these figures as indicators of party organization comes from the fact that in consolidated democracies the recruitment of electoral candidates is commonly carried out through political parties (except where primaries are used).[20] In turn, parties tend to

TABLE 5
ELECTORAL CANDIDATE TURNOVER AND PARTY DISCIPLINE

	Estonia		Latvia		Lithuania
	1992/1995	1995/1999	1993/1995	1995/1998	1992/196
1. Aggregate Candidate Turnover between elections					
a. Repeat Candidates as % of Previous Electoral List	41%	25%	295	35%	33%
b. Repeat Candidates as % of Current Electoral List	21%	17%	25%	32%	18%
2. Average Candidate Turnover within "Established" Parties					
a. Repeat Candidates as % of Previous Electoral List	36%	33%	23%	25%	25%
b. Repeat Candidates as % of Current Electoral List	20%	21%	29%	32%	18%
3. Incumbent MPs					
a. Loyalists	62%	90%	76%	68%	97%
Z Breakaways	38%	10%	24%	32%	3%

develop internal selection procedures that favor personnel continuity and incumbents. Thus the degree of candidate turnover gives a fairly good idea of how successful parties have been in institutionalizing effective recruitment channels.

The figures in Rows 1 and 2 strikingly illustrate the limited institutionalization of recruitment mechanisms among Baltic parties. In each country's second election (1995/1996), over three-fourths of all the candidates were new (Row1b). Moreover, in each country the established parties also showed a high degree of turnover, even though one might have expected these parties to have regularized their candidate recruitment and stabilized their candidate turnover. As Row 2a shows, only about a third or less of candidates selected for the 1992/93 lists were re-nominated for the next round of elections in 1995/96. Compared to parties in established democracies, this rate of continuity was exceptionally low. Indeed, in Estonia's and Latvia's case, these numbers declined still further during 1998/99. To be fair, it should be noted that one reason for this high turnover was that many politicians, who had led the independence fight during the late 1980s, retired from politics during the mid-1990s and returned to their old careers. New candidates therefore took their place.

Furthermore, the second (and third) elections generally saw parties submit more complete candidate lists for the poll, meaning they nominated as many candidates as there were seats in parliament and sometimes even more (in fact, in Estonia this has become an endemic problem, since the personalized PR system means that parties are tempted to throw into the race as many candidates as possible in order to 'fish' for as many votes as possible. Attempts to amend the electoral law during late 1998 to restrict national lists to just 101 members failed. As a result, the Moderates' list in 1999, for example, totalled a whopping 303 candidates because there were combined with the Right-wingers and the Farmer's Party from 1995 and thus needed to offer candidate slots to many more people). These factors further reduced the proportion of repeat candidates (Row 2b). Yet, even if we make allowances for these two factors, it is clear that candidate recruitment among Baltic parties remains weakly institutionalized and wide open to entrepreneurial newcomers.

The third row supports this assertion, particular with regard to Estonia and Latvia. Here we look only at incumbent candidates of the established parties and break them down into loyal candidates who stayed with the same party and breakaway candidates who defected to other parties. These figures provide a further indicator of party organization, since incumbent candidates generally have more to lose from breaking ranks than regular party members. Yet, even on this level, during the 1992–95 period, 38 per cent of Estonian incumbents and 24 per cent of Latvian incumbents still deserted their original parties by the second election. These figures markedly improved in the case of Estonia following the March 1999 elections, however, they actually worsened in Latvia due to the creation of a number of new parties (for example, the People's Party, the New Party).

Admittedly, these latest figures from Estonia and Latvia cast some doubt on the explanatory power of institutions, for ostensibly Latvia's larger district magnitude as well as less ordinal ballot structure should increase party discipline and limit the number of defecting incumbents. By contrast, one would expect Estonia's smaller district magnitude as well as personalized voting to tempt candidates to break away, should they deem it necessary. Yet, in terms of candidate loyalties and party discipline during the 1998/1999 elections, this was not the case. Indeed, quite the opposite: Latvia's numbers got worse, while Estonia's improved. Still, it is clear that in Estonia, the personal vote remains important, if only to judge by the rising number of seats allocated in the first and second tiers of vote counting, and so even though the number of parties themselves appears to be consolidating, future cohesion may still be threatened by entrepreneurial candidates tempted to seek a personal vote during the campaign.

Conclusion

The Baltic electoral and party systems are clearly still in a state of evolution. Their precise paths toward consolidation will take time to emerge. Yet, on a theoretical level, the three cases offer a unique variety of electoral institutions, which differ not only *vis-à-vis* each other, but also in relation to many Western countries (for example, ballot structure, *apparentements*). Of course, in many cases some of the institutions have already been altered, which makes the task of a researcher more difficult. For example, the abolition of *apparentements* in Estonia and Latvia has already provoked a certain number of party mergers and other moves toward consolidation. Each of these changes represents a subtle change in the rules and tactics of the political game, thus making it all the more incumbent upon scholars to understand their intricate patterns. Yet, our research into these cases is also only tentative and much work remains to be done in terms of analysing legislative procedure and concrete party organization. In addition, we will eventually have the results of our survey of Baltic politicians, which will focus specifically on constituency work, campaign tactics, party recruitment and political resources. Only with all this information will we be able to map out fully the patterns of party development in the Baltic states as well as assess their conformity to existing theoretical models.

NOTES

1. Alan Ware, *Parties and Party Systems* (Oxford: Oxford University Press, 1996), pp.1–13.
2. G. Cox, *Making Votes Count: Strategic Coordination in the World's Electoral Systems* (Cambridge: Cambridge University Press, 1997); M. Shugart and J. Carey, *Presidents and Assemblies: Constitutional Design and Electoral Dynamics* (Cambridge: Cambridge University Press, 1992).
3. V. Pettai and M. Kreuzer, 'Party Politics in the Baltic States: Social Bases and Institutional Context', *East European Politics and Societies*, Vol.17 (1999), pp.148–89.
4. For details of Estonian electoral law see Eesti Vabariigi Valimiskomisjon, *Vabariigi Presidendi ja Riigikogu Valimised 1992: Dokumente ja materjale* (Tallinn: Eesti Vabariigi Valimiskomisjon, 1992), pp.8–23; and Eesti Vabariigi Valimiskomisjon, *Riigikogu valimine*, 5 March 1995, p.1–13.
5. R. Taagepera and M.S. Shugart, *Seats and Votes: The Effects and Determinants of Electoral Systems* (New Haven, CT and London: Yale University Press, 1989), pp.35–6, 42–5.
6. R. Taagepera, 'Estonian Parliamentary Elections, March 1995', *Electoral Studies*, Vol.14 (1995), pp.328–1.
7. Both the 1922 and 1992 laws are contained in Latvijas Republikas Centrala Velešanu Komisija, Latvijas Republikas 5. Saeimas Velešanas (Riga: Latvijas Republikas Centrala Velešanu Komisija, 1993), pp.A-10-A-23. For the 1995 law see 'Saeimas velešanu likums', Saeima-Ministru Kabineta, 7 June 1995.
8. For a comparison of electoral systems across Eastern Europe see D.M. Olson, 'Party Formation and Party System Consolidation in the New Democracies of Central Europe', in R. Hofferbert (ed.), *Parties and Democracy: Party Structure and Party Performance in Old and New Democracies* (Oxford: Blackwell, 1998). For research on this specific type of mixed electoral system see R.G. Moser, 'Electoral Systems and the Number of Parties in Postcommunist States', *World Politics*, Vol.51 (1999), pp.359–84.
9. A. Lijphart, *Electoral Systems and Party Systems, A Study of Twenty-Seven Democracies, 1945–1990* (Oxford: Oxford University Press, 1994), p.134.
10. Ibid., pp.134–6.
11. Shugart and Carey, *Presidents and Assemblies*, pp.206–58; Lijphart, *Electoral Systems and Party Systems*, pp.130–4; Cox, *Making Votes Count*, pp.209–12.
12. Shugart and Carey, *Presidents and Assemblies*, p.220.
13. B. Cain, J. Ferejohn and M. Fiorina, *The Personal Vote: Constituency Service and Electoral Independence* (Cambridge, MA: Harvard University Press, 1987), pp.212–29.
14. Lijphart, *Electoral Systems and Party Systems*, pp.118–20; R.S. Katz, 'Intraparty Preference Voting', in B. Grofman and A. Lijphart (eds.), *Electoral Laws and Their Political Consequences* (New York: Agathon Press, 1986).
15. Lijphart, *Electoral Systems and Party Systems*, pp.136–9.
16. *Making Votes Count*, pp.42, 143.
17. Shugart and Carey, Presidents and Assemblies, p.210; G. Sartori, *Comparative Constitutional Engineering* (New York: NYU Press, 1994), pp.11, 69.
18. Cox, *Making Votes Count*, pp.85–6.
19. M. Duverger, *Les partis politiques* (Paris: Armand Colin, 1955).
20. M. Gallagher and M. Marsh, *Candidate Selection in Comparative Perspective* (London: Sage, 1988).

8

Slovakia Ten Years After the Collapse of Communist Rule

GORDON WIGHTMAN

Electoral Landmarks in Slovakia

Almost a decade after the November 1989 Velvet Revolution brought an end to communist rule, Slovakia at last acquired a government favourably disposed towards the consolidation of political democracy, economic transformation and integration with Western Europe. Parliamentary elections in September 1998 brought victory to an unequivocally pro-reform coalition of parties, embracing the right-of-centre Slovak Democratic Coalition (SDC), the left-of-centre Party of the Democratic Left (PDL), a new Party of Civic Understanding (PCU), formed only seven months before the elections, and the Hungarian Coalition Party (HCP) representing Slovakia's half-million strong Hungarian minority.[1] The elections also brought political defeat for the Movement for a Democratic Slovakia (MDS), the political party which had dominated Slovak politics for most of the decade, whose ambivalent stance on reform and the country's geopolitical orientation had been a major obstacle to Slovakia's early accession to NATO and the European Union.[2]

The shift in direction signalled by those elections was, moreover, confirmed eight months later, in May 1999, in presidential elections, held for the first time by popular vote, when Rudolf Schuster, the PCU chairman and the candidate supported by the parties in the new government coalition, defeated Vladimír Mečiar, the MDS leader (see below). Yet, however much those elections created better conditions for democratic consolidation and economic transformation than had existed earlier in the decade, the polarization of opinion evident in those elections and the simultaneous fragmentation of the political scene reinforced fears that Slovakia's democratic transition was far from being consolidated.

Slovakia's Uneasy Path to Democracy

Paradoxically, it could be argued, that Slovakia began the period of transition relatively successfully. The first post-communist parliamentary elections, in

June 1990, witnessed the emergence of what appeared to be potentially durable political parties. Public Against Violence, the broadly-based political movement which had led the campaign against the Communists at the end of 1989 attracted just under 30 per cent of the vote and became the largest party in the new parliament but it faced serious rivals for popular support in the Christian Democratic Movement (CDM), the Slovak National Party (SNP), which had surfaced during the 'hyphen war' over Czechoslovakia's official and popular names in the spring of 1990 and which quickly identified itself with a separatist programme.[3]

Expectations that these parties (along with the parties representing the Hungarian minority and the Communists who, in Slovakia, renamed themselves the Party of the Democratic Left in late 1991) would form the core of a longer-lasting party system proved over-optimistic. The first major casualty was, hardly surprisingly, Public Against Violence. Less than a year after the first parliamentary elections, the leadership of that movement had become increasingly disaffected with the political style and nationalist emphasis of the man they had nominated as Slovak Prime Minister, in July 1990, Vladimír Mečiar. The resulting conflict, which led to the defection of Mečiar's supporters to form the Movement for a Democratic Slovakia in the spring of 1991, moreover, proved extremely bitter, in part because it involved disagreements over policy and personality, and in part because it grew out of fundamental disagreements over Slovakia's future which in their turn were based on divergent views of Slovakia's history.

At the risk of some over-simplification, underlying the disputes over the policies, political style and political ambition of Slovakia's then Prime Minister, Vladimír Mečiar, which led to the split in Public Against Violence, was a fundamental division between groups within the movement who believed Slovakia's future would be best met by continued close association with the Czechs and by the Westernization implicit in the political and economic reform adopted by the federal Czechoslovak government after the 1990 elections and those who believed Slovakia's best interests lay in assertion of its own national identity and adaptation of that reform to Slovakia's circumstances.

Mečiar's gradual swing behind an increasingly near-separatist programme in the run-up to the June 1992 parliamentary elections may have been primarily stimulated by his realization that he could build an effective appeal by establishing for himself an image as a 'defender of Slovak interests' and, following his removal as Prime Minister in April 1991, portraying himself as a victim of Czech-inspired machinations by his political enemies.

Whatever the rationale for Mečiar's behaviour, the break-up of Public Against Violence in 1991 and the increasing emphasis on nationalism and separatism had lasting effects on the party system in Slovakia. The most obvious was the dominance from 1992 onwards of a movement, the MDS, which more closely resembled the loosely-structured and disparate political movements of the immediate post-communist period than an effective political party. The disparate character of the MDS was well depicted by the Slovak scholars Zora Bútorová and Martin Bútora who described it at that time as:

> an 'umbrella organization' in which were to be found anti-Communists and reform Communists of 1968 vintage, proponents of a market economy and advocates of state intervention, former adherents of Czech-Slovak unity and open separatists, pro-Western individuals and Slavophiles, supporters of European integration and xenophobic nationalists. All these people were kept under one roof by Mečiar's forceful personality and, despite its categorization as a movement, the firm discipline associated with a party of the authoritarian leadership type.[4]

That breadth and disparity in composition, combined with Mečiar's aggressive style of leadership and intolerance of colleagues who dared to disagree with him, were a major source of weakness for the MDS. Within eighteen months of the June 1992 elections, from which it emerged only two seats short of an overall majority, the MDS suffered defections which seriously weakened the position of the Mečiar government and, following intervention in March 1994 by Michal Kováč, Slovakia's first President and formerly one of Mečiar's closest allies, Mečiar and his government were forced to resign.

The administration which followed was to be the first example of a phenomenon which became a lasting feature of Slovak politics: a government coalition made up of politically quite diverse parties which seemed the most unlikely potential bedfellows. In this case, that meant the right-of-centre clerical-conservative Christian Democratic Movement, the left-of-centre ex-communist Party of the Democratic Left and two new centre parties formed by defectors from the MDS and SNP, who were later to combine forces to form the Democratic Union.[5]

Yet, however unlikely it had seemed that such politically divergent parties would agree to form a coalition and even though it was understood that that government would remain in power only long enough to call early parliamentary elections (six month later), broad-spectrum coalitions of that kind were to become the norm in Slovakia in the latter half of the 1990s.

The Slovak Party System: Fragmented Polarization

At the time of the parliamentary elections in the autumn of 1994, it was not yet entirely obvious that what were in fact two distinctive, if fragmented, blocs of parties had emerged in Slovakia. Writing in the journal *Quo vadis, Slovensko?* shortly after the 1994 elections, Daniel Balko noted a polarisation between 'two, roughly equally strong groups of political leaders with diametrically opposed views on the meaning of the concept of democracy'.[6] Unfortunately, he concluded, this did not mean that voters had a choice between two clear-cut and equal alternatives. Rather, he argued, voters were faced with a choice between 'a strong MDS on the one hand and as many as five alternatives on the other.'[7]

The polarization of the party system was also hidden, in the 1994 elections, by the decision of the stronger contenders to form electoral coalitions with, or offer places on their lists of candidates to, small parties which, given the operation of a five per cent threshold in parliamentary elections, had no chance of being elected on their own. The Party of the Democratic Left, for example, stood in the elections within a coalition, called Common Choice, which included not only the Social Democratic Party in Slovakia (until then unrepresented in the Slovak parliament), the Green Party and also a Farmers' Party, the last no doubt intended to increase its appeal in rural communities. The Movement for a Democratic Slovakia, in response, formed a formal coalition with the Peasant Party of Slovakia and attempted to improve its ecological image by offering places on its list to a new environmental group, the Green Alternative.

The tactic was not entirely successful, rather the reverse. The PDL, which had expected to obtain around 20 per cent of the vote, came close to electoral defeat when it attracted only a fraction over the higher, ten per cent threshold which was required of electoral coalitions with three or more parties. It lost support, it would seem, in part because of the blandness of the 'Common Choice' label, as well as the defection of traditional PDL supporters who resented its shift towards a more social democratic position and who had an alternative in the more fundamentalist Workers' Association of Slovakia, which had broken from the PDL six months earlier.

However fragmented the 1994 parliament appeared as a result of the representation on its benches of as many as 12 parties, in practice, as Grigorij Mesežnikov argued, the 1994 elections did not create an extreme pluralism but 'a deformed sort of moderate pluralism with strong residues of polarisation' in which were to be seen 'two mutually opposed coalition groupings, which were each comprised of organisations claiming "right-wing", "centrist" and "left-wing" orientations.'[8]

In a later study of political developments in Slovakia, Mesežnikov took that argument further. 'Analysis of the activities of political parties and movements in 1997', he argued, 'confirms the view that the party system in the Slovak Republic is divided into two basic groups of political organization'.[9] What distinguished parties in Slovak politics, he added, was the fact that 'The fundamental axis on which this division has evolved is [a party's] relationship to the norms of modern parliamentary democracy, constitutionalism, the principles of a state based on the rule of law and the values of a democratic political culture.'

On one axis, he argued, were the three parties which formed the government after the 1994 elections: the centrist Movement for a Democratic Slovakia, the extreme right Slovak National Party and the extreme left Workers' Association of Slovakia. These were 'non-standard' parties, parties not easily comparable with mainstream parties in Western democracies. In particular, they:

> maintained an orientation towards a power-seeking and confrontational political style, incompatible with the values of a modern parliamentary democracy, preferred simplified populist methods of addressing the public, evinced a high level of devotion to the values of nationalism (in the case of the SNP and MDS) and egalitarianism (in the case of the Workers' Association of Slovakia).[10]

On the other axis were the parties which found themselves in opposition after the 1994 elections – the Christian Democratic Movement, the Party of the Democratic Left, the Democratic Union and the Hungarian parties. These were what Mesežnikov described as 'standard' parties, closer in most respects to conventional or mainstream parliamentary parties in the West than their 'non-standard' counterparts, the MDS, Workers' Association and the SNP.

Mečiar's new government was, in the view of Peter Schutz, a commentator in a pro-reform weekly, 'a real aberration (unikát)' and something not to be found 'anywhere in the civilised world, at least in a world in which governments come to power on the basis of free and democratic elections.'[11]

There can be little doubt that that government was a coalition born of necessity rather than choice but, however 'abnormal' a coalition of such political disparity might have been and however 'abnormal' the parties comprising it, that coalition survived for the remainder of the four-year term of the Slovak parliament. In that respect, it was the most durable of the three governments presided over by Mečiar between 1990 and 1998 and (it hardly needs saying) the most durable up to that point in post-communist Slovakia.

The 1998 Elections: Prospects for Democratic Consolidation?

Mečiar's third period in office came to an end in the autumn of 1998. Even though the Movement for a Democratic Slovakia remained the largest party in the Slovak parliament after the elections, held on 25 and 26 September, there was simply no way it might concoct some new alliances that would enable it to remain in power. Not only had the MDS and its erstwhile allies in the outgoing government lost their overall majority but the Workers' Association of Slovakia, which had attracted seven per cent of the vote in 1994, failed four years later to come anywhere near the five per cent threshold required to win parliamentary representation (it attracted only 1.3 per cent of the vote). Support for the MDS, however, also declined, from almost 35 per cent in 1994 to 27 per cent four years later while the third member of the coalition, the Slovak National Party, which increased its share from five per cent to just over nine per cent in 1998, failed to compensate for the drop in support for its two allies.

TABLE 1
RESULTS OF THE ELECTIONS TO THE NATIONAL COUNCIL OF THE SLOVAK REPUBLIC, 25 AND 26 SEPTEMBER 1998

Party	%	Seats
Movement for a Democratic Slovakia (MDS)	27.00	43
Slovak Democratic Coalition (SDC)	26.33	42
Party of the Democratic Left (PDL)	14.66	23
Hungarian Coalition Party (HCP)	9.12	15
Slovak National Party (SNP)	9.07	14
Party of Civic Understanding (PCU)	8.01	13
Workers' Association of Slovakia	1.30	–
Others	4.51	–
Turn-out:	84.24	%

Overall, the two surviving coalition parties accounted for only 36 per cent of the vote in 1998 (compared with 47 per cent in 1994 for all three) and were allocated only 56 of the 150 seats in the Slovak parliament (compared with a total for all three of 83 in 1994). Nevertheless, although the MDS remained the most popular party with the highest share of the vote and the largest number of seats, it had obtained less than one percentage point and only one parliamentary seat more than its nearest rival, the Slovak Democratic Coalition (SDC). In those circumstances Mečiar had no hope, as leader of the 'winning' party, of negotiating a new coalition and he was faced with opponents who were united in their hostility towards him and had the further advantage that their combined strength represented not only a simple majority in parliament but the three-fifths majority needed to achieve constitutional reform.

Those opponents, embracing the Slovak Democratic Coalition on the centre-right, the Party of the Democratic Left on the centre-left, a wholly new organization, the Party of Civic Understanding (PCU) and the Hungarian

Coalition Party (HCP) representing the Hungarian minority – were also a rather motley bunch. The SDC, the largest of those parties, and the HCP were in practice – as their names suggest – electoral coalitions which had been forced to 'transform themselves' into parties because of a change in the election law in 1998 which required all parties within an electoral coalition to reach the five per cent threshold to qualify for seats in parliament.

A major strength of the MDS in the past had been the numerical superiority of its parliamentary representation over any single one of its rivals and the fragmented character of the opposition. That had now changed, in part as a result of efforts put in by the centre and right-of-centre parties in the years preceding the 1998 election to collaborate in what was first designated a 'Blue Coalition' and eventually became the Slovak Democratic Coalition.[12] Behind the SDC label were in fact five parties covering a broad enough part of the political spectrum: the right-of-centre Christian Democratic Movement, the neo-liberal Democratic Party (which had failed to enter parliament in the previous two elections, in 1992 and 1994), the centrist Democratic Union, and two small leftist parties – the Social Democratic Party in Slovakia and the Slovak Green Party, which had both decided to abandon the coalition they had formed with the PDL in 1994. The spirit of cooperation created by the formation of the SDC in July 1997 was further enhanced by an agreement reached on 28 August 1998 between it, the PDL and the recently formed Hungarian Coalition Party on the membership of a new government under the PDC's Mikuláš Dzurinda, if they won the elections.[13]

It remained to be seen whether the inclusion of all of these parties would produce stable government over a longer time span, and whether the enforced integration of centre-right parties in the 'party of convenience' which the SDC represented would lead in the longer term to greater consolidation of the party system. But it was clear from the outset that the new government was less equivocal about democratic transition, economic transformation and accession to the European Union and NATO.

Any suggestion, however, that the parties forming the new Dzurinda government were 'standard' parties was less clearly the case. As the Slovak political scientist Miroslav Kusý pointed out in an article on the new government's first 100 days in office, the parties comprising the Dzurinda government were, with one exception, no more 'standard' (or 'normal') parties than their opponents.[14] The Slovak Democratic Coalition, the Party of Civic Understanding and the Hungarian Coalition Party were really 'electoral parties which were created ad hoc', rather than standard parties. Moreover, of those three parties, the Party of Civic Understanding was of very recent vintage. Founded in March 1998, it quickly won the support of a sizeable section of the Slovak population – 14.8 per cent according to a poll by Slovak Radio, cited by Karol Wolf, the Slovak correspondent of the

Czech daily, *MF Dnes* on 10 March 1998, even before it had published its programme. Its success in that respect owed something to the appeal of its leader, Rudolf Schuster, Lord Mayor of the East Slovak city of Košice, the presence within its ranks of a number of prominent politicians like the former Foreign Minister Pavol Hamžík, the trades union leader Marián Mesiarik and the Lord Mayor of the Central Slovak city, Banská Bystrica, as well as two well-known actors. The Party of Civic Understanding's success owed much, too, to strong support from the commercial television station, *Markíza*, and the former Communist Party daily, *Pravda*.

Nor were the Slovak Democratic Coalition and the Hungarian Coalition Party conventional parties. The former was a coalition of discrete parties with their own identities which had recognized the need to integrate at least formally, faced with the change to the electoral law penalizing electoral coalitions. The latter, it has been claimed, succeeded more than the SDC in integrating its constituent parties, and was less susceptible to the danger that such electoral coalitions might be undermined by participant parties' reassertion of their individuality. That risk was made only too clear as early as January 1999 when Vladimír Palko, a leading member of the SDC Presidium, confirmed he planned to return to his mother party, the CDM, and affirmed his belief that survival of the CDM was preferable to the transformation of the SDC into a 'real' party.[15]

The one standard party, in Kusý's view was, paradoxically, the Party of the Democratic Left, whose normality was testified to by its membership of the Socialist International and the European Socialist Party. However, that was a party which, as Kusý put it, 'is a direct descendant of the Communist Party of Slovakia, from which it has acquired a large part of its membership'.

Comprised of parties from right, centre and left, the new government came close to representing a mirror-image of the outgoing coalition. How viable it would prove remained unclear. It had been formed to defeat Mečiar and his allies and, once that was achieved, it remained to be seen whether it would be held together by the more positive shared goals of completing economic transformation, furthering democratic transition and improving Slovakia's chances of 'returning to Europe'.

Eight months after the parliamentary elections, continuing popular support for the parties in the government coalition was made clear in presidential elections which were held for the first time by a direct, rather than parliamentary, poll in line with the government parties' belief that only direct election could avoid the undesirable situation experienced during Slovakia's first months as an independent state (in early 1993) and again for 14 months after President Kováč's term of office came to an end in March 1998, when parliament failed to deliver the required three-fifths majority for the candidates presented to it on several occasions and many of the presidential powers were transferred to the Prime Minister, Vladimír Mečiar.

From the outset, it was clear that the 1999 contest was between Vladimír Mečiar, who had reversed his initial decision to retire from politics after his parliamentary defeat, and the chairman of the Party of Civic Understanding, Rudolf Schuster, who also had the support of the SDC and the PDL. Of the ten contenders in the first round of those elections on 15 May 1999, only one – apart from Mečiar and Schuster – had much chance of attracting a sizeable vote: the actress Magda Vášáryová, who had served as Czechoslovak ambassador in Austria in the early 1990s, and appealed to neo-liberals in the electorate who were less than ready to fall in line immediately behind Schuster, because of his successful career during communist rule (he had first become mayor of Košice in 1983 and was later elected to the Slovak Communist Party Central Committee.)

TABLE 2
SLOVAK PRESIDENTIAL ELECTIONS, MAY 1999

Candidate	First round Votes	15 May 1999 %	Second round Votes	29 May 1999 %
Rudolf Schuster	1,396,950	47.37	1,727,481	57.18
Vladimír Mečiar	1,097,956	37.23	1,293,642	42.81
Magdaléna Vášáryová	194,635	6.60		
Ivan Mjartan	105,903	3.59		
Ján Slota	73,836	2.50		
Boris Zala	29,697	1.00		
Juraj Švec	24,077	0.81		
Juraj Lazarčík	15,386	0.52		
Ján Demikát	4,537	0.15		
Michal Kováč*	5,425	0.18		
Total	2,948,402		3,021,123	

Turn-out: 73.89 % (15 May 1999); 75.45% (29 May 1999).

Source: Slovak Statistical Office Election website – http://volby.statistics.sk/volby99/

* Although Kováč, President of Slovakia between March 1993 and March 1998, withdrew from the contest a week before the first round his name remained on the ballot-paper. Of the unsuccessful candidates, Mjartan had worked for Slovak Radio before serving as Slovakia's first ambassador in Prague; Slota was chairman of the Slovak National Party and Švec a former Rector of Comenius University, Bratislava (The Slovak Spectator No. 18, 10-16 May 1999; http://www. slovakspectator .sk/).

Vášáryová's attraction of 6.6 per cent of the vote certainly helped prevent Schuster winning in the first round. Nevertheless, his share – at 47.37 per cent – was remarkably close to the majority he needed. The subsequent straight fight between Schuster and Mečiar in the second round, on 29 May, brought an increased absolute vote for both candidates, reflecting not only the transfer of some votes from defeated contenders to both candidates but also a two per cent rise in the turn-out, to 75.45 per cent, which reflected above all the strength of feeling (commitment as well as hostility) towards Mečiar. Nevertheless, if the 42.8 per cent of the vote Mečiar won in the second round was higher than the 38 per cent given to the MDS, SNP and Workers' Association in the September 1998 elections, Schuster's 57.2 per cent of the vote was close to the 58 per cent the parties in the government coalition won in the parliamentary elections (see Table 1 above).

Historical Antecedents

The presidential elections confirmed the polarisation evident in the 1998 parliamentary election. Shortly after the first round in the presidential contest, the daily *Sme* observed how strongly the election results confirmed suggestions of two distinctive political cultures in the country, with support stronger for Schuster in contiguous districts in western, southern and eastern Slovakia and favouring Mečiar in the northern and central regions.[16]

Any explanation of the origins of that polarisation and of that dual political culture and its reflection in the party system must take into account the legacy of Slovakia's past. As Daniel Balko noted, that legacy was not to be found in any claimed links between contemporary Slovak parties and those of the pre-communist era.[17] The neo-liberal Democratic Party of the late 1990s, for example, bore little resemblance to the post-war party of that name which had attracted two-thirds of the Slovak vote in the 1946 elections, two years before the communist take-over in Czechoslovakia. In the 1990s there was, as Balko pointed out, little hope of reviving that party following the eradication of its traditional supports among the peasant and artisan strata during communist rule. Nor could the SNP of the post-communist period claim genuine links with the Slovak National Party of the pre-war years. The older party (whose origins dated back to the nineteenth century) had been a socially conservative Protestant party in the inter-war years which had favoured autonomy within Czechoslovakia and was opposed in particular to the wartime Slovak state by which the modern-day SNP lay such store.[18] 'The one party', Balko noted, 'whose continuity with its predecessor was incontrovertible – the Communist Party of Slovakia – paradoxically attempted to shake off that continuity by changing its name to PDL'.

Yet, however strong the institutional discontinuity, 'every relevant political party', as Balko noted, 'must incorporate in its programme values of the population which are for the most part formed by environment and family and through which continuity with the traditional political thinking of any specific society is maintained'.[19] Slovak parties in the 1990s were no exception. A 'tendency to exploit the allegiance of a section of the Slovak population to historically and culturally conditioned traditional ideas', Mesežnikov noted in his 1997 study of the Slovak party system, was to be found not only in the mobilisational activities of the Workers' Association of Slovakia with their emphasis on socialist collectivism but also in other parties.[20] The SNP's defence of the Slovak wartime state was only one example of a more widespread 'attachment to outdated historical traditions' found also, if less overtly, among other Slovak parties, including 'standard' and 'non-standard' parties. The MDS, Mesežnikov suggested, 'attempted to exploit the residues of pre-war national-conservative authoritarianism and perceptions of reality typical for the communist period' and even the CDM displayed 'a leaning towards the values of religious traditionalism (morality, family, faith) and partly towards orthodox conservatism from the inter-war period'.[21]

One measure of Slovak parties' receptiveness to democratic ideas and Europeanisation were attitudes to the wartime Slovak state and its President, Jozef Tiso. For the Slovak National Party in the 1990s, both the wartime state and Tiso were symbols of Slovak nationhood which should be revered. Tiso, in their eyes, was 'a martyr for the defence of the nation and Christianity, against Bolshevism and liberalism'.[22] The position of the MDS on those issues, on the other hand, appeared to be contradictory. In a broadcast for Slovak Radio in March 1997, Mečiar dissociated himself and the MDS from the wartime Slovak regime, which he described as a fascist state 'they' had no intention of rehabilitating. Six months later, Mečiar made no comment on a visit by a number of his party's deputies to Tiso's villa that suggested a more sympathetic stance for that politician. In June that same year, the MDS spokesman, Vladimír Hagar, praised a controversial and much criticised *History of Slovakia and Slovaks* by Milan Stanislav Ďuric, which portrayed the wartime regime in a positive light, and recommended its use in schools. The Dzurinda government, by contrast, sought to distance itself from the wartime state in a statement issued to mark the sixtieth anniversary of its creation in March 1939 which denied any link between present-day Slovakia and a state 'created in circumstances determined by the Nazis' plans for total control over Europe'.[23]

It is tempting to see a polarization in Slovak political culture – and in the modern-day party system – between what might be called Westernisers and Slavophiles. Criticisms in the post-war years of excessive centralisation in pre-war Czechoslovakia, its failure to concede some form of Slovak autonomy and misguided attempts to forge a single Czechoslovak nation – as well as the break-up of Czechoslovakia at the end of 1992 – have tended to obscure from view the contribution made to the creation of that state by Slovaks who shared the pro-Western outlook of that state's Czech founders, T.G. Masaryk and Edvard Beneš. Many Slovaks were equally committed to the formation of a Czechoslovak state — and among them there were even those willing to accept the notion of a single Czechoslovak nation, not least Masaryk and Beneš's closest colleague in the independence struggle, M.R. Štefánik.

Few in 1990s' Slovakia would have argued for a unitary state comparable with Czechoslovakia in the 1930s but, once the break-up of Czechoslovakia had occurred, popular expectations provided little possibility of its restoration. Commitment to democratic values and identification with western Europe nevertheless remained a legacy of that pre-war republic shared by Slovaks as much as Czechs. Such features were as central to the party programmes and identities of some contemporary Slovak parties just as much as they had been an integral component of parties in the Czech Republic.

For most of the twentieth century Slovak society was polarized between those who saw Slovakia's place in western Europe, whether as part of a unitary Czechoslovakia or in a state in which Slovakia had been granted some form of autonomy, and those who placed greater emphasis on Slovakia's separate national development. That division was still evident among supporters of different parties in the 1990s. Opinion polls carried out by the Institute for Public Affairs in Bratislava in 1997, for example, showed a marked dichotomy in attitudes towards critical historical events in their country's history between supporters of the Slovak Democratic Coalition, the Hungarian Coalition Party and the Party of the Democratic Left and those favouring the Movement for a Democratic Slovakia and the Slovak National Party. Not only did those who intended to vote for the SDC and its allies see the last years of Mečiar's government in a black light while their opponents regarded that period highly, but the two groups of respondents held quite contrasting attitudes towards earlier periods in Slovak history.[24]

In an assessment of these polls, Zora Bútorová and Martin Bútora noted that SDC supporters,

> clearly define the following periods as brighter times in the history of Slovakia: November 1989, the Slovak National Uprising, and the first Czechoslovak Republic. On the contrary, the darker times were as follows: the fifties, the seventies, the eighties, and the wartime Slovak State.

Supporters of the MDS, they observed,

> believe differently. The Slovak National Uprising marks a positive historic movement for them, followed by November 1989. However, the third most appreciated period is the wartime Slovak State. For SNP adherents, the Slovak National Uprising ranks first and the wartime Slovak State even second. Paradoxically, adherents of the two [then] ruling coalition parties place the Slovak State and the Slovak National Uprising on the same side of the value spectrum. On the other hand, for

PDL and SDC adherents these two periods are evidently incompatible.[25]

Equally interesting were attitudes to historical figures in Slovak and Czechoslovak history. Slovak politicians associated with the Czechoslovak state (Štefánik; Dubček) were rated highly by supporters of all parties while there was a sharp divergence in relation to Czech politicians and to Slovak politicians such as Tiso. Among SDC and HPC supporters, the Czech politicians Masaryk and Havel were rated highly while their rating among SNP and MDS voters was much lower. The wartime Slovak leader, Jozef Tiso, conversely, was rated highly by supporters of the SNP and, to a lesser degree, the MDS (reflecting the ambivalence of that party itself) and rated poorly by adherents of other parties.

Yet, as the authors noted, comparison of the 1997 poll with one taken four years earlier, just after the break-up of Czechoslovakia, indicated that

> important changes in historic consciousness have taken place over the past several years. First, the attitudes toward Havel and Masaryk – the two politicians representing democratic traditions in former Czechoslovakia – have improved. Second, the images of Tiso, Husák and Mečiar, who embody three different types of undemocratic regime in Slovakia's modern history, have worsened.
>
> These shifts indicate that the historic consciousness of Slovak citizens has not been influenced by the frequent attempts of the [1994–1998] coalition representatives to emphasize the independent line in Slovak traditions and to downgrade the references to the common Czech and Slovak history (ibid., p.197).

Initial comparison with a poll carried out in October 1968 suggests that Slovaks' regard for the pre-war First Republic had also increased in the intervening 30 years. In 1997, 42 per cent regarded it as a positive period in Slovakia's history, eight per cent negative and 14 per cent as both positive and negative. In 1968, 17 per cent of respondents, asked to refer to at most two periods they regarded as the most glorious in their nation's history, cited the First Republic, putting it in fourth place after the Age of Štúr (the period when a Slovak literary language was established), the 1968 Prague Spring and the Slovak National Uprising, while only five per cent regarded it as the least glorious period in their nation's history.[26] Only 13 per cent then regarded the Slovak wartime state as the most glorious period in their nation's history and as many as 44 per cent the least glorious.

Slovak politicians were not the first in Central European to see their state as a potential 'bridge between East and West' but the inclusion of that perception in the programme of the SNP in the late 1990s seemed somewhat out-of-place at a time when most Central European ex-communist states were focused almost exclusively westwards, on accession to the European Union and NATO. SNP hostility to whose institutions was not shared by many of the population as a whole. Polls carried out in October 1997 and April 1998 by the Institute for Public Affairs indicated that roughly three-quarters of Slovak citizens favoured integration into the European Union and just over half supported integration in NATO.[27] Surprisingly enough in the case of the EU, in October 1997, over 60 per cent of adherents of all parties favoured Slovakia's integration. By contrast, support for adhesion to NATO was strongest among supporters of the SDC and the Hungarian parties (80 and 79 per cent), weaker among adherents of the PDL (48 per cent) and weaker still in the case of supporters of the MDS, SNP and WAS (33, 31 and 36 per cent respectively).[28]

Conclusions

The 1998 parliamentary elections and the 1999 presidential elections in Slovakia produced an important shift towards parties and politicians more favourably disposed towards consolidation of political democracy, transformation of the economy and Slovakia's integration in Western institutions. Nevertheless, that shift in power did not mean a certain end to the problems Slovakia faced in the 1990s in that respect. The party system remained highly polarized and it remained open to question whether the experience of cooperation among the parties in the new Dzurinda government would lead to a reduction in the excessive fragmentation among those parties and the emergence of a more 'normal' party system.

The polarization, and fragmentation, of the parties reflected a polarization and fragmentation in society, not only in relation to events in Slovakia's past but also over current issues (including notably attitudes to Slovakia's Hungarian and Roma minorities). It seems unlikely to disappear completely. Nevertheless, the elections of 1998 and 1999 have given Slovakia a new chance to renew its endeavours to build a democratic and prosperous Slovakia.

NOTES

1. J. Fitzmaurice, 'The Slovak elections of 25th and 26th September 1998', *Electoral Studies*, Vol.18 (1999), pp.271–300.
2. I have changed the Slovak abbreviations used in this book for English equivalents for the sake of consistency in this chapter as well as easier comprehensibility.
3. G. Wightman, 'The Czech and Slovak Republics. In Developments in East European Politics', in S. White, J. Batt and P.G. Lewis (eds.), *Developments in East European Politics* (London: Macmillan, 1993), pp.54–6; K. Henderson and N. Robinson, *Post-Communist Politics: An Introduction* (London: Prentice Hall,

1997), pp.135-8.
4. Z. Bútorová Z. and M. Bútora, 'Political Parties, Value Orientations and Slovakia's Road to Independence', in G. Wightman (ed.), *Party Formation in East-Central Europe* (Aldershot: Elgar,1995), p.125.
5. G. Wightman, 'The 1994 Parliamentary Elections in Slovakia', *The Journal of Communist Studies and Transition Politics*, Vol.11, No.4 (1995), pp.384–5.
6. D. Balko, 'Päť' rokov politickej slobody – päť' rokov zápasov o demokraciu', *Quo Vadis, Slovensko?*, Vol.1 (1995), p.5.
7. Ibid., pp.33–4.
8. G. Mesežnikov, 'Štrukturácia systému politických stran: stav a trendy', in S. Szomolányi (ed.), *Slovensko. Problémy konsolidácie demokracie* (Bratislava: Slovenské zdruenie pre politické vedy a Nadácia Friedricha Eberta,1997), p.27.
9. G. Mesežnikov, 'Vnútropolitický vývoj a systém politických stran', in Martín Bútora and Michal Ivantyšyn (eds.), *Slovensko 1997. Sœhrnná správa o stave spoločnosti a trendoch na rok 1998* (Bratislava: Inštitít pre verejné otázky, 1998), p.93.
10. Ibid., p.60.
11. *Domino Efekt*, No.4 (1995).
12. On these events, see Mesežnikov, 'Vnútropolitický vývoj', pp.90–2.
13. The composition of that government was published on the SDC Website – http://www.sdk.sk/.
14. *Domino Forum*, No.8 (March 1999).
15. *Sme*, 7 Jan. 1999.
16. *Sme*, 18 May 1999.
17. D. Balko, 'Päť' rokov', p.10.
18. J. Lettrich, *History of Modern Slovakia* (Toronto: Slovak Research and Studies Center, 1985), pp.81 ff.
19. D. Balko, 'Päť' rokov', p.10.
20. Mesežnikov, 'Štrukturácia systému politických stran', p.28.
21. Ibid.
22. Mesežnikov, 'Vnítropolitický vývoj', p.70.
23. *Sme*, 15 March1999.
24. Z. Bútorová and M. Bútora, 'Events and Personalities in Slovak History,' in Z. Bútorová (ed.), *Democracy and Discontent in Slovakia* (Bratislava: Institute for Public Affairs, 1998), p.194.
25. Ibid.
26. A. Brown and G. Wightman, 'Czechoslovakia: Revival and Retreat', in A. Brown and J. Gray (eds.), *Political Culture & Political Change in Communist States* (London: Macmillan, 2nd edn, 1979), pp.168–9.
27. Z. Bútorová and M. Bútora, 'Slovakia and the World', in Z. Bútorová (ed.), *Democracy and Discontent in Slovakia* (Bratislava: Institute for Public Affairs, 1998), p.180.
28. Ibid., p.181.

9

Perspectives on Democratic Party Development in Belarus

ELENA A. KORASTELEVA

Introduction

After a decade under a new regime, at least a 'minimal' definition of democracy may be applied to the majority of the new states within central and eastern Europe. This presumes, first, freely contested elections with full suffrage and the absence of massive fraud; secondly, effective guarantees of civil liberties (freedom of speech, assembly and association); and finally, government accountability and system legality.[1] But some countries do not even fit this minimal definition. Belarus reflects such a failure of post-communist democratisation, but nevertheless shows some signs of party development. This chapter seeks to analyse the specific, but limited, role parties play in post-communist Belarussian politics.

Belarus officially declared independence from the former Soviet Union on 25 August 1991 and became – for only the second time in its history (a short-lived National Republic having been established in 1918) – an independent sovereign state. However, its move to democracy was short and largely unsuccessful. The first parliamentary elections to the existing Supreme Soviet in March-April 1990 (held within the framework of the Soviet Union) resulted in a short-term success for the democrats, who established the first 'Democratic Club' with nearly one-third of all deputies. However, they were overruled by a communist majority which continued a counter-reform course similar to that of the pre-*perestroika* period. In 1992 nationalists initiated a call for new parliamentary elections, which was widely supported by the electorate but ignored by the resolutely conservative parliament. The latter was finally replaced in 1995 by a new multi-party legislature after the first truly competitive elections.

While its external appearance changed, though, parliament remained largely the same internally: there still was a majority of non-partisan (48 per cent) and left-oriented deputies – the latter composed of communists (22 per cent) and agrarians (17 per cent) – and very few others. Its democratic tenure was also brief. The parliament was dissolved in 1996, following the introduction of a new constitution by President Alexander Lukashenka. It nevertheless continued to meet and was still recognized by all major international authorities on the basis of the 1994 constitution. According to the latter, President Lukashenka's term of office also expired in July 1999, although he refused to recognize this. Internationally, therefore, Belarus has remained in a form of political limbo, and Belarussian politics has continued to be a constitutional battleground.

In 1999, Belarus was therefore in its tenth year of 'transition', although it showed little democratic achievement when compared with neighbouring states like Poland, Ukraine, Lithuania and even Russia. The reasonably popular president, Alexander Lukashenka, continued to control the 'representative' institutions of parliament and the constitutional court as well as the state bureaucracy. Political parties – the basis of an effective democratic system – have only fought one election and had little opportunity for independent development. The power balance has remained heavily weighted towards the president and away from parliament. The main focus of this chapter will be to analyse the degree of party development in Belarus that has occurred. The first section outlines the main aspects of party development and demonstrates the importance of cleavage structures in relation to early post-communist voter alignments. The second section outlines the problems encountered in further party development. The concluding section evaluates perspectives for further party development.

Social Cleavages and Early Party Differentation

Historical analysis suggests some continuity between pre- and post-communist periods in terms of cleavage structures, and these are likely to have exerted an influence over recent Belarussian politics. Such conflicts and controversies may foster party system formation by polarizing the political environment and anchoring emerging voter preferences.[2]

In Belarus at the beginning of the century a centre-periphery divide, associated with nationalist calls for independence and sovereignty, dominated the pre-communist range of political conflicts. The activity of independent nationalist movements in Belarus formally began in 1902 with the emergence of the Belarussian Revolutionary Hramada, renamed the Belarussian Socialist Hramada in 1903. Indeed, the idea of nationhood had been dominant before the beginning of the century with the emergence of mass nationalist movements such as 'Land and Freedom' and 'Talk'. The Belarussian Socialist Hramada, though, was the first exclusively Belarussian party with a definite programme and clear nationalist stance. It mobilized most of the population of Belarus, of whom 75 per cent were said to consider themselves Belarussians, in a temporary alliance with the communists to secure national statehood.[3] In the revolutionary period after 1917 other nationalist political parties and organizations, such as the Belarussian People's Hramada, the Belorussian Autonomous Union, and the Christian Democratic Union, were founded.

Inter-war Belarus covered two major periods: pre-Soviet Belarus (which included a year of independent statehood) and the 1919–39 period, when Belarus was divided into eastern and western parts. In 1921 Belarus was formally partitioned between Poland (which took the western part) and Russia (which formed the Belarussian Soviet Socialist Republic: BSSR in 1922), after which the nationalist politics of different parts of the country took a different form.

In the *eastern* part of Belarus (BSSR) the New Economic Policy of the 1920s made concessions to national sentiments in a form of 'Belarussification'. The extent of official use of the Belarussian language by early 1927 was almost 100 per cent amidst the legislature and most of the executive, and 30–50 per cent among other commissariats. 81 per cent of the population recognised Belarussian as their native and official language. But with Stalin's succession to power a purge of the Belarussian National-Democrats was made, and by 1937 'the Belarussians comprised only 15 per cent of the professional staff of the higher educational institutions of BSSR'.[4] Urbanization played a significant role in the Russification of the nation. By 1939 25 per cent of the population were urban Belarussians, and they were dominated by the spreading influence of Russia. The relation between occupation/social status and nationality was a further sign of national change. In 1897 fewer than one-fifth of one per cent of Belarussians was engaged in professional occupations, due to the low level of literacy and education amongst. In 1926 15.7 per cent of the population of the BSSR were classified as office and professional workers, among whom were 8.4 per cent urban Belarussians. As Belarussians entered an urban and more mobile environment they also became highly susceptible to Russianisation: 'in the Soviet Union urbanisation and Russianisation run hand by hand'.[5]

In 1922 the Belarussian Peasants' and Workers' Association, a popular peasant movement, represented the *western* part of Belarus in the Polish parliament: it held 11 seats in the lower House and 3 in the upper (Zaprudnik, 1993, p.238).[6] At this time it was the largest political party with an anti-Soviet and pro-Belarussian ideological background, and its nationalist stance later deepened with the repression of national minorities in Poland. The second largest political party was the Belarussian Christian Democratic Party, whose adherents were almost exclusively Roman Catholics, and the Greek Orthodox Belarussians. The official program of the party was nevertheless based on the principle of unification of Belarussian lands and recognition of its independence. On this basis the centre-periphery cleavage

143

remained the most prominent dimension of political differentiation in Belarus as a whole after reunification in 1945 within the Soviet Union.

The beginning of strong nationalist protest and demands for the restoration of the Belarussian cultural heritage and language in the late Soviet period can be dated to 1987. It started with a collective petition from the Belarussian intelligentsia to President Michael Gorbachev and an unauthorised rally in Minsk. This was preceded by the emergence of an extensive informal youth organization in the republic during early the 1980s. In 1989 the Belarussian Popular Front (BPF) was registered and defined itself as 'a mass socio-political movement' whose goal was 'to create a society and to renew the identity of the Belorussian nation ... guaranteeing the irreversibility of reforms in the BSSR'.[7]

In July 1990 a Democratic Opposition group consisting of 27 Belarussian Popular Front members and seven other democrats formally identified itself within the Supreme Council of the BSSR. At the initiative of BPF about 100 deputies also set up a 'Democratic Club' to oppose the conservative majority. In 1992 the Belarussian Popular Front initiated a signature-gathering campaign to organize a referendum on the dissolution of the Supreme Soviet, in which the ex-Communists made up 86 per cent of its deputies. Despite the fact that the referendum campaign collected more than the required number of votes, the Supreme Soviet rejected the initiative by 202 to 35 votes. This did little to alleviate conflict between the nationalists – who were calling for a new republic – and the socialist old guard.

The 1990 legislature was finally replaced by a new parliament in 1995 on the basis of freely contested elections. Despite the relatively large number of parties then in existence, which by 1995 exceeded 30 (see Appendix), only a dozen of them entered the newly-elected democratic parliament. Amongst the 198 deputies the majority of mandates were won by non-partisan candidates (48 per cent). Six parliamentary factions were established: Communists, Agrarians, the Social Democratic Union, Union of Labour, Civic Action (composed of liberal parties) and Accord (the pro-presidential wing).

Despite subsequent ideological and political disarray, the Communists have remained the largest party organization (with 9,300 members in 1999) and continue to base their programme on principles of socialist economic organization and the public ownership of land. They have been the primary agent for economic and political alliance with Russia. They initiated the Minsk agreement on the Confederation of Independent States in 1991, as well as a collective security pact and monetary union in 1993. They continued to call for economic reunion with Russia in the 1996–98 period. Workers' associations and trade unions – which number more than 38 according to recent official figures – strongly buttress this traditional left. The Labour Party, and independent trade unions associated with it, have promoted similar issues but not collaborated with the communists because of doubts about their old-fashioned and rather confused political style. The BPF has remained the most influential and the second largest party organization in Belarus, with 5,100 members as well as more occasional supporters. With leadership change two opposing wings emerged: one liberal (involving figures like Kchadiko, Viachorka, Barscheyski) and another radical (with such activists as Pazniak, Krivorot, Siychik).

The party structure has remained characterized by a fixed distribution of political parties along the left-right spectrum. The left bloc has traditionally advocated issues of reform moderation, state social protection, and reunion with Russia. Liberal/nationalist parties, articulating pro-European and nation-building issues, have provided the right-wing opposition and been accompanied by a range of small parties with vague ideological stances representing the centre. Since 1996, however, a new divide reflecting pro- and anti-Lukashenko positions has emerged. This introduced a second major focus of party competition, thus creating the possibility of a multi-dimensional space for political competition.

The Presidency and Constitutional Conflict

The events of November 1996 added a new dimension to party politics when a new constitution was introduced and the largely oppositional 1995 parliament was dissolved according to its provisions. Seventy per cent of the Belarussian electorate voted in a referendum on 24 November in favour of expanding the powers of the president and accepted his draft of a new constitution. President Lukashenko signed it into effect on 28 November, thereby terminating the authority of all 'old' deputies. For more than a week Belarus literally had a situation of dual power as ousted oppositional MPs continued formally to meet whilst the new legislature began to exercise authority under Lukashenko's regime.

This fundamental issue of state power produced sharp divisions within parties, as well as turning many against the politics of the president. As an example of the first tendency, a splinter communist party (CPB) emerged in 1996 composed of the president's supporters. While mainstream former communists advocated policies of social libertarianism and expressed moderate support for market policies in line with the neo-socialists, the splinter Communist Party of Belarus (headed by V. Chikin) pursued a clear non-market socialist stance. The main demarcation line underlying such conflicts nevertheless concerned political support for or opposition to the repressive policies of the president. The majority of other political parties in Belarus also reflected this conflict.

In 1994 the Agrarian Party had grown into the third largest, 'class' party representing the Belarussian peasantry, but it also split and ceased to exist on the national level after the institutional crisis of 1996. Internal conflict emerged in response to the presidential actions against the 1995 Parliament and completely destroyed party unity. The second largest class party – the Belarussian Peasant Party, registered in 1991 as a more radical and right-wing force – also later withdrew from the electoral market after a subsequent restrictive presidential decree on 'The order of registration of political parties, trade unions and public organisation in the republic' in 1999.

Social democratic and liberal parties continued to play a more active role in the electoral arena, the 'Narodnaia Hramada' (SDP), United Civic Party (UCP) and the centre-right Liberal-Democratic Party (Gaidukevich) being the most prominent examples of this group. They have also been more concerned with issues of legality and the country's democratic deficit rather than their original programmatic appeals in terms of market reform and integration with the West. After breaking away from its party family, the Belarussian Social-Democratic 'Hramada' (BSDH), under the leadership of Stanislav Shushkevich (the former Parliamentary spokesman, 1991–92), has aligned with the right-wing BPF. Due to this, its future as a credible political player remains uncertain.

Religious issues have also been widely promoted by the nationalist opposition. The Belarussian Christian-Democratic Union, founded in 1991 as a continuation of the party which existed in west Belarus in the 1920–30s, was the only one to receive significant support from the electorate. Religious values were also promoted by smaller parties, including the Christian-Democratic Movement of Women (founded in 1992), the Belarussian Christian-Democratic Party (1994), Christian-Democratic Choice (1995), and a number of others. Like many other small parties, they all ceased their activity in accordance with the presidential decree issued in January 1999, which requires compulsory party registration and an official membership of 1,000.

The new parliament established under President Lukashenko's constitution of 1996 was composed of a new bicameral legislature: the House of Representative (lower house) and the Council of the Republic (upper). Of the 110 deputies in the lower house 47.3 per cent were from the Accord faction, 21.8 per cent from that of the Agrarians, and 19.2 per cent from both communist parties. The new legislature was politically compliant and not empowered to take initiative action, acting as a rubber-stamp for all presidential proposals.

The main goals of most Belarussian parties are now state independence, the establishment of a law-governed system, and political democracy. This has united them under a single protest movement known as 'Democratic Opposition against the President', whose central organ is the Constitutional Coordination Council. This development demonstrates the full entrenchment of the second major dimension of party competition, according to which parties are aligned in response to presidential authoritarianism on the basis of opposition to or support for presidential policies. The joint effort of political opposition, however, has not overcome internal conflict or weakened the influence of personal political ambition within the parties.

Although (at the time of writing) no free elections have been held since beginning of the constitutional crisis in 1996, surveys give an indication of popular support for the different parties. Preliminary analysis of public preferences from opinion polls conducted on average three to four times a year show divisions between potential voters. Urban residents tend to cast their preferences for the right-wing democratic parties. Younger, professionally trained groups in small towns are inclined to support nationalist appeals, whereas the middle-aged intellectuals of Minsk and regional centres normally choose social democrats and the UCP liberals. The communists find their principal supporters among the rural and less educated elderly population. In occupational terms, the cluster of potential democratic voters is mainly composed of the self-employed, unemployed (students, housekeepers, etc.) and those surviving on state benefits. Amongst the conservatives and those whose seek reunion with Russia are pensioners, and full or part-time workers with low incomes.

Generational analysis, conducted on the basis of the division of respondents into cohorts according to the year they were first socialised into politics, also shows a growing tendency towards support of nationalist issues and against presidential claims. Younger groups are likely to have more radical views, especially those socialised after 1996 and the president's violatation of the constitution. This suggests that Lukashenka has failed to make converts of the young and other social strata which are usually more open to political influence.

Party Outcomes

The above analysis shows that there is some potential basis on which parties might develop, in view of the informal legitimacy of existing parties and their acceptance by the majority of the public. In addition, manifestations of some regularity in popular attitudes and partisanship suggests that prospects exist for eventual democratization. The overall tendency in Belarussian politics since 1995, however, has been towards authoritarianism and the entrenchment of conditions that are highly unfavourable for party development. No more free elections were held to accelerate institutional evolution or assist the emergence of clearer party identity. The results of a Multiple Scaling Analysis confirm the validity of this view. Due to the large number of contemporary parties voters perceive them as a complex political miasma. There are clear signs that voters have difficulties distinguishing

TABLE 1
GENERATIONAL EFFECT CALCULATED ON THE BASIS OF VOTERS' SEPARATION
INTO COHORTS ACCORDING TO THE ELECTION YEAR WHEN THEY BECAME
SOCIALIZED INTO POLITICS

Attitudes	GM	1	2	3	4	5	6	7	8	9
To the return to communist rule										
1994	0	0	0.67	0.33	0	0.38				
1995	0.13	0	0.36	0.29	0.77	0.13	0.46			
1998	0.1	20	0.17	0.18	0.48	0.48	0.19	0.59	0.44	0.44
*1998	0	0	0.41	0.27	0.34	0.31	0.33	0.72	0.57	0.57
To the socialist economy of 1989										
1994	-0.50	0	0.44	0.25	0	0				
1995	-0.90	0	-0.13	0	0	0	0			
1998	-0.61	0	0.33	0	0.16	0	0.31	0.16	0.28	0.56
*1998	0	0	0.13	0	0	0	0.41	-0.39	-0.26	0
To the communist economy										
1994	-0.25	0	0.57	0	0	0.25				
1995	0.8	8	0	0	0	0	0	0		
1998	-0.30	0	0.15	-0.17	0.35	0.59	0.17	0.25	0.52	0.18
*1998	0.11	0	0.17	0	0	0.33	0.33	-0.15	0.11	-0.22
To the necessity of multipartism and freely contested elections										
1994	-0.25	0	0	0	0.32	0.25				
1995	-0.19	0	0	-0.30	0.54	0.15	0.19			
1998	0.13	0	-0.17	0	0.17	0	-0.30	-0.13	0.28	0
*1998	-0.10	0	0	0	0.31	0.10	0	0.10	0.51	0.27
To the introduction of direct presidential rule had political unrest occurred										
1994										
1995	-0.24	0	0	0	0.66	0	0.12			
1998	0	0	0.29	0	0.36	0.37	0	0.17	0.22	0.12
*1998	-0.23	0	0.21	0	0.20	0.13	0.23	0.44	0.49	0.40

Note: There are 1000 (100%) respondents included in each election year. The year *1998 consists of 3000 (100%) cases, based on a combined matrix. The entries in this table are MCA coefficients, which show the average distance between each group and the average voter (GM) in the data set. Negative coefficients indicate more left-wing groups, positive coefficients relatively right-wing groups. Only statistically significant differences are shown. The 'intake' technique (numbers in columns) is allocated around the null hypothesis of no discernible difference between different sections of the electorate socialised under various political events, including first presidential election. This was achieved by separating groups of cohorts into discrete years. The first intake would occur in 1990 being socialised prior to the year 1991. The 1991 intake will consist of two intakes respectively – 1990 and 1991. By 1998 the intakes will comprise nine in total.

Source: Centre of Social and Political Research, BSU, Minsk. The author was a co-ordinator of the project.

most parties from one other, despite the fact of some popular capacity for party identification. Only a handful of parties appear to stand out as clearly separate from the general political blur. According to respondents' perceptions these are the Communists (PCB), the Nationalists (BPF), Narodnaia Hramada (SDP), United Civic Democrats (UCD) and the Agrarians (AP).

148

FIGURE 1
PERCEPTION OF PARTIES BY THE BELARUSSIAN ELECTORATE,
OCTOBER–NOVEMBER 1996

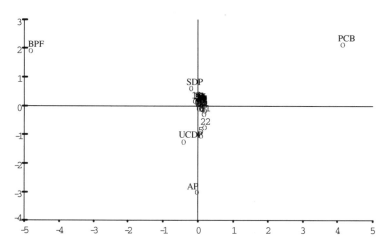

Note: Configuration of 31 parties is derived from the question 'Whom would you vote for, if election were tomorrow?'. Euclidean distance model is used to indicate statistical similarity/difference between parties as variables in the two-dimensional solution. Kruskal's stress test is less than 0.001 (significance).

This chart is designed to indicate a linear model of the Belarus political spectrum. After rotation horizontal dimensions may be interpreted as 'market liberals, nationalists' on the left to 'populists, social-democrats' on the right. Vertical dimensions did not receive a meaningful elaboration, for most of variables spread along X-axis. List of parties is presented in the Appendix.

Source: Public opinion survey, conducted by the Centre of Social and Political Research, BSU, Minsk in October-November 1996 (the author was a co-ordinator of the project). Stratified nation-wide sample included 1500 respondents with 95% confidence probability, representing all adults over 18.

A second reason for the weakness of party development in Belarus is the lack of interest in party politics shown by voters even during apparently key periods of political change. Even during the first freely contested parliamentary elections in 1995, three rounds of voting had to be held to fill the necessary 76 per cent of deputies' seats. In 1996, too, 70 per cent voted in favour of the president's proposal to amend the constitution and extend his personal power. To this extent the national political situation may be characterised as one of 'delegative' democracy. By this O'Donnell designated regimes characterized by executive practice, electorally empowered to act in whichever ways it deems appropriate.[8] This kind of 'democratic' regime is inevitably hostile to the patterns of heterogeneous representation and the emergence of functional political institutions, including parties as the prime agency of mobilisation and popular activity. Even such a restrictive democratic definition underplays the authoritarian tendencies that have come to prevail in contemporary Belarus as President Lukashenka showed great reluctance to permit any form of electoral activity at all.

NOTES

1. S.P. Huntington, *The Third Wave: Democratization in the Late Twentieth Century* (Norman, OK: University of Oklahoma Press,1991); G. O'Donnell, 'On the State, Democratisation and Some Conceptual Problems: a Latin American View with Glances at Some Postcommunist Countries', *World Development*, Vol.21 (1993), pp.1355–69.
2. S.M. Lipset, and S. Rokkan, 'Cleavage Structures, Party Systems, and Voter Alignments: an Introduction', in S.M. Lipset, and S. Rokkan, (eds.), *Party Systems and Voter Alignments* (New York: Free Press, 1967), pp.1–57.
3. S. Guthier, 'The Belorussians: National Identification and Assimilation, 1897–1970', *Soviet Studies*, Vol.29 (1977), pp.37–61 and 270–83.
4. I.S. Lubachko, *Belorussia Under Soviet Rule, 1917–1957* (Lexington: University Press of Kentucky,1972), pp.85, 111.
5. Guthier, *The Belorussians*, pp.46, 283.
6. J. Zaprudnik, *Belarus: At a Crossroads in History* (Boulder, CO: Westview Press, 1993).
7. Zaprudnik, *Belarus*, p.51.
8. O'Donnell, 'On the State', pp.1355–69.

APPENDIX

POLITICAL PARTIES AND ORGANIZATIONS IN BELARUS
(LIST USED IN OPINION POLLS AND SURVEY ANALYSIS)

Party acronym or name	Full English name of party	Blocks of Spectrum
1. AP	Agrarian Party	Left
2. BHP	Belorussian Humanitarian Party	Ceased to exist (Centre Right)
3. BPP	Belorussian Peasant Party	Right
4. Green World		Centre Right
5. Hope	Belorussian Party of Women	Centre
6. LP	Belorussian Labour Party	Centre Left
7. BRP	Belorussian Republican Party	Centre
8. BEP	Belorussian Ecological Party	Centre
9. BPF	Belorussian Popular Front	Right
10. BMPD	Belorussian Movement for People's Defence	Ceased to exist (Centre Left)
11. MDR	Movement for Democratic Reforms	Ceased to exist (Centre Right)
12. MSPJ	Movement for Social Progress and Justice	Ceased to exist (Centre Left)
13. CDM of Women	Christian-Democratic Movement of Women (united with CDU)	Centre Right
14. LDP	Liberal-Democratic Party	Left

15. Otechestvo	People's Patriotic Movement 'Motherland'	Right
16. BNP	Belorussian National Party	Right
17. NDP	National Democratic Party of Belarus	Right
18. UCP	United Civic Party	Centre Right
19. PBUC	Party of all-Belorussian Unity and Consensus	Ceased to exist (Centre Left)
20. Green Party		Centre
21. PCB	Party of Communists of Belarus	Left
22. Beerlovers	Party of Beerlovers	Centre Right
23. PSIP	Party of Scientific-Industrial Progress	Ceased to exist (Centre)
24. PLJ	Party of Labour and Justice	Left
25. Belorussian Women	Political movement	Ceased to exist (Centre Right)
26. RP	Republican Party	Centre Left
27. White Russia	Political Party	Right
28. Narodnaia Hramada	Social Democratic Party	Centre Right
29. SP	Socialist Party	Left
30. CDU	Christian Democratic Union	Centre Right
31. Yabloko	Belorussian Popular Movement	Centre Right

Source: Ministry of Jurisprudence.

10

Strands of Conservative Politics in Post-Communist Transition: Adapting to Europeanization and Democratization

KENNETH KA-LOK CHAN

Introduction

The political economy of post-Communist transition has been centred on what might be called a US-style neo-liberal conservatism discourse that, in turn, helped successive governments to legitimize the introduction of strict pro-market, monetarist policies.[1] However, the fall of the Communist regimes in Europe and the Soviet Union did not lead to 'an end of ideology'.[2] While Communism had been discarded, there remained a large ideological void to fill. Indeed, the introduction of free electoral competition in the region has encouraged a proliferation of parties and political groupings with wide-ranging ideological profiles.[3] Democratization presented an unprecedented opportunity for contenders to shape the trajectories of post-Communist transformation. Some of the groupings tried to provide a coherent set of values and policy guidelines; but most of them could only present ambiguous and overlapping 'visions' of one kind or another. The emergent party systems showed a marked propensity for factionalism and fragmentation. Since most of the parties lacked solid implantation in society, few were able to attract a large number of members and sympathisers, and there was serious confusion of roles between parties, pressure groups and social movements. This situation thus brought new hopes but also serious anxieties to societies not used to having a 'free market of ideas'.

Political labels, however, are necessary; without them it would be difficult for the citizens to develop long-term political identification and voting patterns in the complex world of politics. In the post-Communist transitional period, emergent political parties have had to shape and re-shape their images to muster support in an electoral market that has necessarily been very volatile. So far as the development of transnational party cooperation is concerned, party labels provide the basic information to highlight similarities between party families in different states.[4]

The aim of this chapter is to explore the politics of ideology formation in relation to the emerging democracies and market economies in the post-Communist world. It will examine the formation of a multitude of 'conservative' tendencies against the backdrop of marketization, democratization and European integration of the region. The basic premise of this preliminary study is that, contrary to the rhetoric that there is no alternative to neo-liberal economic dogma, post-Communist transition has generated a distinctive ideological competition between socialist, neo-liberal and traditional concerns. The analysis sheds light on the conditions for the emergence and re-orientation of the various ideological tendencies at the level of political practice, and the prospects of consensus politics from the ideological perspective.

The Dominance of Neo-Liberalism in Post-Communist Transition

The collapse of Communism in 1989 was hailed by many commentators as 'Back to Europe' or 'the victory of liberalism'.[5] There was a widespread feeling of the historical inevitability of Western-style capitalist democracy extending to the post-Communist world. Economic prosperity and political freedoms in west European countries, it was widely felt, not only exposed the failings of Communism in the east, but also became a superior model for the peoples of the post-Communist world.

Amidst revolutionary elation, people expected quick material improvements and prosperity on the west European market model. However, the dogmas of the command economy had ruled out both a robust private sector and a capitalist class. What was left behind was an unwanted legacy of notorious shortages, corruption, inefficiency, a distorted industrial structure, fiscal crisis and heavy debts. The partial exceptions here were Hungary and Romania; the former had a functioning 'second economy', whereas the latter's foreign debt was negligible.

In the face of a harsh economic environment, Jeffrey Sachs described his experiences as economic advisor to governments in East Central Europe and Russia as about 'life in the emergency room'.[6] His neo-liberal 'shock therapy' was therefore recommended to all post-Communist countries to cure all the problems at one stroke. Since the 'left' was discredited, few had the courage then to advocate social democracy as an alternative to the newly emerged neo-liberal orthodoxy. The dramatic turn to the Anglo-Saxon type of neo-liberal conservatism, which prevailed at the time, was seen as an unmistakable sign of total rejection of Communism in the region.

Even though in some countries a gradualist approach was initially preferred over a radical 'big bang', as the decade progressed, country after country appeared to have embraced neo-liberal, monetarist policies in order to combat macroeconomic problems. Since 1989, successive governments were told to implement trade liberalization, privatization, wage control, labour market flexibility, welfare reduction and restrictive monetarist policies in order to revive the ailing economy. By the mid-1990s, the EU and international financial institutions, which had played a deterministic role in bringing about market-oriented reforms in Central Europe and the Baltic region, began to enjoy some leverage with the governments in south-eastern Europe, particularly in Romania and Bulgaria, with the accession of more pro-Western coalitions to power. Consequently, there has appeared to be in recent years a broad acceptance that there is no alternative to the central tenets of Reaganomics and Thatcherism, although minor policy adjustments might still be possible.

With regard to the pervasiveness of neo-liberalism in the post-Communist world, two rational choice explanations are in order. One may argue that what matters for the post-Communist transitions is the presence and absence of some feasible alternatives. In the past decade, many of these countries have remained convinced that democracy and the market economy are, to paraphrase the famous words of Winston Churchill, preferred as the lesser evil among the known forms of political and economic system. Another possible explanation for this concerns the widely-prevalent notion of globalization. In an era of globalizing capitalism, it is argued, expansionary macroeconomic policies and generous social models would discourage foreign investment and hamper trade with advanced western economies.

Yet in most cases governments had little autonomy of action and had to accept strict criteria on budget deficits and inflation imposed by the World Bank, the International Monetary Fund and holders of the country's debt in order to qualify for debt reduction agreements, as well as western funds to back restructuring plans in the financial and industrial sectors. Thus, adapting to painful austerity measures based on the neo-liberal model was considered a price one must pay for Western acceptance and assistance.

Consequently, in the last decade, East Central Europe witnessed the rise of a neo-liberal conservatism, whose dominance has been felt most strongly in the economic sphere. Arguably, many of the post-Communist governments were prisoners of a harsh economic reality which required them to implement radical measures aimed at ensuring the introduction of free market. In practice, neo-liberal conservatism is a 'revolutionary' ideology that seeks to redefine radically the relationship between state, market and civil society.

However, it is a mistake to suggest that there can be only one brand of conservative politics. In the post-Communist context, one finds not one strand of conservative politics, but three. As a result, the choice is not a simple two-way one. Obviously, context matters for our understanding of the various conservative tendencies. Thus, the following section considers the background against which three strands of 'conservatism' can be explained.

The Politics of Ideology Formation in the Aftermath of Communish

The first problem in the articulation of any party ideology is to define one's terms. In the post-Communist world, however, the search for political identities has been a particularly vexed issue. To begin with, the barriers against party and party system development in the aftermath of Communism were already complex and onerous:[7] the submergence of multi-party competition under protracted Communist rule, an inauspicious political culture that held political parties and ideology in low esteem, the short history of the parties, the novelty of competitive elections, the lack of charismatic leadership and the absence of trained cadres, activists and the like.

Meanwhile, the end of Communism created a fluid and unsettling political environment as the countries in question were undergoing rapid changes on all fronts. As a corollary, public opinion was very much in flux, which was reflected in the high level of electoral volatility.[8] One distinctive feature of the post-Solidarity groupings in Poland was the dominance of personality, and the shunning of attempts to present clear-cut alternative policies to the electorate. While cleavage fault lines were hard to define, most political parties adopted catch-all strategies to appeal for support from different sections of the population. Ideological confusion inevitably grew as a result of a proliferation of political groupings that did not seem to be sufficiently differentiated by their manifestoes, which carried programmatic statements and doctrinal declarations which were often misleading or deliberately vague.

When the profiles of the parties are still in the nascent, formative stage, the application of terms like 'left' and 'right' will help little to clarify the political scene. Rather, one expects to see endless disputes over their core attributes and meaning. Jeffrey Goldfarb recalled a joke from Poland, 'How can you tell the difference between a leftist and a rightist? Answer: The leftist will maintain that the distinctions between left and right no longer make sense, whereas the rightist will maintain that they do.'[9]

Naturally, there are significant country-specific differences. For example, the Czech Republic displays a dominant left versus right spectrum in the area of economic policy equivalent to that in Western Europe. Here, the right espouses strong individualistic, pro-market values in opposition to the left's egalitarian orientations. However, Richard Sakwa contends that the traditional left/right distinctions 'provide little insight' into Russia's volatile political environment.[10] Interestingly, in Russia and most of the former

Soviet republics, the left supports market and democratic reforms, while in the Baltics the left opposes reforms. In Poland, the centrists have been the most persistent advocates of market-oriented reforms, while the left and the right both have demanded 'reforms with a human face'. Within the post-Communist world, therefore, generalization of political labels, whose meanings are contingent and time- and space- specific, is inherently difficult.

Contextualizing Conservative Politics in Post-Communist Transition

In the West, the ideological and programmatic contents of conservatism vary over time and across nations. According to Nigel Ashford and Stephen Davies,

> French conservatism is very different from the Anglo-Saxon variety both in style and content. It is more abstract and logical, far more uncompromising and extreme. It has for much of its history an intransigent, fundamentalist quality not found in conservatism in Britain or most of the United States ... In recent years a more recognizably Anglo-Saxon type of conservatism is emerging, combining social conservatism with economic liberalism.[11]

Historically speaking, conservatism was an outgrowth of conflict with liberalism and later on, with socialism.[12] It abhorred the utopianism of the rival ideologies, and reacted to that with a corresponding defence of the past or the existing institutions and practices. 'To be conservative', Michael Oakeshott explained, 'is to prefer the familiar to the unknown, to prefer the tried to the untried, fact to mystery, the actual to the possible, the limited to the unbounded, the near to the distant, the sufficient to the superabundant, the convenient to the perfect, present laughter to utopian bliss'.[13]

In the post-Communist context, where enormous changes are expected to take place, conservative politics cannot be politics of the *status quo*. Of course, almost every party draws on 'the past' to some extent in its attempt to build an ideological profile.[14] However, there does not seem to be a set of definitive criteria to determine which elements from 'the past' are worth preserving in the new order. For one thing, confusion is inevitable in countries where a host of right-wing groupings compete with one other for leadership. For another thing, consistent ideological labelling is particularly hard to achieve when ex-Communists and left-wing parties claim a share of the conservative tradition of social concern and evolutionary change. Thus, the concept can refer to both Communist and anti-Communist tendencies.[15] One consequence is the politicization of historical issues relating to the region's history and destiny.

Having said that, since 1989 post-Communist politics has been characterized by a two-dimensional political space. First of all, a strong

156

Communist versus anti-Communist divide was already observable in the first elections of the post-Communist era. On the one hand, parties associated with the *ancien régime* – the (ex-) Communist parties and the former satellite parties – were discredited and were therefore held in very low esteem in many of the countries. On the other hand, anti-Communist umbrella organizations had stronger appeals to citizens with their transformational promise. Such a divide, which reflected much deeper historical, attitudinal and cultural dilemmas for the peoples who once lived under Communism, would become the first salient dimension of political competition in post-Communist democracies.

Once the initial revolutionary elation subsided, however, the market transition generated a second dimension of political competition, which further divided parties into those espousing free market values and those embracing statist-egalitarian ones. In many countries, market-oriented reforms had resulted in very high inflation, falling output, falling real incomes, an unprecedented level of unemployment, rising inequality and sharp cut-backs in welfare provisions. Indeed, the first experience of the free market for the majority of citizens was one of profound bewilderment and insecurity. The 'fast track to Europe' that the post-Communist regimes courageously embarked on was so fraught with difficulty that the early confidence of success soon looked premature. There seemed to be no way of avoiding passing through the 'vale of tears' of economic transformation.

This shift of focus from historical to economic issues and the social cost of transition opened a window of opportunity for (ex-) Communist groupings and paved the way for their full re-legitimization and restoration to mainstream politics. This stage was also characterized by the instability of many of the grand anti-Communist coalitions such as Poland's Solidarity movement, the Czech Civic Forum and Bulgaria's Union of Democratic Forces. Within the incipient party systems, ideological differentiation gathered pace along with this pro-market versus pro-welfare dimension.

Thus, each post-Communist democracy has at least a basic two-dimensional ideological structure, which can be further supplemented by other divisive issues over religion and politics, EU and NATO memberships, decommunization and lustration (settling accounts with the past), and the rights of ethnic minorities.[16] With the help of an ideological map, it should now be possible to determine with some precision the ideological and programmatic contents of the three strands of conservatism in post-Communist democracies.

Communist/Ex-Communist Conservatism

To begin with, Communist and ex-Communist parties have in recent years frequently been described as 'conservative' because of their scepticism towards market-oriented reforms and democratization.[17] 'Communist/ex-

Communist conservatism' began to grow in the late 1980s in reaction to Gorbachev's *glasnost* and *perestroika*, as hard-line Communists who opposed change in the Soviet Union were called conservatives. Krasnodar Krai, which lies in the far south of Russia, has been described as a 'conservative community ... ruled by a conservative, pro-communist political elite.'[18] In June 1990, Ivan Polozkov, the Krasnodar regional Party Secretary and a long-term critic of Gorbachev's reforms, was elected First Secretary of the newly formed Russian Communist Party. Under pressure from conservative opposition, Gorbachev was said to be 'drifting to the right'.[19]

In post-Communist Russia, leaders who adhere to an anti-Western stance in combination with strong anti-capitalist positions on economic issues represent this strand of conservatism. As Leslie Holmes has observed in Russia:[20]

> Reformist implies that a party seeks substantial change from the communist period, which in turn suggests a very laissez-faire approach in economics and politics. It implies an outward looking approach, in which a given country is seen as part of the large world and global economy ... *Conservative*, in contrast, implies here that a group believes in high levels of state involvement in economics and politics. It also often implies a relatively high level of nationalism ... Among the best-known parties in this group were the Communist Party, led by Gennadi Zyuganov, the Agrarian Party, and the misleadingly titled Liberal Democratic Party which was neither liberal nor democratic, led by Vladimir Zhirinovskii (Italics added).

The Communist Party of the Russian Federation (CPRF) is an upholder of not only the Soviet myths about the October revolution and the achievements of the Soviet Union, but also Russia's great power status in the post-cold war period. For the Russian Communists, the East-West divide did not end with the collapse of the Communist regimes and the dissolution of the Warsaw Pact. Rather, they fear that the eastern enlargement of the European Union (EU) and NATO will lead to a new political demarcation in Europe. The resurgence of strong nationalism and neo-imperialism is thus a response to the perceived threat from the West. But ex-Communists in countries where there are large ethnic minorities have also appropriated anti-Westernism-cum-nationalism. This is the case in many of the Balkan states.

Economically, this brand of conservatism pays merely lip-service to reforms. In their opinion, although the private sector should be allowed to grow, the state claims ultimate control over the economy. Looking back, the Communist era appears to them to have been stable and people knew what to expect. Essentially, state ownership and central planning are still regarded as a viable model of economic development. This nostalgic mood has been particularly dominant in the distressed regions of the post-Communist world.

Communist/ex-Communist conservatives, who appeal to those who rate the previous regime higher than the present order, have always been the laggards in democratization. It is their flirtation with nationalism in the Balkans and the former Soviet Union that has put regional stability and security in extreme jeopardy.

Traditional Conservatism

There is also a 'traditional conservatism', which draws on the heritage of dissent and opposition but harks further back to the pre-Communist period. For the traditional conservatives in Eastern Europe, Communism was an alien ideology imposed on them by force. For more than four decades, the so-called People's Republics were sustained by terror and coercion. Moreover, the Soviet economic model distorted the economies and the structure of production to the detriment of the peoples' welfare. The 1989 'revolution' was thus hailed as a national liberation from the Soviet-Russian control; an opportunity to return to the nation's authentic traditions. To begin with, therefore, traditional conservatives called for thorough decommunization and for banning former Communists from public office. On the economic front, the key items were re-privatization and property restoration.

One of the traditionalists' fears is the destruction of all authority in the aftermath of Communism. Since the sudden fall of Communism created considerable uncertainties, law and order naturally became their prime concern, as did the newly-won state independence and national security. In the area of social policy, traditional conservatives hold highly stubborn views on family, nation, religion and culture, and they talk tough on crime and juvenile delinquency. Many of them are Eurosceptics because of their strong sense of nationalism; their vision of European integration is limited to that of a 'European Union of Nations'. In multi-ethnic states traditional conservatism portends a politics strongly polarized along ethnic lines.

While the traditionalists appear to be uncompromising on socio-political issues, their attitudes towards marketization and privatization are more ambivalent, reflected in carefully chosen notions such as 'social market economy' and 'social partnership'. This strand of conservatism does not oppose changes, but traditional conservatives are concerned about what they regard as the fundamental values that underpin the very nature of their societies. Therefore, a conservative political philosophy requires what Peter Murrell calls 'an extreme skepticism concerning the workability of any blueprint for a new society'.[21] In general terms, a traditional conservative is a pragmatist who prefers gradual piecemeal changes to radical measures.

In Hungary, Christian national, national peasant, religious-fundamentalist and nationalist parties are the standard-bearers for the traditionalists' policy agenda. In 1989, the Hungarian Democratic Forum (MDF), a mixture of

159

Christian-conservative-populist tendencies, won the first election on a statist platform. Under the MDF-led government from 1990–94, politically trouble-some reforms were postponed, state intervention in the economy and society actually increased and privatization proceeded with great circumspection.[22]

In Poland, where Roman Catholics account for more than 90 per cent of the population, the Catholic Church and its teachings provide traditional conservatives with the elementary frame of reference.[23] Thus, the leading groupings amongst the traditionalists, the Christian National Union (ZChN) and the fundamentalist Polish Family (RP), manifest a continuing belief in the appropriateness of Catholic theology for politics and traditional political values such as nation, family and religion. They are very vocal in their opposition to secularization, divorce and abortion. Moreover, they are characterized by anti-Communism as well as anti-liberal rhetoric. In both countries traditional conservatives found it difficult to tolerate criticisms levelled against them by the independent media. This culminated in the 1991 media war in Hungary, during which the Head of the Hungarian Television and Radio was dismissed by the MDF government. One year later the Olszewski government in Poland appointed their own man to 'clean up' the news division of the public television, while Catholic traditionalists in parliament sponsored laws that obliged the media to respect 'Christian values'.

Thus, for the traditionalists, the notion of liberal democracy and the market economy provide inadequate protection for moral and national values deemed essential for national survival. The paternalistic authoritarian stance on socio-political issues of the traditionalists stems from a rejection of individual self-determination and a mistrust of free market ideology.

Neo-liberal Conservatism

Of course, there is a 'neo-liberal conservatism', which complements its rejection of the recent past with a strong commitment to the modernization of the post-Communist economic systems on strict *laissez-faire* lines. Leszek Balcerowicz of Poland, Václav Klaus of the Czech Republic and the Young Democrats of Hungary (Fidesz) have all claimed to support neo-liberal market reforms. In Russia, political groupings which belong to this strand of conservatism, such as Democratic Choice-United Democrats and Yabloko, are often referred to as 'progressives'.

In sharp contrast to their ex-Communist and traditional counterparts, the neo-liberal conservatives do not eschew radicalism. Rather, they deliberately forge a radical image by calling for a big jump to the market economy and by proclaiming an ideological blueprint for a new society. Radical neo-liberal conservatives think they know what is best for their society. Their search for a quick-fix has led them to endorse some kind of 'shock therapy' for many of the problems in the aftermath of Communism.

Although neo-liberal conservatism remains a Western import whose local roots are weak compared with the other two brands of conservatism, it is privileged by extensive Western support. Advocates of neo-liberalism do not believe they are promising a new utopia, but rather something which has been proven to work in Western Europe. In truth, the neo-liberals have found in the British Conservative Party under Margaret Thatcher a model for emulation. Their values and beliefs therefore include monetarism, sound money, a free market and individual enterprise, reduction of state intervention, cuts in public spending, rejection of egalitarianism, and 'conviction' politics as opposed to 'consensus' politics.[24] In the face of strong competition from the other two strands of conservatism, the neo-liberal domination in post-Communist politics is far from complete. However, an ambitious vision for the future and a corresponding aversion towards the old order has rendered some neo-liberal conservatives arrogant and intolerant towards dissenting views.

In the post-Communist context, therefore, one can observe the formation of different strands of conservatism, each offering a peculiar ethos and identity on the basis of the countries' past and current developments. The first strand places special emphasis on the positive legacies of Communism, the second one on nation, traditions and religious values, and the third one on market-oriented reforms. This should not surprise us. Uniformity, not diversity, should. However, in spite of the different points of departure, each strand of manifests a measure of authoritarianism and is 'in some way antagonistic to the introduction and functioning of liberal democracy'.[25] Therefore, the main features of the conservative orientations which emerged after Communism were their multiplicity and their dubious democratic credentials.

At the Crossroads: Adapting to Europeanization and Democratization

Since 1989, the EU has played a vital role in the development of democracy and market economy in countries whose foreign policy priority is to 'rejoin Europe'.[26] At the systemic level, the EU is concerned about the quality of the emergent democratic and economic order in the prospective member states. At its meeting in Copenhagen in June 1993, the European Council set the conditions for EU accession as:[27]

> stability of institutions guaranteeing democracy, the rule of law, human rights and respect for and protection of minorities; ... a functioning market economy, as well as the capacity to cope with competitive pressure and market forces within the Union; [and] the ability to take on the obligation of membership, including adherence to the aims of political, economic and monetary union.

At the party level, EU-based transnational party groupings have exerted a positive socialization effect on the emergent party families in the post-Communist states.[28] The Socialist International, the Liberal International, the European People's Party, the European Democratic Union and the European Union of Christian Democrats have developed ties with no less than 70 parties in the region, particularly those with a clear commitment to democratization-cum-Europeanization (see Table 1). Many of these parties regard such European/international ties as necessary in order to gain power and international respectability.[29] The main activities of transnational party cooperation consist of assistance with party organizational development and electoral engineering. Evidently, this kind of transnational party networks has helped mould the identities of parties at their formative stages. Thus, the democratization-cum-Europeanization of party ideologies should come as little surprise. With time, such voluntary adaptation of ideology amounts to a fundamental change 'from inside, in their mentality and institutions',[30] in order to overcome authoritarian tendencies in post-Communist politics. Subsequently, the ex-Communists and the traditionalists have come to terms with the market and democratic transitions, whilst the neo-liberals have become more sensitive about the costs of transition inflicted on the people.

Although there is growing transnational party cooperation which certainly provides normative guides for the emergent ideological tendencies, elections provide instructive evidence of the perceived constraints on the political actors and the manner in which they have shaped their ideological positions in relation to others. As long as elections remain by and large free and fair, the parties are given plenty of opportunities to address the most important questions facing the country, to refine their programmes, to signal their policy positions, to influence public opinion, to participate in policy-making and, last but not least, to demonstrate leadership or the lack of it.

In practice, voters in these countries have exercised their rights by removing from power parties that were considered not to have done enough to ensure that their country stayed in the good books of the international financial institutions or to have responded adequately to the social costs of transition. The confrontation of a group's core beliefs and values with actual public attitudes towards those beliefs provoked, from the early 1990s onwards, an ongoing political learning process for the political elite. It has been seen that electoral victory legitimizes beliefs, whereas electoral defeat may trigger a crisis of faith. In the latter case, ideological adaptation is most likely to follow when political leaders came to the conclusion that their parties will not survive, let alone win elections, without some degree of ideological repackaging and image regeneration. In fact, the series of elections and changes of government that began in 1989 has not only helped to delimit the issue dimensions of party competition, but also helped to select the most adaptive parties.

TABLE 1
TRANSNATIONAL PARTY AFFILIATIONS IN POST-COMMUNIST EUROPE: MEMBERS OF CHRISTIAN DEMOCRATIC INTERNATIONAL (CDI), EUROPEAN DEMOCRATIC UNION (EDU) AND EUROPEAN PEOPLE'S PARTY/EUROPEAN UNION OF CHRISTIAN DEMOCRATS (EPP), SOCIALIST INTERNATIONAL (SI) AND LIBERAL INTERNATIONAL (LI), JUNE 2000

Country/Party Name	Membership
Albania	
Democratic Party of Albania (PDS)	EDU, EPP
Christian Democratic Party (PDKS)	EPP, CDIo
Social Democratic Party of Albania (PSD)	SI
Socialist Party of Albania (SPA)	SIc
Armenia	
Christian Democratic Union of Armenia (ACDU)	CDIa
Armenia Socialist Party (ARF)	SIc
Azerbaijan	
Social Democratic Party of Azerbaijan (SDPA)	SIo
Belarus	
Belarussian Popular Front (BPF)	CDI
Belarussian Social Democratic Party (BSDP)	SIo
Bosnia-Herzegovina	
New Croatian Initiative-Sarajevo (NCIS)	CDI
Liberal Party (LS)	LIo
Social Democratic Party of Bosnia and Herzegovina (SDPBiH)	SI
Bulgaria	
Union of Democratic Forces (ODS)	EDU, EPPo, CDI
United Christian Democratic Centre (OHDZ)	EDU
Democratic Party (DP)	EDU, EPP, CDI
Bulgarian National Peasant Union (BZNS-NP)	EPP, CDI
Bulgarian Social Democratic Party (BSDP)	SI
Liberal Democratic Union	LIo
Centre New Policy (LSNI)	LIo
Europe Left (EL)	SIo
Croatia	
Croatian Democratic Union (HDZ)	EPP
Croatian Peasant Party (HSS)	EPPo
Croatian Christian Democratic Union (HKDU)	EPPo
Croatian Social Liberal Party (HSLS)	LI
Liberalna Stranka (LS)	LIo
Social Democratic Party (SDP)	SI
Czech Republic	
Civic Democratic Party (ODS)	EDU
Civic Democratic Alliance (ODA)	EDU, EPPo
Christian Democratic Union (KDU-CSL)	EPPa, CDI
Freedom Union (US)	EPPa
Free Democrats-Social Liberal Party (SD-LSNS)	LI
Czech Social Democratic Party (CSSD)	SI

TABLE 1 (cont.)
TRANSNATIONAL PARTY AFFILIATIONS IN POST-COMMUNIST EUROPE: MEMBERS
OF CHRISTIAN DEMOCRATIC INTERNATIONAL (CDI), EUROPEAN DEMOCRATIC
UNION (EDU) AND EUROPEAN PEOPLE'S PARTY/EUROPEAN UNION OF CHRISTIAN
DEMOCRATS (EPP), SOCIALIST INTERNATIONAL (SI) AND LIBERAL
INTERNATIONAL (LI), JUNE 2000

Country/Party Name	Membership
Estonia	
Fatherland Union (Isamaaliit-PPU)	EDU, EPPo, CDI
Estonian Reform Party (ER)	LI
Estonian Coalition Party (EK)	LIo
Estonian Social Democratic Party (ESDP)	SI
Moderates (M)	SI
Georgia	
National Democratic Party of Georgia (NDPG)	CDI
Christian Democrat Union of Georgia (CDUG)	CDI
People's Party of Georgia (PPG)	CDI
New Democrats (ND)	CDI
Citizens Union of Georgia	SIo
Hungary	
Hungarian Democratic Forum (MDF)	EDU, EPP, CDI
Christian Democratic People's Party (KDNP)	EDU
Independent Smallholders Party (FKGP)	EDU
Alliance of Free Democrats (SZDSZ)	LI
Federation of Young Democrats (Fidesz)	LI
Hungarian Socialist Party (MSZP)	SI
Hungarian Social Democratic Party (MSZDP)	SIc
Kosovo	
Albania Christian Democratic Party of Kosovo (PSHDK)	CDI
Liberal Party of Kosovo (PLK)	CDI, LIo
Latvia	
Latvian Christian Democratic Union (LKDS)	EPPo
People's Party (TP)	EPPa
Latvia's Way Alliance (LC)	LI
Latvian Social Democratic Workers' Party (LSDSP)	SI
Lithuania	
Conservative Party of Lithuania (LK)	EDU
Lithuanian Christian Democratic Party (LKDP)	EPPa, CDI
Lithuanian Centre Union (LCS)	LIo
Lithuanian Liberal Union (LLS)	LIo
Lithuanian Social Democratic Party (LSDP)	SI
Macedonia	
Liberal Democratic Party (LDP)	LI
Moldova	
Popular Christian Democratic Front	
Social Democratic Party of Moldova	SIo

TABLE 1 (cont.)
TRANSNATIONAL PARTY AFFILIATIONS IN POST-COMMUNIST EUROPE: MEMBERS
OF CHRISTIAN DEMOCRATIC INTERNATIONAL (CDI), EUROPEAN DEMOCRATIC
UNION (EDU) AND EUROPEAN PEOPLE'S PARTY/EUROPEAN UNION OF CHRISTIAN
DEMOCRATS (EPP), SOCIALIST INTERNATIONAL (SI) AND LIBERAL
INTERNATIONAL (LI), JUNE 2000

Country/Party Name	Membership
Montenegro	
Liberal Alliance of Montenegro (LSCG)	LI
Social Democratic Union of Montenegro (SDUM)	SIo
Social Democratic Party of Montenegro (SDPM)	SIc
Poland	
Solidarity Electoral Action (AWS)	EPPa
Conservative-Peasant Party (SKL)	EPPa
Freedom Union (UW)	EDU, EPPa, CDI
Democratic Left Alliance (SLD)	SI
Labour Union (UP)	SI
Romania	
National Peasant Christian Democratic Party (PNTCD)	EDU, EPPo, CDI
Democratic Alliance of Hungarians in Romania (RMDSZ)	EDU, CDIo, EPPo
Hungarian Christian Democratic Party of Romania (RMKDP)	CDI, EPP (permanent guest)
National Liberal Party (PNL)	LI
Democratic Party of Romania (PD)	SI
Romanian Social Democratic Party (PSDR)	SI
Russia	
Christian Democrat Union-Christians of Russia (CDU-CR)	CDI
Yabloko	LI
Slovakia	
Christian Democratic Movement of Slovakia (KDH)	EDU, EPPo, CDIo
Hungarian Christian Democratic Movement (MKDM)	EDU, EPPo, CDIo
Hungarian Civic Party (MPP)	LI
Democratic Union (DUS)	LI
Political Movement Coexistence (ES)	LI
Social Democratic Party of Slovakia (SDSS)	SI
Party of Democratic Left (SDL)	SI
Slovenia	
Slovenian Christian Democrats (SKD)	EDU, EPPa, CDI
Liberal Democracy of Slovenia (LDS)	LI
United List of Social Democrats (ZLSD)	SI
Ukraine	
Christian People's Union	CDIa
Ukrainian Christian Democratic Party	CDIa
Liberal Party (LPU)	LIo

Sources:
Christian Democratic and People's Parties International <http://www.idc-cdi.org/>,
European Democratic Union <http://www.edu-ude.at/edu/>,
European People's Party <http://www.evppe.org/party/index.html>,
Socialist International <http://www.dsausa.org/si/si.html>,
Liberal International <http://www.worldlib.org/index.shtml>.

EPPo, CDIo, LIo, SIo: observer parties
SIc: Socialist International consultative parties
EPPa, CDIa: associate/other parties

At the level of party competition, making and keeping the parties electable should be a powerful reason for ideological adaptation. Generally speaking, the logic of electoral competition and coalition formation has compelled party leaders to mix their core values with those of their rivals in an interlocking fashion. However, as we shall see below, what is important is that in some cases such a process has helped to tame the aforementioned 'authoritarian temper' in post-Communist politics and has encouraged a more pragmatic and accommodative strategy of change. Thus, the ex-Communists have rejected their past connections with totalitarianism, whilst the traditionalists and the neo-liberals have rejected their connections with ultra-nationalism and paternalistic elitism respectively. All this has proved to be conducive to further democratic and market transitions in many of the post-Communist regimes in East Central Europe.

Social-democratization of Communist/Ex-Communist Conservatism

For example, in Hungary and Poland, the reform experience before the 1989 breakthrough had the effect of 'deideologizing' the Communist leaderships, leading to their rapid social democratization and increasing acceptance of the basic principles of free market economy and democracy in the new era. Both the Hungarian Socialist Party (MSZP) and its Polish counterpart, the Democratic Left Alliance (SLD),[31] were umbrella formations of social democrats, trade unionists, and former communist cadres with business interests; their leaders thus embraced traditional socialist pledges for higher wages and better welfare as much as pro-market policies. Importantly, both groupings were determined to repudiate Communism and undertook 'social democratization' in order to acquire a legitimate role in the incipient party system. The revamped social democrats are nowadays members of the Socialist International.[32]

Notably, the return of the successor parties to power in subsequent elections did not signify an adoption of policies against the market or a return to more explicitly pro-welfare budgetary policies. In Poland, the ex-Communist social democrat-peasant coalition that governed from 1993–97 maintained disciplined budget and monetary policies, but to keep its constituents happy the government was forced to postpone difficult public sector reforms and to increase state involvement in the agricultural sector. In Hungary, however, we saw how a socialist-liberal coalition implemented a radical adjustment programme, the Bokors Package, in response to economic stagnation and current account instability. The Prime Minister, Gyula Horn, was reported as saying to a Western audience: 'To appreciate what we have done you must realize that we have abolished what Hungarians grew up to accept as sacred rights'.[33]

Even so, the absence of a traditional Communist alternative rendered such a rightward move largely free of trouble. The Hungarian and Polish ex-

Communists have thus far achieved a workable ideological balance between the demands of neo-liberal reforms and the need for political gestures towards the concerns of the ordinary people. Ideological reorientation and the retention of their predecessors' resources helped ensure the ex-Communists' dominance on the left of the political spectrum. Although in both countries there are other left-leaning labour-oriented parties–the Hungarian Social Democratic Party (MSzDP), the Polish Socialist Party (PPS) and the Labour Union (UP), they have not been able to consolidate their electoral base in the face of strong competition from the ex-Communists.

However, it would be wrong to assume that all the ex-Communist parties in East-Central Europe and Russia have undertaken similar path of ideological modernization.[34] In fact, in Russia and most of the former Soviet republics we observe a large, unreformed Communist elite that appeals to large parts of the electorates who remained attached to the old Soviet values. The CPRF, for instance, has so far rejected the path of social democratization. The largest Communist party in the post-Communist world is indeed a coalition of orthodox Marxist-Leninists, Marxist reformers and left-wing patriots in the Soviet sense. None of the three main tendencies expect to take the lead in order to bring about an ideological revamp along social democratic lines. Rather, as long as the CPRF remains popular among Russian voters, there is not much to gain from a rightward shift away from its hitherto statist, Slavophile, populist and anti-Western profile.[35]

In some parts of the region, particularly the Balkan countries, the successor parties were unable to modernize themselves and chose to maintain a strong anti-reform position. The ex-Communist Bulgarian Socialist Party, with its over-gradual 'Third Road' reform programme, stayed in power for six years until a financial crisis in early 1997 brought it down through massive public demonstrations. In Romania the political dominance of Ion Iliescu and the ex-Communist Social Democracy of Romania (PDSR) until 1996 was a major stumbling block to the country's democratic and market-oriented reforms.[36] It should be pointed out that before 1989, Romania, Bulgaria and Czechoslovakia were amongst the most monolithic regimes in the Eastern bloc. Unlike Poland and Hungary, these countries had categorically rejected 'liberalization'. For all practical purposes, the Communist dictators neglected reforms whilst the level of repression was high. Consequently, there was no strong reformist wing in the Party that might have initiated change after the fall of Communism.

In the Czech lands, the anti-capitalist Communist Party of Bohemia and Moravia (KSČM) continued to attract more than ten per cent of the votes. The communists' electoral strength not only signified widespread uncertainty about far-reaching political and social transformation in large parts of society, but also prevented the Czech Social Democrats (ČSSD), a historical party refounded after 1989 and a member of the Socialist International, from taking on a more pro-market stance in the area of economic and monetary policy. The left-leaning party has been critical of Klaus's political style and his neo-liberal policies. In particular, political controversy evolved around issues concerning the proper role of the state in promoting production and the provision of infrastructure, education, services and social welfare. The ČSSD concentrated its efforts on charging the neo-liberals with an inadequate response to the economic crisis that erupted in 1997. The question was, of course, how to obtain new resources in the face of the fiscal pressure. In the area of foreign policy, the ČSSD and the KSČM have shared their scepticism towards the EU and have not welcomed Czech membership of NATO. After the indecisive general election in 1998, the Social Democrats formed a weak minority government. However, for almost two years, the government has had great difficulty in formulating a coherent and credible socio-economic strategy to restore public confidence in the economy.

Christian Democracy and Modern Conservatism

Meanwhile, there is some sign in the region of the emergence of modern Christian Democracy that underscores the importance of national or religious traditions without being fundamentalist. Christian Democracy has also emerged with different degrees of electoral success in Albania, Bulgaria, Croatia, the Czech Republic, Hungary, Latvia, Lithuania, Romania, Slovakia, Slovenia, as well as the former Soviet republics of Georgia, Armenia and Russia. In Romania, for example, such a moderate tendency is represented by the Romanian National Peasant Party/Christian Democracy (PNTCD). The PNTCD is one of the best-organized parties in Romania, with the aim of establishing a functioning market economy. The Christian Democrats were instrumental in the formation of a grand electoral coalition the Democratic Convention of Romania (DCR) which included social democrats, liberals, the Hungarian minorities and various ecological parties.[37]

In some cases Christian democrats, moderate conservatives and traditionalists had little choice but to join forces in the face of a strong ex-Communist opponent. In Poland, there are two smaller moderate pro-Church conservative parties, the Conservative-Peasant Party (SKL) and the Conservative Coalition (KK), and the Party of Christian Democrats (PChD).[38] However, in the Solidarity Electoral Action (AWS), the moderate conservatives and Christian democrats remain numerically weaker than the more traditional pro-Church groupings. The latter have exercised considerable influence within the AWS.[39] While the AWS embodied a strong traditional conservatism, it formed a centre-right government with Balcerowicz's Freedom Union (UW) after winning the 1997 general election. The governing circles were therefore characterized by a pro-reform pragmatism. Yet the conservative-liberal partnership ended in June 2000 with the departure of the junior partner after a series of complaints about the populist and anti-liberal tendencies of the AWS. Though the AWS may still prove to be yet another transitional phenomenon, its persistence will at least help to build up a stable right-of-centre conservative constituency and reduce electoral volatility in the long run.

Challenges to the rise of Christian Democracy and modern conservatism come less from traditionalists than from the far right of the political spectrum in the form of nationalist fundamentalism, xenophobia and right-wing extremism. Across the region, the rise of parties and leaders professing anti-minority, anti-Semitic, anti-Romany and quasi-fascist views is hardly conducive to stability, consensus-building and constructive opposition.[40] While they are shunned by the mainstream parties, the Czech Republican Party (SPR-RSČ), the Hungarian Justice and Life Party (MIÉP) and the Liberal-Democratic Party of Russia (LDPR) managed to gain enough votes to enter parliament in recent elections. What these parties shared is the exploitation of national chauvinism and economic populism to their own advantage. Romania also witnessed cooperation between the ex-Communist PDSR and the ultra-nationalist National Unity Party in the form of a 'red-brown' coalition. In the former Yugoslavia, people proved to be even more susceptible to populist and xenophobic incitement. In circumstances of economic dislocation, even mainstream parties could develop traits of anti-democratic, authoritarian tendencies. For example, the Hungarian Smallholders' Party (FKGP), which campaigned for the re-privatization of land to re-establish a Hungarian agricultural sector, was suspended from membership of the European Union of Christian Democrats in 1996 because of its increasingly nationalist-populist standpoint.[41]

Neo-liberal Pragmatism

Last but not least, the logic of electoral competition has had the effect of compelling some of the neo-liberals to not only re-visit the idea that 'the state should intervene where the market fails', but also to pay more attention to the concerns raised by traditionalists and socialists.

In fact, neo-liberal stabilization measures invariably caused further hardships before the possible benefits of the market could fully materialize. As the social costs of economic change were running too high for many, it became more difficult to achieve and maintain broad social consent for consistent market-oriented reforms. In fact, the New Democracies Barometer surveys indicated that there was less support for the new economic systems in comparison with the former planned economies.[42] What is more, neo-liberal politicians were often accused of allegedly putting IMF/overseas debtors' interests ahead of domestic interests. Yet, if the self-proclaimed neo-liberal 'conviction' politicians continued to ignore or failed to accommodate social demands, impatient citizens would be drawn towards populist parties that claimed to know painless ways of dealing with pressing economic problems. Eventually, democratic elections would provide the opportunity to undermine the reforms.

Therefore, the neo-liberal Young Democrats (Fidesz) first shifted to a pro-welfare position in response to the market shocks between 1994 and 1998. Then, following the weakening of the Hungarian conservative parties, the party successfully captured the traditionalist constituency under the leadership of Viktor Orbán and changed its name to Hungarian Civic Party (Fidesz-MPP). As a result, the Fidesz has transformed itself from a radical neo-liberal party into a moderate conservative force.[43]

Political realism also guided market-oriented reforms in the Czech Republic, despite Václav Klaus's own pledge to build 'an unconstrained, unrestricted, full-fledged, unspoiled market economy' as quickly as possible.[44] As Seán Hanley argues, Czech-style neo-liberalism in practice embodied a more pragmatic, statist and corporatist approach.[45] This explains the apparent contradictions between Klaus's radical neo-liberal rhetoric and his willingness to protect jobs in loss-making state enterprises using state subsidies. The success of this approach was largely responsible for helping sustain support for reforms in the early stages of the transition. However, the political domination of Klaus's Civic Democratic Party (ODS) ended in 1997 when the leader was forced to resign as Prime Minister amidst a spate of political funding scandals and an economic crisis.

In Poland, where advocates of the shock therapy successfully implemented macroeconomic stabilization measures, the same neo-liberals also demonstrated a certain degree of social sensitivity and agreed to slow the pace of privatization of state-owned enterprises and incorporated workers' concerns into the privatization programme. UW leader Balcerowicz, who gained 17,994 more votes than AWS leader Krzaklewski in the Katowice district during the 1997 election, seemed to have some success in shedding the image of the unloved architect of Poland's shock therapy.[46]

In all, we observe in the post-Communist region not only the existence of the three strands of conservatism, but in some countries also their successful democratization-cum-Europeanization. Merely ten years after the collapse of the Communist regimes, many of the countries have seen several national elections and local government elections, as well as the peaceful transfer of power between different parties at all levels. Emergence, polarization and democratization-cum-Europeanization: these are the phases by which the ideological tendencies in question progress in their realization of the crucial tasks of democratic and market transitions. To the extent that the three ideological blocs have closed the gaps between one other, policies adopted by governments led by the ex-Communists do not differ radically from those of the traditionalists and the neo-liberal conservatives.

It is at this point, when the initial ideological polarization is being replaced by partial convergence regarding fundamental beliefs in political economy and the direction of key policy areas, that consensus politics can further develop. In theory, and depending on the circumstances, such a development offers each strand a choice of partners on both sides. Meanwhile, there is still room for genuine doctrinal competition for dominance between 'welfarism', 'traditionalism' and 'free enterprise' within the new consensus. For instance, the Hungarian socialists formed a stable pro-reform coalition with the liberal Free Democrats (SZDSZ) from 1994 to 1998. But as shown in the break-up of the AWS-UW government in Poland, mutual rapprochement will not be effective without rejecting 'conviction' politics in favour of a more moderate and tolerant style.

Such an approach is particularly popular among some intellectual circles in East Central Europe. In Poland, for instance, Adam Michnik has argued pithily that 'there is a need for the presence of a socialist care for the poorest, a conservative defence of tradition, and a liberal reflection on efficiency and growth.'[47] In the same vein, Marcin Król has put forward the idea of 'liberal conservatism' to combine notions of progress and tradition and re-construct diverse themes into a coherent discourse.[48] In his words:

> ... a conservative attitude is needed to oppose destruction by the modernizing forces of nationalism, socialism, and liberalism ... *Poland has to produce a liberal animal with a nationalist background and remnants of a socialist mentality*, it does not necessarily have to destroy the important achievements of Poland's past. It does not have to destroy positive national traditions ... [but it has] to rescue everything that is worthy of being kept ... liberal conservatism [is] liberalism with good taste, liberalism with a memory of our national past, liberalism with a strong idea of our homeland. (Italics added)

However, one must not underestimate the inherent difficulty of the exercise. The transition from Communism is exceptional and unprecedented in terms of scale and complexity, for it is knotted with radical attempts to establish the foundations of a modern political-economic system. Also, whether or not such convergence is irresistible depends in large measure on whether it is broadly felt to be desirable. Across the region, there are situations in which hard-line Communists and ultra-nationalists have refused to learn from the positive changes elsewhere in the post-Communist world since 1989. At the party level, many of the leading political parties in Russia and the Balkan states are not adequately institutionalized or democratized to qualify for EU-based transnational party links. In particular, there remain greater cultural and ideological barriers for the successor parties in the Balkans and the former Soviet republics to overcome. Thus, the EU has encountered certain difficulty in drawing Russia and the Balkan states into its sphere of influence. Thus, there is nothing inevitable in the democratization-cum-Europeanization of the three strands of conservatism.

Table 2 reports the electoral performance of main political parties and groupings in Bulgaria, the Czech Republic, Hungary, Poland and Romania. Clearly, the ideological transformations in the post-Communist region are far from complete. One may contend that the centripetal ideological movement of parties has had the entirely predictable result of opening up a large political space on both ends of the political spectrum. What is certain, however, is that a multitude of anti-democratic ideological tendencies will continue to exert centrifugal pressures on the political centre, which will have the effect of obstructing the development of consensus politics.

TABLE 2

ELECTORAL PERFORMANCE OF MAIN POLITICAL PARTIES AND POLITICAL GROUPINGS IN BULGARIA, THE CZECH REPUBLIC, HUNGARY, POLAND AND ROMANIA

Country/Party Name	Election Performance (Votes)			
Bulgaria	**1990**	**1991**	**1994**	**1997**
Bulgaria Socialist Party (BSP, Post-Com)	47.2	33.1	43.5	22.1
Union of Democratic Forces (ODS: grand coalition of Christian Democrats, peasants, liberals, social democrats, and ethnic groups)	36.2	34.4	24.2	52.3
Volatility		27	31	49
Czech Republic		**1992**	**1996**	**1998**
Communist Party of Bohemia and Moravia (KSCM, Post-Comm)		14.0	10.3	11.0
Czech Social Democratic Party (CSSD, Soc. Dem.)		6.5	26.4	32.3
Civic Democratic Party (ODS, Lib. Cons.)		29.7	29.6	27.7
Freedom Union (US, breakaway from ODS, Lib. Cons.)		-	-	8.6
Civic Democratic Alliance (ODA, Soc. Lib.)		5.9	6.4	-
Christian Democratic Union (KDU-CSL, Christ. Dem.)		6.3	8.1	9.0
Association for the Republic/ Republican Party (SR-RSC)		6.0	8.0	3.9
Volatility			38	NA
Hungary		**1990**	**1994**	**1998**
Hungarian Socialist Party (MSZP, Post-Com)		10.9	33.0	32.9
Hungarian Social Democratic Party (MSZDP, Soc. Dem.)		3.6	0.9	0.1
Alliance of Free Democrats (SZDSZ, Lib.)		21.4	19.7	7.6
Young Democrats/ Civic Party (Fidesz, Lib. Cons.)		9.0	7.0	29.5
Hungarian Democratic Forum (MDF, Cons.)		24.7	11.7	2.8

TABLE 2 (cont.)
ELECTORAL PERFORMANCE OF MAIN POLITICAL PARTIES AND POLITICAL GROUPINGS IN BULGARIA, THE CZECH REPUBLIC, HUNGARY, POLAND AND ROMANIA

Country/Party Name	Election Performance (Votes)		
Christian Democratic People's Party (KDNP, Christ. Dem.)	6.5	7.0	2.3
Independent Party of Smallholders (FKGP, Agrarian)	11.7	8.8	3.1
Hungarian Justice and Life (MIEP, Extreme Right)	-	1.6	5.5
Volatility		48	NA
Poland	**1991**	**1993**	**1997**
Democratic Left Alliance (SLD, Post-Com)	12.0	20.4	27.1
Solidarity of Labour (SP)/ Labour Union (UP, Soc. Dem.)	2.0	7.3	4.9
Polish Peasant Party (PSL, Agrarian)	8.7	15.4	7.3
Congress of Liberal Democrats (KLD, Lib.)	7.5	4.0	[UW]
Democratic Union (UD, Lib.)	12.3	10.6	[UW]
Freedom Union (UW, Lib.)	-	-	13.4
Solidarity trade union (Christ. Nat.)	4.9	[AWS]	
Christian National Union (ZChN, Christ. Nat.)	8.7	6.4	[AWS]
Centre Alliance (PC, Christ. Dem.)	4.4	[AWS]	
Solidarity Election Action (AWS: grand coalition of Solidarity trade union, conservatives, peasants, Christian nationals, Christian democrats and nationalists)	-	-	43.7
Movement for Reconstruction of Poland (ROP, Cons. Nat.)	-	-	5.6
Confederation for an Independent Poland (KPN, Nat.)	7.5	5.8	[AWS]
Volatility		56	59
Romania	**1990**	**1992**	**1996**
National Salvation Front (FSN, Post-Com)	66.3	-	-
Democratic National Salvation Front (FDSN)/Social Democracy) Party of Romania (PDSR, Post-Com)	-	27.7	21.5
Democratic Party (PD-FSN, Soc. Dem.)	-	10.2	[USD]
Social Democratic Union (USD, Soc. Dem.)	-	-	15.5
Romanian Social Democratic Party (PSDR, historical Soc. Dem.)	0.5	[DCR]	[USD]
National Peasant Christian Democratic Party (PNTCD)		2.6	[DCR]
Democratic Convention (DCR, a grand coalition of Christian Democrats, liberals, social democrats, greens and agrarians)	-	20.0	30.2
Democratic Alliance of Hungarians in Romania (UDMR, ethnic)	7.2	7.5	6.6
Greater Romania Party (PRM, Extreme Right)	-	4.7	5.6
Romanian National Unity Party (PUNR, Extreme Right)	-	8.8	5.3
Volatility		9	22

Sources:
Richard Rose, Neil Munro and Tom Mackie, *Elections in Central and Eastern Europe Since 1990* (Glasgow: Centre for the Study of Public Policy, University of Strathclyde, 1998).
See also <http://www.strath.ac.uk/Departments/CSPP/partiesframe.html>.

Conclusion

The above analysis shows that the emergence of conservative politics in the post-Communist states took place under specific sets of circumstances that did not allow for a straightforward definition of the term. In fact, the nature of conservative reactions to the system change since 1989 has varied considerably: Sometimes it has been outright opposition, considering the Communist model of governance to be still perfectly viable. Alternatively, it can take a 'reactionary' form, attempting to restore national and religious traditions. Last but not least, it can also look to the experience of the West for ready-made models of advancing the free market and democracy. In truth, there are numerous expressions of conservatism that vary across the political spectrum. Against the specific politico-historical situation in the post-Communist region, this study has identified three strands of conservatism: (ex-) Communist conservatism, traditional conservatism and neo-liberal conservatism. In the post-Communist world, therefore, 'conservatism' can be used in conflicting and confusing ways to refer to a mystified past as much as a promising future.

It may well be that an unequivocal conception of conservatism will never be attainable in the post-Communist world. Rather, conservatism in this region will always be a hybrid of some sort. One view is that in the post-Communist era the political elite should take a pragmatic approach to ideologies, in the sense that a balance can be found between neo-liberalism and its rivals by combining appropriate elements from a broad range of ideologies including socialism, liberalism, conservatism and so on. In practice, that involves (1) accepting that the scope for full-fledged realization of the core beliefs of each strand of conservatism is limited and (2) finding a way of accommodating the opponents' beliefs alongside the essential core of their own values. The resultant consensus politics, contrary to the neo-liberal economic dogma and the various forms of 'conviction' politics, is a politics of tolerance and accommodation, which is open to cooperation across strict doctrinal or confessional lines. Last but not least, a consensual style of politics helps establish a credible dialogue with the people in order to sustain electoral and social support for far-reaching reforms.

However, it must be noted that the new consensus politics is not as invulnerable as it may seem to be. For one thing, die-hard Communists, ultra-nationalists and doctrinaire neo-liberals will not tolerate it. It will sometimes be difficult for moderates not to yield to extremist pressure. For another thing, there are virtually no actions or policies available to the leaders that will please all sections of the population. Both factors lead to tensions within the newly emerged consensus, a consensus that offers the best hope for the region's political and economic transformation.

Having said that, the western rim of the post-Communist world, in particular Poland and Hungary, is in a better position to put a new style of consensus politics into effect than several other countries in the region. Here, reversals of parliamentary majorities have not disrupted the reform process but have merely adjusted the pace of reforms in response to the people's will. By and large, developments in the two countries concur with the above discussion about the partial convergence of the various conservative forces in connection to broader processes of democratization and European integration.

It is hoped that this brief exploration of the subject has shed some light on the nature of the various ideological tendencies in the post-Communist world and helped to chart the dynamics of changing beliefs against the backdrop of far-reaching systemic transformations.

NOTES

1. See, for example, Anders Åslund, *Post-Communist Economic Revolutions: How Big a Bang?* (Washington, DC: The Centre for Strategic and International Studies, 1992), Jozef M. van Braban, *The Political Economy of Transition: Coming to Grips with History and Methodology* (London and New York: Routledge, 1998) and John Pickles and Andrian Smith (eds.), *Theorising Transition: The Political Economy of Post-Communist Transformations* (London and New York: Routledge, 1998).

2. Jerzy Wiatr, *Four Essays of East European Transformation* (Warsaw: Scholar Agency, 1992), pp.88–102. See also Christopher G.A. Byrant and Edmund Mokrzycki (eds.), *The New Great Transformation? Change and Continuity in East-Central Europe* (London and New York: Routledge, 1994).

3. Richard Rose, Neil Munro and Tom Mackie, *Elections in Central and Eastern Europe Since 1990* (Glasgow: Centre for the Study of Public Policy, University of Strathclyde, 1998).

4. Pridham is right to point out that 'labels alone do not automatically tell us much of substance, although admittedly individual party self-identification with a Western European type of party family may denote an element of conviction, or otherwise, opportunism'. But he also argues that 'taking self-identified and de facto members of European party families together does nevertheless allow us some scope for cross-national comparison'. Thus, this paper will shed light on the implication of transnational party cooperation for political ideological development in the post-Communist states. See Geoffrey Pridham in the next chapter of this volume (Chapter 11).

5. See, for example, Francis Fukuyama, *The End of History and the Last Man* (London: Hamish Hamilton, 1992).

6. Jeffrey Sachs, 'Life in the Economic Emergency Room', in John Williamson (ed.), *The Political Economy of Policy Reform* (Washington, DC: Institute for International Economics, 1993), pp.501–24.

7. Peter Mair, 'What is the Different about Post-Communist Party Systems?' in

Peter Mair, *Party System Change: Approaches and Interpretations* (Oxford: Oxford University Press, 1997), pp.175–98.

8. Rose, Munro and Mackie, *Elections*, p.119.

9. Jeffrey Goldfarb, *After the Fall: The Pursuit of Democracy in Central Europe* (New York: Basic Books), p.29. See also Jeffrey Goldfarb, 'What's Left, What's Right?', *Social Research*, Vol.60, No.3 (1993), pp.415–32.

10. Richard Sakwa, 'Left or Right? The CPRF and the Problem of Democratic Consolidation in Russia', in John Löwenhardt (ed.), *Party Politics in Post-Communist Russia* (London and Portland, OR: Frank Cass, 1998), p.129.

11. Nigel Ashford and Stephen Davis (eds.), *A Dictionary of Conservative and Libertarian Thought* (London and New York: Routledge, 1991), pp.102–6. See also Michael Gallagher, Michael Laver and Peter Mair, *Representative Government in Western Europe* (New York: McGraw-Hill, 1992), pp.70–5.

12. Michael Freeden, *Ideologies and Political Theory: A Conceptual Approach* (Oxford: Clarendon Press, 1996), pp.333–67. See also Brian Girvin, *The Right in the Twentieth Century: Conservatism and Democracy* (London and New York: Pinter, 1994), pp.1–23.

13. Michael Oakeshott, *Rationalism in Politics and Other Essays* (London: Methuen, 1967), p.169.

14. Michael Waller, 'Party Inheritances and Party Identities', in Geoffrey Pridham and Paul Lewis (eds.), *Stabilising Fragile Democracies: Comparing New Party Systems in Southern and Eastern Europe* (London and New York: Routledge, 1996), pp.23-43.

15. Jakub Karpiński, Polska, *Komunizm, Opozycja – Słownik* (London: Polonia, 1985), p.106.

16. Fritz Plasser, Peter A. Ulram and Harald Waldrauch, *Democratic Consolidation in East-Central Europe* (London: Macmillan, 1998), pp.147-63.

17. Sakwa, p.128. See also M. Steven Fish, 'The Advent of Multipartism in Russia, 1993–95', *Post-Soviet Affairs*, Vol.11, No.4 (1995), p.348.

18. Mary McAuley, *Russia's Politics of Uncertainty* (Cambridge: Cambridge University Press, 1997), p.115.

19. Karen Henderson and Neil Robinson, *Post-Communist Politics: An Introduction* (London: Prentice Hall, 1997), pp.100–8.

20. Leslie Holmes, *Post-Communism: An Introduction* (Cambridge: Polity Press, 1997), pp.146–7.

21. Peter Murrell, 'Conservative Political Philosophy and the Strategy of Economic Transition', *East European Politics and Society*, Vol.6, No.1 (1982), pp.3–16.

22. Erzsébet Szalai, 'The Power Structure in Hungary after the Political Transition', in Bryant and Mokrzycki, pp.120–43.

23. Kenneth Ka-Lok Chan, 'The Religious Base of Politics in Post-Communist Poland: A Case of Bounded Secularisation', in David Broughton and Hans-Martien ten Napel (eds.), *Religion and Mass Electoral Behaviour in Europe* (London and New York: Routledge, forthcoming).

24. See, for example, Leszek Balcerowicz, *Socialism, Capitalism, Transformation* (Budapest: Central European University Press, 1995), pp.340–69 and Václav Klaus, 'Transition? An Insider's View', *Problems of Communism*, Jan.–April 1992, pp.73–5. See also Adam Przeworski, 'Neo-Liberal Fallacy', *Journal of Democracy*, Vol.3, No.3 (1992), pp.45–59.

25. George Schöpflin, 'Conservatism in Central and Eastern Europe', in János Mátyás Kovács (ed.), *Transition to Capitalism? The Communist Legacy in Eastern Europe* (New Brunswick, NJ and London: Transaction Publishers, 1994), pp.192–4.
26. Ten post-Communist states have applied to join the EU. They include Hungary, Poland, the Czech Republic, Slovenia, Estonia, Romania, Slovakia, Bulgaria, Latvia and Lithuania.
27. European Council, *Conclusions of the Presidency* (Copenhagen, June 1993).
28. See, for example, Geoffrey Pridham, 'Transnational Party Links and Transition to Democracy: Eastern Europe in Comparative Perspective', in Paul Lewis (ed.), *Party Structure and Organization in East-Central Europe* (Cheltenham: Edward Elgar, 1996), pp.187–219. Also, Geoffrey Pridham, 'Regime Change, Democratic Conditionality and Transnational Party Linkages: The Case of Eastern Europe', paper presented at the ECPR Joint Sessions of Workshops, Berne, Switzerland (1997).
29. For example, 'European way – European manner' was one of the pro-European slogans used by the ex-Communist Hungarian Socialist Party during the 1998 general election.
30. Attlia Ágh, *The Politics of Central Europe* (Beverly Hills, CA: Sage Publications, 1998), p.65.
31. Originally established to be a loose coalition of ex-Communist parties and groupings, the SLD finally registered as a political party in the summer of 1999.
32. Michael Waller, 'Adaptation of the Former Communist Parties of East-Central Europe: A Case of Social-democratization?' *Party Politics*, Vol.1, No.4, pp.473–90. See also Michael Waller, Bruno Coppieters and Kris Deschouwer (eds.), *Social Democracy in a Post-Communist Europe* (London: Frank Cass, 1994).
33. 'Hungarian Survey', *Financial Times*, 21 Nov. 1995, p.1.
34. Kate Hudson, *European Communism since 1989: Towards a New European Left?* (London: Macmillan, 2000).
35. Sarah Oates, 'Party Platforms: Towards a Definition of the Russian Political Spectrum', in Löwenhardt (ed.), *Party Politics in Post-Communist Russia*, pp.76–97.
36. See John D. Bell, 'Democratization and Political Participation in "Postcommunist" Bulgaria', in Karen Dawisha and Bruce Parrot (eds.), *Politics, Power, and the Struggle for Democracy in South-East Europe* (Cambridge: Cambridge University Press, 1997), p.393. See also Vladimir Tismaneanu, 'Romanian Exceptionalism? Democracy, Ethnocracy, and Uncertain Pluralism in Post-Ceausescu Romania', ibid., p.441-3.
37. Wendy Hollis, *Democratic Consolidation in Eastern Europe: The Influence of the Communist Legacy in Hungary, the Czech Republic, and Romania* (New York: Columbia University Press, 1999), p.230–33.
38. See, for example, Partia Konserwatywna, *Dokumenty Partii Konserwatywnej* (Warszawa, 1993) and Koalicja Konserwatywna, *Konserwatyzm na Prawicy: Pięć Lat Koalicja Konserwatywnej* (Warszawa, 1998). See also *Spór o Polskę. Z Aleksanderem Hallem rozmawiają Ewa Polak I Mariusz Kobzdej* (Warszawa: RYTM, 1993), pp.131–41 and Kazimierz M. Ujazdowski, *Prawica dla Wszystkich* (Warszawa: ARARAT, 1995), pp.54–62.

39. Michael Wenzel, 'Solidarity and Akcja Wyborcza "Solidarność". An Attempt At Reviving the Legend', *Communist and Post-Communist Studies*, Vol.31, No.2 (1998), pp.139–56. See also 'AWS-Trzy filary I czwarty obserwator', *Rzeczpospolita*, 5 March 1999.
40. See, for example, Janusz Bugajski, Nations in Turmoil: Conflict and Cooperation in Eastern Europe (Boulder, CO: Westview Press, 1995).
41. See Pridham, 'Patterns of Europeanization and Transnational Party Co-operation' (Chapter 11, this volume).
42. Richard Rose and Christian Haerpfer, *Change and Stability in the New Democracies Barometer: A Trend Analysis* (Glasgow: Centre for the Study of Public Policy, University of Strathclyde, 1996), p.51. Also Geoffrey Evans and Stephen Whitefield, 'The Politics and Economics of Democratic Commitment: Support for Democracy in Transition Societies', *Europe-Asia Studies*, Vol.25, No.4, p.497 and Gábor Tóka, 'Political Support in East Central Europe', in Hans-Dieter Klingeman and Dieter Fuchs (eds.), *Citizens and the State* (New York: Oxford University Press, 1995), p.360.
43. András Körösényi, *Government and Politics in Hungary* (Budapest: Central European University Press, 1999), pp.42–4.
44. Quoted in Jerzy Szacki, *Liberalism after Communism* (Budapest: Central European University Press, 1995), p.147.
45. Seán Hanley, 'The New Right in the New Europe? Unravelling the Ideology of "Czech Thatcherism"', *Journal of Political Ideologies*, Vol.4, No.2 (1999), pp.163–89.
46. Kenneth Ka-Lok Chan, 'The Polish General Election of 1997', *Electoral Studies*, Vol.17, No.4 (1998), p.564–5.
47. Adam Michnik, *Letters From Freedom: Post-Cold War Realities and Perspectives* (Berkeley, CA: University of California Press, 1998), p.325.
48. Marcin Król, 'Being a Conservative in a Postcommunist Country', *Social Research*, Vol.60, No.3 (1993), pp.601–7ff.

11

Patterns of Europeanization and Transnational Party Co-operation: Party Development in Central and Eastern Europe

GEOFFREY PRIDHAM

Introduction

Nearly a decade since the fall of Communist regimes in Central and Eastern European countries (CEECs), the still relatively new party systems have not yet clearly settled into stable patterns – either in terms of durable or principal party actors or levels of individual party support. It would appear therefore that party development in CEECs has been undergoing a long transition period without, as yet, firm signs of moving into system consolidation. That conclusion would broadly fit with the general view about regime change there. At the same time, cross-national variation is increasingly evident not merely between regions like East-Central Europe and the Balkans, but also among the countries in each of these regions – a point that may be said also about party systems in the CEECs.

However, this is not to say that new party system stabilization and democratization march automatically in conjunction, for the former may be autonomous. This article explores party system development in the CEECs while recognising difficulties of comparison with Western Europe. It does this by, first, considering familiar methods of cross-national comparison of party systems, especially the ideological, before looking at the question of Europeanization. It then concentrates on an analysis of transnational party co-operation as a focused way of evaluating the Europeanization dynamic in party development in the new democracies in Central and Eastern Europe in contrast with the more descriptive approach of identifying party families across Europe. In examining transnational party co-operation (TPC), the paper draws on elite interviews with party leaders and senior officials in a variety of CEECs .[1]

Patterns of Party Development in Central and Eastern Europe

Party system stabilization is undoubtedly affected by the democratization process in a variety of ways. The generally difficult transitions in the CEECs warn against making anything more than a tentative characterization of their party systems. The fact that economic transformation and, in many cases, state and nation-building have accompanied political change reinforces that conclusion. But the party systems are also affected by historical inheritances including any significant pre-authoritarian experience of democratic rule.

This leads to our first consideration for, much more than the post-war European and the Southern European transitions, those taking place in the CEECs have revealed weak historical backgrounds in party development. Historical parties like the Social Democrats did not perform well in the first free elections in 1990, leaving the way open for new parties to dominate the political stage although, in the second phase of party development, many former regime parties successfully converted themselves from Communist into democratic Socialist or Social Democratic parties. By and large, the four decades of Communist rule left greater discontinuities in party development than was the case in the earlier two experiences of European democratization. Hence, party identification has taken longer to emerge.

There are additional reasons for this problem. The initial dominance in several transitions of anti-Communist umbrella movements inhibited the ready occurrence of political pluralism expressed through the medium of organised parties along recognizable ideological lines. The continuing importance of Solidarity is one reason for the belated flowering of full competitive politics in Poland, and similar problems were encountered with Civic Forum and Public Against Violence in both parts of the soon-to-split-Czechoslovakia. Analogous movements in Bulgaria and Hungary – the United Democratic Front and the Hungarian Democratic Forum – were however more obviously identified with the centre-Right in the political spectrum. But even they had to transform themselves into organized parties, the UDF much more successfully than the MDF, which ultimately fell from grace. Party development in the CEECs has furthermore been marked by a distinct focus on parliamentary activity and a tendency towards elite control. At the same time, a pattern of splits and recombinations has persisted in party formation.[2] As a whole, parties in these new democracies have often demonstrated weak organisational links with the public.[3]

Do these problems of party system settledness mean that identifying patterns of party development is particularly difficult? To some extent, this must be so, although after a decade interim assessments are possible, while growing cross-national variation – with some party systems more stabilized than others – does invite comparison. So what does such comparison show?

Given that party systems are multi-level in their development, there is the matter of which criteria to adopt. The most obvious is the ideological – which look at party families and how far these are replicated in the CEECs. In a recent survey of party development, the following patterns were identified:[4]

- the scarcity of modern conservative parties, with a notable exception in the Czech ODS;
- a pattern of centre-Right parties settling in the Liberal camp; with traditional authoritarian parties on the right in certain countries (Hungary, Poland and Slovakia);
- strong Left parties as modernized successors to the former Communist regime parties or, alternatively, in the form of Social Democratic parties (notably, the CSSD in the Czech Republic);
- the failure of Green parties to establish themselves despite their initial impact during the fall of Communism;
- and, the absence of agrarian parties except in Poland and Hungary.

This snapshot may not be ephemeral, since longer-term patterns can be distinguished. This is especially so with respect to the first and fourth patterns, while the third suggests some similarity – except the modernized left parties derived from former regime parties in CEECs. In Western Europe they often tended to be in opposition and, in any case, had long practice of operating in a pluralist environment. It should be noted, however, that Segert underrates the importance of centre-right parties including those of the Christian Democratic tendency.

But there are limitations to this exercise in party families. It offers some descriptive value with restricted mileage for cross-national comparison. Labels alone do not automatically tell us much of substance, although admittedly individual party self-identification with a West European type of party family may denote an element of conviction, or otherwise, opportunism. Thus, the two types of left parties are the clearest case of transnationally identifiable forces, as are the Christian Democrats on the centre-right in some countries, such as the Czech and Slovak republics. But there are many examples in the CEECs of parties that do not adopt transnational nomenclature, although in terms of ideological precepts they may approximate to one party family or the other. This is true of other parties on the centre-Right in particular, such as the Civic Democratic Party (ODS) in the Czech Republic and the Hungarian Democratic Forum (MDF) and their allegiance to conservative or Christian Democratic parties. Taking self-identified and de facto members of European party families together does nevertheless allow us some scope for cross-national comparison.

But there are obvious deficiencies, as even in Western Europe conventional ideological labels are very broad and their meaning may not be transferable to the CEECs. According to Agh, this is not just because their local connotations are idiosyncratic but also because parties in the CEECs often have obscure profiles.[5] The last may alter with time as transition progresses, although the first problem reflects possible differences of political culture and, given the quite different political experiences in Eastern and Western Europe since the Second World War, one should expect there to be significant problems of culture-boundness when comparing ideological labels cross-nationally.

Similar to this exercise is the categorisation of parties into 'standard' and 'non-standard', terms initially applied to the Slovak party scene.[6] 'Standard' parties are those related without too much difficulty to the Left/Right spectrum in European politics; while 'non-standard' parties fail to do so because of their propensity to national and social populism, authoritarianism, radicalism and extremism as well as a confrontational and charismatic approach – the archetype of the latter being Meciar's Movement for a Democratic Slovakia (HZDS). This categorization of 'standard' parties furthermore stresses 'compatibility with international party structures', and thus overlaps with the exercise of party family alignment.

Whatever approach is adopted, it has to be recognized that there are in CEECs different types of party not usually found in Western Europe. This is because of cleavage fault lines which are particular to CEECs or individual states in the region. The most obvious example is ethnic parties like the Hungarian parties in Slovakia (now united in the SMK) as well as the similar Hungarian Democratic Federation of Romania (HDFR) in Hungary and the Turkish Movement for Rights and Freedoms (MRF) in Bulgaria. Olson calls into question the resemblance of party systems in East-Central Europe to their counterparts in Western Europe precisely because of issue alignments being different or sufficiently so as to rule out any congruence.[7]

There are further levels of party system that may highlight broad developmental differences between the CEECs and Western Europe. Thus, Olson goes on to note the organizational pattern of cadre parties in the former compared with the greater prevalence of mass parties in the latter. These cadre parties are distinguished by strong elite control and focus on parliamentary life combined with catch-all electoral appeals, this being possible through the instruments of mass communication. Olson argues therefore that leaders of these parties need not recapitulate the developmental sequences of Western Europe but rather they may leapfrog directly into a mass communications video age.[8] This may have influenced the degree to which leader personalities have been important in early party development in CEECs.[9] Such a pattern is not uncommon in democratic transitions, as shown in previous regime changes in Europe. Whether these features of party life in Central and Eastern Europe become permanent remains to be seen.

It is clear, therefore, that familiar comparative concepts may be applied to the new democracies in the Eastern half of Europe, but only to a restricted degree. In particular, they encounter not merely differences of historical experience but there are also problems in trying to compare unsettled party systems with long-established ones. With one or two exceptions, the CEECs have suffered from the debilitating effects on civil society of long Communist rule; and it would be surprising if that inheritance had not inhibited party development. Notwithstanding these difficulties, they have developed into vital and central actors in the new democracies of the CEECs.

Patterns of Europeanization: Multi-Level Approaches

In the evolution of new democracies, Europeanization tends to have different meanings although they may be connected and often have a common focus in terms of the accession to European organizations. Above all, Europeanization involves a basic policy reorientation towards institutionalized European co-operation – in terms primarily of the organizations of European integration but also some others like NATO and the Council of Europe. The European framework has allowed countries exiting from non-democratic rule to start anew in international relations. In doing so, Europe has became associated with liberal democracy and thus acquired a symbolic value – one which is underlined by the democratic requirements for entry to the EU.[10] But in Central and Eastern Europe the question of Europeanization has assumed a rather broader meaning. First, it has a distinct historical edge in that these countries, to varying degrees, emphasize the need to reconnect with mainstream European politics as in the catchphrases 'Return to Europe' or 'Back to Europe'. The concrete process of joining the EU thus represents an historical mission. Linked with this, Europeanization also carries a cultural or modernizing message as it involves the basic transformation of these countries into civil societies, indeed ones that will underpin the whole process of democratization.[11]

Clearly, there are different dimensions to Europeanization – economic (in terms of marketization) as well as social and cultural.[12] It is, however, the political which provides a systemic pressure in that the established form of political regime in Western Europe – that of parliamentary democracy – becomes the model for new democracies in the East. And the dictates of democratic conditionality seek to ensure that this model is not adopted merely in formal but also qualitative terms. There are, however, obstacles to this process of Europeanization – for it is not automatic despite the Europeanizing dynamic of the EU and its conditional promise of eventual membership. Insofar as this dynamic depends essentially on an overriding motive in new democracies to achieve EU entry, then political pressures and influences from Brussels but also individual EU member states are likely to be effective. If, on the other hand, this aim is clouded or contested domestically, then accordingly the scope for political Europeanization is reduced. That is most noticeable in those CEECs where traditionalist or nationalist attitudes hold sway among elites. But, also, mentalities carried over from predecessor Communist regimes can restrain the advance of elite understanding of the Western norms, practices and procedures that facilitate Europeanization. The very overload of everyday and systemic tasks in transition and transformation may also add to this problem.

It is here that we should turn to Europeanization patterns in party development. For it is against this background of EU promise and pressures that political elites in the CEECs and their parties are most likely to approximate to Western European ideological tendencies. This may take two forms. First, there is a diffuse sense of following European models of party development. This is not always directly related to the EU and may be influenced either by cross-national trends in Western Europe or be stimulated by particular national models there.

This pattern has been most noticeable on the Left with the Social Democratization of former regime parties in the CEECs. Reform Communists looked consciously to European models, and the domestic motivation was evident in their desire for legitimation with recognition by the Socialist International (SI) being the most obvious external accolade. This influence of European models on the Left was most pronounced in the case of the newly proclaimed Hungarian Socialist Party, whose leaders and activists made frequent visits to Western Europe in the early transition years.[13] But it was later evident, too, in other former Communist parties. The Slovak party changed its name in 1990 to Party of the Democratic Left (SDL) with Peter Weiss, its new chairman, deliberately aiming to create a modern European left party. In particular, it was the Italian Democratic Party of the Left (PDS) – the former PCI – that acted as a national model for the European left. It had a strong influence on the SDL in both strategic and organizational ways.

There are, therefore, different levels at which the Europeanization of party development can take place. These may be typed as identity and ideology, programme, organization, electoral politics and personnel. It is in all of these respects that transnational party co-operation may impact on party development in new democracies; and that is the second form of approximation to West European ideological tendencies. It exerts real, sometimes regular, pressures or influences through inter-elite socialization between countries in both halves of Europe and through a variety of channels that act in parallel and are in some cases linked. They are: the party groups in the European Parliament (EP) as well as in the Parliamentary Assembly of the Council of Europe, the different EU party federations related to these party groups such as the Party of European Socialists (PES), the European Liberal, Democrat and Reform Party (ELDR), the (Christian Democratic) European People's Party (EPP) and the conservative European Democratic

Union (EDU), the traditional party internationals such as the Socialist and the Liberal and, not to be omitted, bilateral links between parties in different countries, a growing pattern all the more significant when it involves those belonging to the EU party organizations. Such bilateral links followed a pattern of dividing tasks between member parties in Western Europe with a view to both vetting closely candidate parties but also influencing their own evolution. Often geographical proximity was the basis. For instance, Austrian parties concentrated on other, usually neighbouring, countries in Central Europe; just as Scandinavian parties paid special attention to new parties in the Baltic states. The German parties spread their contacts more broadly throughout the CEECs.

There are recognisable barriers to the impact of TPC, just as there may be political ones if elites in new democracies are either uninterested or mistrustful. They operate primarily via party leaders and organizations although to some extent the latter has included local or regional branches as well as national party headquarters. Activity has involved election training as well as policy and organizational advice and has sometimes included financial support. Whatever its limitations, transnational party co-operation provides a convenient and pertinent mechanism for assessing how far party development in the CEECs has in reality been determined by Western European models whether in an integral or partial form. In this sense, it is unique and should therefore be utilized as a specific method in the comparative analysis of political parties.

Transnational Party Co-operation and the Central and East European Parties

In one obvious way, TPC accords strongly with the categorization into party families. Parties from new democracies interested in joining transnational party formations have to declare an adherence to one or other official ideological tendency. This is not merely nominal as even this decision may entail some ideological adjustment or certainly a sharpening of party identity – at presumably a formative stage of individual party development, except possibly in the case of historical parties. The process of being accepted has been tightened up by most formations in response to the wave of new parties seeking membership in the 1990s. This policy was on the Left determined by the problem of how to deal with applications from former regime parties; but it also reflected general difficulties that emerged early on of identifying the correct or acceptable partner parties in the CEECs. Finally, once parties have joined, they are subject to various pressures to conform to TPC programmes and policy positions. These are, admittedly, largely platonic given that transnational party formations do not transform policy positions into political action; but the very process of policy debate has its own mild dynamic effects.

One may generalize in this way, but in the end the impacts of TPC are likely to be quite party-variable and under certain conditions also nationally variable. We now explore these impacts more specifically under a number of headings. In doing so, an attempt will be made to answer two questions: how really influential has involvement in TPC activity been for party development in the CEECs; and, can one in any way draw conclusions about the impact of European models of political parties? At the same time, attention will also be given to difficulties encountered in transnational party relations between EU member states and the CEECs.

Party identification initially proved a major problem for TPC, especially in the first year or two. There was time pressure to find partner parties because the first free elections were called within only a few months of the fall of Communist regimes. Ideological labels sometimes turned out to be misleading; transnational actors occasionally discovered more ideological sympathy with tendencies within rival parties than with their formal fraternal partners; and, there was some element of opportunism in dealings with transnational actors since there was a dire need of election training and support.[14] While in the course of time a greater familiarity with the party scene in the different CEECs developed on the part of transnational actors, some problems of party identification persisted due to the instability of political parties in CEECs or the fact that East/West cultural differences were imprinted on ideological terms.

The greatest problems were found on the centre-Right of the political spectrum. Among the Christian Democrats, the problem was not so much ascertaining which parties were de facto CD without their using the title but rather trying to draw a line to exclude those holding hard Right views. According to the adviser on Eastern Europe to the chairman of the EPP group in the European Parliament, the European Union of Christian Democrats (EUCD) had become more careful about scrutinizing party programmes before admitting new parties into the first stage of formal links. This followed some dilemma over contacts with Christian parties in Poland which were rather right-wing and even anti-Semitic.[15] In one case at least, the Hungarian Smallholders' Party, a party was suspended from membership of the EUCD because of its increasingly nationalist-populist standpoint.[16]

The same problem was faced by conservative parties looking for reliable partners in the CEECs. Party terminology was particularly difficult since 'conservative' was a rare name in these countries and in some of them was associated with reactionary tendencies. Instead, parties of this ilk displayed myriad and sometimes idiosyncratic names. The usual way of sifting them out was to study party programmes to test their conformity with standard centre-right views, for programmes were seen as a form of basic commitment.[17] There was the same problem of self-demarcation from the hard Right, the main difficulty concerning parties with nationalist tendencies. These were tested for their views on patriotism and soundings could produce a negative response, as became clear in a reluctance to pursue further talks with the Croatian Democratic Union (HDZ) – the party of Franjo Tudjman. Human rights and treatment of minorities were generally major issues in keeping certain parties at a distance from transnational organisations.[18]

On the positive side, however, there were many cases on the centre-right of especially Christian Democratic parties in CEECs that found no difficulty in aligning themselves with these transnational formations. This was, for instance, true of Christian Democratic parties in the Czech Republic, Slovakia, Hungary, Poland, Romania and Slovenia. Some like the Slovak Christian Democratic Movement (KDH) took slightly divergent lines, such as in taking a fundamentalist standpoint on religious matters.[19] That reflected a relatively strong religious presence in Slovak society but did not put it out on a limb transnationally, for the KDH's record on human and minority rights was clear-cut. These Christian Democratic parties from the CEECs went on to play a fairly active part in the transnational organisations, this being facilitated by a strong support for the values of European integration – their most salient sympathy being with standard Christian Democratic parties in Western Europe.

The European Liberals encountered severe problems at first of identifying partner parties, although their opportunity for influencing party development was, in individual cases at least, if anything greater than with conservative and Christian Democratic parties. As the deputy secretary-general of the Liberal group in the EP noted,

> Everybody called themselves liberals at the time of the revolutions, so it was not an easy task to identify [these parties]; and so we made mistakes, so we headed into uncharted waters, we didn't have fixed points; we didn't know whether he or she was a liberal, whether the party set up was a true liberal party and so on. What we did: we travelled extensively to meet with these people, and some of them we discarded immediately afterwards as we saw they were nationalist, for example. I even remember that Zhirinovsky's [extreme right-wing] party was invited to a Liberal International congress in Helsinki. Of course, quickly we discovered that this was not a happy event![20]

The situation was that much more fluid for Liberals since the tradition of Liberalism was generally not strong in the CEECs. But, eventually, this provided transnational actors of this tendency with a special scope for helping to establish if not mould new parties. One can see this in the Slovak case. The Slovak Democratic Union (DU) was established late in transition, shortly before the parliamentary elections of 1994. Electoral pressure was therefore a factor in explaining the DU's strong reliance on advice from European Liberals. It drew on their own programmes not least as 'liberalism doesn't have a long tradition in Slovakia', so that 'we have to implement the experience of our partners and make this work in our Slovak conditions', this being an 'important source of information but also of inspiration'. In particular, specific programmatic tenets like devolution of power to the local level were mentioned.[21] To this extent, the DU's early identity formation was significantly determined by standard European Liberal ideas. It also reflected the general pattern in Slovakia during the 1994–98 parliament when opposition parties placed that much more importance on transnational linkages as a defence mechanism against authoritarian pressures from the then Meciar government.

A major obstacle to the development of transnational linkages were the umbrella movements that emerged from opposition to Communist rule. They were ideologically diverse and therefore did not relate to the transnational organisations which operated along conventional ideological lines. With Polish Solidarity during 1989–90, Bronislaw Geremek – one of its leading figures – noted that contacts were made with all the main internationals – Socialist, Christian Democratic and Liberal – and with parties of different political tendencies in various West European countries. He explained: 'My conclusion is that in 1989 the leadership of Solidarity tried to preserve a social movement, in which all these political tendencies would be preserved without a very clear definition of political colour, of political behaviour, ideological attitude ... it was very difficult to translate the psychological problem of the parties in terms of Western political structures'.[22]

Eventually, different parties emerged from Solidarity's ranks but they did not always form transnational links. In the Polish Democratic Union (DU), internal debate about whether it should follow a centre-left or centre-right direction continued. The DU did not really wish to relate to European party families, for the party bureau took a formal decision not to pursue transnational links as there was a fragile balance in the DU that might have been disturbed by any priority over such links. DU leaders kept open links with different transnational organisations for some while. Eventually, the DU merged with the Liberal Democratic Congress (KLD), which had already joined the conservative EDU and maintained good links with European Democrats, to form the Union of Freedom (UW). This new party later joined the Christian Democratic EPP. In general, the party scene in Poland was fragmented, complicated and slow to crystallize. This undoubtedly explained why transnational actors often found it difficult to settle on firm partners there.[23]

Transnational actors played a waiting game but kept open contacts in these umbrella movements. When they split, the way was open for more serious consideration of longer-term links. In Czechoslovakia, Civic Forum divided in 1991 into the Civic Democratic Party led by Klaus and the Civic Movement led by Dienstbier. While the former allied with European Conservatives in the EDU; the latter, renamed Free Democrats, joined the Liberal International. In Slovakia, Public Against Violence split into a couple of small parties, but the bulk of its support went to Meciar's Movement for a Democratic Slovakia (HZDS). But the HZDS as a populist-nationalist force contained mixed and some contradictory elements, including anti- and pro-reform Communists, advocates of a market economy and state intervention, and others who were pro-Western or Slavophile.[24] This composition really prevented the HZDS from establishing viable transnational links with Western Europe. The main problem was its ideological diversity, but European doubts about Meciar's dubious democratic credentials also played a part, as did attitudes within the HZDS itself.[25]

Altogether, therefore, a fairly clear pattern had emerged during the first half of the 1990s whereby 'standard parties' in the CEECs had declared themselves in relation to transnational membership it was also apparent that a line of demarcation was drawn on the right excluding parties that were nationalist, racialist or ideologically extremist. On the political Left, there was much less of a problem in identifying parties as party nomenclature was familiar. The problem was how to respond to former Communist regime parties that had now converted themselves into parties called Socialist (as in Hungary and Bulgaria), Social Democratic (as in Poland) or Democratic Left (as in Slovakia). Their new programmes tended to adopt centre-left policies and policy lines like support for EU entry and economic reform, although in some cases offering a milder version of it. This was often combined with leadership change involving generational turnover. Continuities nevertheless remained at the level of party activists, electoral support and strong organization. The initial response of the SI at the time of the 1990 elections was to favour the old reconstituted Social Democratic parties, but they did not perform impressively in political terms. Only very gradually, however, did the SI – and later the PES – come round to considering former regime parties as members. This required a long process of vetting candidate parties, a practice applied by all transnational organizations and one that employed a fairly strict form of democratic conditionality at the party-political level. In the case of the ex-Communists, it demonstrated the degree of influence that could be exerted by transnational actors.

The procedure in all cases is similar in that an emphasis is placed on accurate information gathered from a variety of sources. These include: party programmes, public statements by leaders, confidential reports by West

European embassies in the country of the candidate party, 'missions' by transnational organizations to the party headquarters, and often invitations to party delegations to come and visit the transnational party offices, usually in Brussels, for detailed discussions of policy matters. Personal impressions have invariably influenced decisions on requests for membership. The SI was the most assiduous of these organizations and it also investigated the way parties handled their own past, clearly this having particular reference to former Communists. The latter sought links with the SI and it soon became clear their motivation was international legitimation. These parties were closely scrutinized over several years, and it helped that several of them were elected to national government during 1992–94. They lobbied hard for a formal link but did not disclose the high priority they accorded this. By the mid-1990s, the parties in Hungary and Slovakia (HSP and SDL) were recommended for membership and observer status was offered the two Polish parties – the Social Democrats (SLD) and Union of Labour (UP). But some cross-national differentiation was evident in the SI approach. Doubts were expressed over the Slovak party and, more seriously, over the Bulgarian Socialist Party (BSP).

The SDL was a fervent applicant to the SI and regular visits were paid to Brussels. However, the SI remained hesitant for a time owing to internal divisions in the SDL and the crisis which hit the party after its serious loss of support in the 1994 election. Concern was also expressed over an interest by some SDL leaders in a deal with the Meciar government, thus raising doubts about the party's firm democratic commitment. This phase passed and SI membership was confirmed. The SDL had chosen to lean in particular on the Italian PDS to press its case because of close leadership-level links that had developed between the two parties. The Italian party had also acted as a guide to the Slovak one over such matters as election campaigning and policy matters, so it is possible to speak of the PDS as something of a model for the SDL.[26]

The BSP proved more difficult to handle as it was deeply divided – and it eventually split – but also as the Bulgarian transition was for some time in doubt, not least as a result of the BSP's own questionable policies while in government during 1995–97. Even in the mid-1990s, SI circles in Brussels were not sure as 'we still don't know if it is a reformed party or if it still has very strong tendencies of a Communist party'; but there was a willingness to keep open contact with the BSP and to involve it in policy discussion.[27] Its success in the 1994 election helped here as a legitimacy factor, for one consideration in the SI was encouraging strong parties to facilitate Bulgaria's democratization and the party's mass base could encourage centre-left inclinations as part of that.[28] But the divisions in the BSP persisted and included a Social Democratic faction (Alliance for Social Democracy) and one attached to traditional Communist ideals (Marxist Platform). The former placed a high priority on links with the SI. One of its leaders explained:

> The importance of these international contacts – not only contacts but recognition and legitimization of the BSP by its counterparts in Europe … important from the point of view of belonging in real terms to a set of values which are also the values of the EU – this is the democratic mentality … belonging to the SI will bring about new kinds of commitments which are important for the general education, maturing of the BSP to what the actual 'Socialist' ideal stands for, because in this country there is a very mixed and erroneous perception of socialism, both on the part of the opposition and on the part of many of the members of the BSP. Socialism is equivalent to Communism to many of the politicians of today, which is the result of the misuse of the term in the past. So, this is an important challenge to restore socialism, its new value and new respect.[29]

This was an explicit acknowledgement of the strategic importance of TPC for redefining ideology and hence party identity. But it was one that did not work for the BSP as a whole. Problems were already present in differences between the factions over SI membership together with reservations among activists, due in part to lack of knowledge about the International but also suspicion over criticisms of the BSP by some West European parties.[30] Finally, in 1997 the BSP split with the Social Democrats and left to form the Euro-Left, which became thereby freer to pursue transnational links.

The European Left and the SI in particular thus played a fairly significant part in the establishment of a viable Left in the new democracies of the CEECs. Clearly, other factors were influential and these related both to internal party affairs but also, more broadly, to the political culture emerging in these countries. In Hungary, for instance, there was no trace of wariness towards transnational involvements as evident in Bulgaria as well as in Slovakia, where the links of opposition parties were attacked by the ruling HZDS. As one close observer of the Hungarian scene from the PES, present during the 1990 election, noted:

> My impression was that the average Hungarian in the street was probably aware of the fact that there were all these foreign politicians from whichever party involved in the campaign. To that extent, there was a very large sense of occasion: they were one of the first (in Eastern Europe], they were able to construct a multi-party system without any internal revolution – a very smooth transition, they were very proud of that. To that extent, there was a sense of Hungarians opening their arms to all colours, especially from Western Europe.[31]

This undoubtedly helped account for Hungarian parties of different

191

tendencies being to the fore among the CEECs in initiating and developing transnational links. And, in turn, once accepted into these organizations, they played a part as sponsor for parties in other CEECs.

There were two other ways in which TPC affected the prospects for party development in the CEECs converging with established patterns in Western Europe. The first concerned the inheritance from the Communist period and therefore reflected directly on a major difference between both parts of Europe. Several respondents among transnational actors commented on some differences of understanding and mentality in dialogue with party representatives from the CEECs, especially in the first years after transition began. To some degree, it was due to an unfamiliarity with democratic techniques and competitive politics, but the problems could go deeper. The Czech Social Democratic Party (CSSD) was an historical party and, therefore, there were no ideological obstacles to affiliation with the SI and other transnational organisations of the same tendency. But complications arising from experience under Communist rule were present For instance, complications were evident in internal disputes over the party's role in 1948 when it merged with the Communists; but they also arose over dislike for returned exiles and former dissidents as their presence made people feel guilty because of compromises made with the Communist regime. However, in the course of time European links – such as attending party congresses abroad and involvement in transnational policy projects – helped to instil more confidence among the party elite, all the more once the party's popular support rose.[32]

Such problems tended to diminish with time. Political and electoral experience was acquired first hand as well as vicariously through transnational actors; while, it could be said, increasingly routine contact with the latter created patterns of socialization that also helped reduce the pull of inheritances from the Communist period. There was, as noted by interview respondents, some differentiation between different regions and sometimes countries from the former Communist world. This was particularly marked between the CEECs and republics from the former Soviet Union, with the possible exception of the Baltic states due to their own European background and close party links with Scandinavia and Sweden in particular. But there was another factor that impinged – and increasingly so – on TPC and its influence on party development in the new democracies; and that was the prospect of EU membership. This second way in which TPC evolved became more and more evident during the course of the later 1990s.

Transnational organizations and contacts came to be viewed by party leaders from the CEECs as a non-official channel for networking in favour of EU accession. Some figures in transnational organizations were also ministers in EU member governments, while opposition politicians could be in office at some future time when entry negotiations proceeded. Such transnational party fora were a relatively informal occasion for cultivating personal contacts. It could generally be said that the greater the possibility of eventual EU membership, the more it was likely that parties from CEECs would be ready to conform with European party political patterns, subject to obvious constraints in domestic politics. Clearly, one cannot view this relationship in isolation from other developments – of which the most important was the state of regime transition, which in turn affected both party systems and decisions in Brussels about opening entry negotiations.

Many interview respondents remarked on significant differences between East-Central European and Balkan countries when it came to TPC. In some cases, these responses appeared to convey culturalist preconceptions; and it is therefore important to take account of cross-national variation within both regions. All the same, links with parties in Balkan countries proved difficult for a number of reasons. They were basically non-existent with republics in the former Yugoslavia until the Dayton peace agreement of late 1995, with the one exception of Slovenia. Since then, the SI and its member parties in Western Europe have begun to show an interest in these republics but there has been little progress in countries like Serbia and Croatia because of their authoritarian regimes. Milosevic's Socialist Party of Serbia (SPS) is distinctly a pariah party in transnational circles, but links have developed with parties in Macedonia and Montenegro.[33]

Among centre-right parties, it was found much easier to find Christian Democratic parties in East-Central Europe than in the Balkans for confessional reasons (Slovenia here counted among the former), save for a few small parties like the Hungarian Christian Democrats in Romania.[34] This was a clear admission that the cultural divide between Catholic and Orthodox countries imprinted itself on party development. Nevertheless, transnational links were most developed with Romania and particularly Bulgaria judging by the membership of the SI, LI and EUCD by the mid-1990s.[35] The various German political foundations were more active and influential in Bulgaria than in any other Balkan country; and there was evidence they competed to support the different political tendencies inside the Union of Democratic Forces (UDF).[36] In Albania, the Democratic Party had formal links with the EDU and EUCD, becoming a full member of the latter in 1995, but these were not established without difficulty. Some parties in the EUCD were opposed to accepting it because of ethnic tensions, complaints having been received from the Greek minority, and because of doubts about its democratic commitment – it was the party of President Berisha, whose authoritarian practices were becoming controversial. But the Democratic Party's desire for international acceptance was such that outside pressure for Albania to negotiate with Athens were successful. Special account was also taken of difficult conditions in Albania, including inheritances from the oppressive Hoxha Communist regime.[37]

Overall, transnational links with Balkan countries were less intensive than with those in East-Central Europe. Geographical distance may have influenced this, but more important was the problem in matching West European party formations with viable partner parties in countries that were undergoing, in many cases, difficult and uncertain transitions. The greater incidence of ethnic problems in the Balkan countries also played a part, ethnic nationalism and authoritarian tendencies being – as noted above – a basic obstacle to TPC. These same factors explained why transnational links with Russia were threadbare if not non-existent for a long time, as many interview respondents pointed out. Russia's party system was simply too unstable and peculiar with many individual parties often undefinable in West European ideological terms. Furthermore, hostility in Russia towards foreign influence proved a major disincentive to developing transnational links. According to a former head of the Naumann Foundation office in Bulgaria, 'Russian people are suspicious of any foreigners trying to intervene in their political life; even for Westernizers it was difficult to co-operate more closely with the Naumann Foundation'.[38] All the same, some *ad hoc* contacts have slowly developed in the last few years. In August 1998, the EPP organised a conference in St. Petersburg for its West European member parties to engage in dialogue with parties in Russia and some other states like the Ukraine, Moldavia, Armenia, Georgia and Belarus; and a further conference was planned for 1999 in Kiev.[39]

Behind these regional differences lay the issue of EU entry for the CEECs. Differences in prospects here influenced TPC to the extent that transnational actors in Brussels were more prepared to invest resources as well as time in countries that had better chances of membership. The future balance of party group representation in the EP following enlargement was one major consideration. This differentiation was moreover influenced by progress or the lack of it with democratization. Transnational actors were as a whole more cautious about developing close links with countries where the outcome of regime change was difficult to predict, although in some cases they did choose to make a special effort to support allied parties precisely to help democratization along. Clearly, both factors – EU entry prospects and transition outcomes – were related and tended to mean that the most meaningful TPC was with countries in East-Central Europe rather than elsewhere among the CEECs, a pattern reinforced by the fact that party systems in the former were more compatible with those in Western Europe. In this context, TPC was dependent on these factors, although its own importance was significantly enhanced by the issue of EU entry.

In conclusion, TPC while influential was undoubtedly secondary to domestic factors in party development. This is shown, in particular, by the fate of umbrella movements, which succumbed to the dynamics of political competition in their own countries. It was only then that transnational organizations started to relate effectively to their successor parties. TPC was also constrained, where applicable, by cultural reservations towards outside influence and these included nationalism, which proved a very firm deterrent to transnational activity. European party leaders kept nationalist forces or those with authoritarian tendencies at a distance, although there is not much evidence that this exclusion had any effect in changing their outlook.

At the same time, there were different ways in which TPC could help influence party development. In some individual cases, transnational support could have a fairly decisive effect in the formative stage of parties. Otherwise, influence was particularly evident at elite levels. It was party leaders and senior officials who were most directly concerned with TPC, but they themselves were in a position to mould their own parties given that these were often top-down in their structural life. Policy training and advice on election campaigns could also have wider effects within parties. Interview respondents remarked frequently on the sense of belonging to international groupings – there was undoubtedly a feel-good factor emanating from involvement in transnational meetings. And these were not simply regarded as tame events, since they had a European and particularly EU focus so that serious political messages were transmitted via these organizations. Recognition proved a valuable encouragement to party development, and in the case of the political Left the legitimation this accorded was given top priority.

Conclusion: Towards 'Standard Parties' in Central and Eastern Europe?

Transnational party co-operation between EU member states and the new democracies in the CEECs has substantially assisted the emergence of identifiable party families as transnational organizations offer various advantages to these parties and, at the same time, apply conditions for acceptance that can have a secondary influence on their development. This is quite evident in the fact that, with some exceptions, parties in the CEECs have overwhelmingly sought links with parties – whether transnational, or national – in Western Europe rather elsewhere in the CEECs. There has been some tendency in recent years for various regional associational networks to develop among parties in different parts of the former Communist world, including conferences on common interests. Some of these have developed with the assistance of transnational organizations, and included a regional body of Socialist parties from the Visegrad countries sponsored by the SI with plans to repeat this model for parties from the Balkan countries and from the Baltic states.[40] Thus, overall, the pattern in the 1990s has been for

West European party-political habits and attitudes to imprint themselves on parties from the CEECs with little sign so far of the opposite effect. Whether in the course of time distinct national influences from new member parties in the CEECs start to influence transnational organisations is likely, all the more if they come from successful entrants to the EU. One may therefore speak of a pattern of Europeanization, but it has been one-sided in its effects.

Europeanization through TPC has concentrated on the major political forces in European politics to the exclusion of certain categories. Namely, it has been parties that are Christian Democratic, Conservative, Liberal and Socialist that have benefited from this activity. Greens have a weak form of TPC and, in any case, they are not very strong in the CEECs. However, parties that are nationalist or populist or ethnically hostile have been shunned, just as have parties with authoritarian leanings. Ideological or systemic objections have, combined with the transnational organizations' own version of democratic conditionality, seen to the exclusion of such parties. In this way, therefore, TPC has tended to draw a fairly clear distinction between standard and non-standard parties and to deepen the divide between them. It is difficult, however, to argue that TPC has actually helped to weaken the standing of non-standard parties especially if they draw on political cultures that are, at least in part, not friendly towards outside influences.

In different ways, TPC has been strengthened by factors less present in previous phases of democratic transition in post-war Western Europe. First, the parties that emerged in post-Communist countries had much weaker historical roots than those in post-Fascist and Southern European states. To that degree, therefore, transnational organizations have had more opportunity to exert a formative influence on party development in the CEECs. Secondly, the impact of the international environment has been so much greater in the transitions of the 1990s compared with those of the 1970s in Southern Europe. And, most of all, this has been present in the desire to join the EU. This link between EU entry and TPC will almost certainly increase in the near future, with continuing effects on party development. However, also likely is greater cross-national variation in this pattern, as has already become evident in the last few years.

For all these different reasons, the comparative study of political parties in Central and Eastern Europe will encounter greater differentiation. It will, therefore, make less and less sense to view them in contradistinction to parties in Western Europe. And that conclusion will be further supported the more party systems in the CEECs become stabilized and therefore, individually, are more comparable to those in countries in Western Europe.

NOTES

1. These interviews were conducted for the project on Regime Change in East-Central Europe funded under the East/West Change Programme of the Economic and Social Research Council. The interviews were carried out during 1993–96 in Hungary, Poland, the Czech Republic, Slovakia and Bulgaria as well as with parties in Western Europe in Austria, Germany and the UK. Update interviews were conducted in Slovakia in 1998.
2. David Olson, 'Party Formation and Party System Consolidation in the New Democracies of Central Europe', *Political Studies*, special issue on Party Structure and Party Performance, Vol.46, No.3 (1998), pp.433–35.
3. Geoffrey Pridham and Paul G. Lewis (eds.), 'Introduction', to *Stabilising Fragile Democracies: Comparing New Party Systems in Southern and Eastern Europe* (London: Routledge, 1996), pp.17–18.
4. Dieter Segert, 'Party Politics in the Process of Europeanisation – is there a special way for party development in Central Eastern Europe?', in M. Szabo (ed.), *The Challenge of Europeanisation in the Region: East Central Europe* (Budapest: Hungarian Academy of Sciences, 1996), pp.226–7.
5. Attila Ágh, 'The End of the Beginning: the Partial Consolidation of East-Central European Parties and Party Systems', Budapest Papers on Democratic Transition, No.156 (Budapest University of Economics, 1996), p.22.
6. G. Meseznikov, 'The Parliamentary Elections 1994: A Confirmation of the Party Systems in Slovakia,' in S. Szomolanyi and G. Meseznikov (eds.), *Slovakia: Parliamentary Elections 1994* (Bratislava: Slovak Political Science Association, 1995), pp.105–13.
7. Olson, 'Party Formation and Party System Consolidation', pp.447, 461–2.
8. Ibid., p.445.
9. Petr Kopecký, 'Developing Party Organisations in East-Central Europe: What Type of Party is Likely to Emerge?' *Party Politics*, Vol.1, No.4 (1995), pp.528–9.
10. Geoffrey Pridham (ed.), *Encouraging Democracy: the International Context of Regime Transition in Southern Europe* (Leicester: Leicester University Press, 1991), Ch. 11.
11. Attila Ágh, 'The Europeanisation of ECE polities and the emergence of the new ECE democratic parliaments', in Attila Ágh (ed.), The Emergence of East Central European Parliaments: the First Steps (Budapest: Hungarian Centre of Democracy Studies, 1994), pp.9–10.
12. Ibid., pp.18–19.
13. Attila Ágh, 'Partial Consolidation of the East-Central European Parties: the Case of the Hungarian Socialist Party', *Party Politics*, Vol.1, No.4 (1995), p. 493.
14. Geoffrey Pridham, 'Transnational Party Links and Transition to Democracy: Eastern Europe in Comparative Perspective', in Paul G. Lewis (ed.), Party Structure and Organization in East-Central Europe (Cheltenham: Edward Elgar, 1996), p.199.
15. S. Biller, Representative of European People's Party group, European Parliament, Interview (Brussels: Jan. 1996).
16. K. Welle, Secretary-General of the European People's Party (EPP) and the European Union of Christian Democrats (EUCD), Interview (Brussels, Jan. 1996).

17. A. Wintoniak, Executive-Secretary of the European Democratic Union (EDU), Interview (Vienna, Nov. 1995).
18. R. Normington, International Office of the British Conservative Party, Interview (London, Jan. 1996).
19. J. Kohutiar, International Secretary of the Christian Democratic Movement (KDH), Interview (Bratislava: Nov. 1995).
20. B. Jensen, Representative of Liberal Group in European Parliament, Interview (Brussels, Jan. 1996).
21. E. Kukan, Chairman of Democratic Union, Interview(Bratislava, Sept. 1998).
22. B. Geremek, Chairman of the International Affairs Committee in the Polish Sejm, Interview (Warsaw, Sept. 1994).
23. S. Gebethner and R. Gortat, 'Pan-European Co-operation Between Political Parties; the Polish Case', paper for European Dialogues (Brussels, Feb. 1995), p.1.
24. Z. Butorova and M. Butora, 'Political Parties, Value Orientations and Slovakia's Road to Independence', in G. Wightman (ed.), *Party Formation in East-Central Europe* (Aldershot: Edward Elgar, 1995), p.123.
25. G. Pridham, 'Complying with the EU's Democratic Conditionality: Transnational Party Linkages and Regime Change in Slovakia, 1993-98', *Europe-Asia Studies*, Vol.51 (1999).
26. Ibid.
27. B. Toresson, Secretary-General of the SI Forum for Democracy and Solidarity, Interview (Brussels, Jan. 1996).
28. D. Kanev, Head of Research Department in the National Assembly of Bulgaria, Interview (Sofia: Sept. 1995).
29. E. Poptodorova, National deputy of the Bulgarian Socialist Party, Interview (Sofia, Sept. 1995).
30. Ibid.
31. P. Brown-Pappamikail, Party of European Socialists, Interview (Brussels, Jan. 1996).
32. S. Navarova, Head of International Office in the Czech Social Democratic Party, Interview (Prague, Nov. 1995).
33. Country Updates for Macedonia (September) and Federal Republic of Yugoslavia (January), SI European Forum for Democracy and Solidarity (Brussels, 1997 and 1998).
34. Wintoniak, Interview of 1995.
35. Pridham, 'Transnational Party Links', pp.217–19.
36. I. Krastev, Programme Director of Centre for Liberal Strategies and former head of Friedrich Naumann Foundation office in Bulgaria, Interview (Sofia, Sept. 1995).
37. Welle, Interview of 1996.
38. Krastev, Interview of 1995.
39. European People's Party, EPP News No. 157 (Brussels, 1998).
40. I. Puskac, International Secretary of the Party of the Democratic Left (SDL), Interview (Bratislava, Sept. 1998)

12

Conclusion: Party Development and Democratization in Eastern Europe

PAUL G. LEWIS

Democratization in Post-Communist Eastern Europe

In post-communist eastern Europe as a whole democratization has made patchy progress.[1] It has made most advances in east-central Europe. Pluralist party development has been significantly stronger in Hungary, Poland, Slovakia, Slovenia and the Czech Republic where viable political communities and civic order have been maintained (the dissolution of the Czechoslovak state into its constituent parts occurred peacefully and was conducted according to agreed constitutional procedures), the dismantling of the centrally administered, state-dominated economy has proceeded quite swiftly (although by no means without major social dislocation), and democratic norms have increasingly taken root (a feature initially affirmed by the accelerated EU accession procedures agreed in 1997 with four of the five countries concerned).

Three democratic elections, as outlined in Chapter 1, have been held in all countries of the region and power has changed hands on more than one occasion in most of them. Left-wing voters in east-central and south-eastern Europe far more than in the FSU have, Chapter 2 demonstrates, firmly switched their allegiance from traditional communist parties to the democratic socialist alternative. The successor parties in east-central Europe contribute more, in the light of the analysis presented in Chapter 3, to democratic consolidation than in the less advanced countries of post-communist Europe. More detailed analysis of the party processes that contribute to this higher level of democratic development was presented in Chapters 4–6. The influence of the broader European context (and particularly the European Union) has been strong on the countries of east-central Europe, and distinctive processes of Europeanization were examined by Kenneth Ka-Lok Chan and Geoffrey Pridham in Chapters 10 and 11 respectively.

The only major doubts to surface in east-central Europe have concerned Slovakia, where the style of government employed by Vladimír Mečiar as much as its actual content raised concerns in the EU (which issued several negative appraisals, or 'démarches'), and the international community more generally. The defeat of Mečiar both in the parliamentary election of 1998 and the subsequent presidential contest, combined with the acceptance by Mečiar and his still numerous supporters of the legitimacy of these defeats, provided a broad reassurance of the fundamentally democratic trajectory of political change in Slovakia. This was explored in Chapter 8.

Despite weaknesses in structural consolidation and continuing political fluidity, the Baltic states of Estonia, Latvia and Lithuania have also made considerable progress in building new parties and developing a broadly democratic system. A strong national consciousness, relatively high levels of socio-economic development and a shorter period of encapsulation within the Soviet Union all helped them cope with the problems of post-communist transition more successfully than other areas of the FSU. The challenge of incorporating the large Russian minorities in Latvia and Estonia into a democratically organized political community caused considerable problems but has been met with increasing success, while the traditions of inter-war independence have provided a reasonably solid basis for contemporary democratic practice. Details of this process were presented in Chapter 7.

One major weakness in the Baltic region has been the continuing fluidity of party structures, the tendency of parties to split and reform with disconcerting frequency, and the dominance of individuals and political leaders over party structures (a feature perhaps linked with the size of these mini-states and the personalized character of the political community). Such problems have been less pronounced in Lithuania, where features of a two-party system have been emerging, and both electoral volatility and parliamentary fragmentation showed signs of reducing in later elections in Latvia and Estonia.

Throughout the countries both of the rest of the former Soviet Union (FSU) and the Balkans democratization has made only limited progress (a generalization from which Slovenia may now be wholly excluded as being part only of the former Yugoslavia and effectively having lost its Balkan identity; Bulgaria also appears to have developed quite strongly in this area since the change of government in 1997). The absence of democratic conditions for party development have been particularly marked in Belarus, where only one post-communist election was held throughout the 1990s (whose outcome was by no means clear) while President Lukashenka grew increasingly opposed to independent parties and unconstrained parliamentary activity in general. Chapter 9 explored the roots of this process.

Serbia has also experienced major limitations on democratic practice during the unbroken period of leadership of Slobodan Milošević, the only east European leader to have stayed in power since 1987 during the communist period, although it should also be noted that the Serbian opposition has not always been strongly committed to promoting a more democratic alternative. Democratic party development has not been opposed so resolutely in the other countries of the Balkans and the FSU, but neither has it been pursued with great enthusiasm either by government leaders or the political elite – or, it must be said, by much of the population as a whole. Mass attitudes and the weak development of a civic culture also play an important part throughout the region. Only in the two other areas of eastern Europe have conditions overall been more favourable for party development.

But while the conditions for party development have been more positive in east-central Europe than in other parts of the post-communist area, that does not necessarily mean that the course of such development has run smoothly or met all initial expectations. The prime weaknesses may be seen primarily as those of institutionalization. This involves the accretion by organizations of value and stability, qualities as central to the consolidation of a democratic regime as to any other form of political order.[2] The complexities involved in estimating levels of democratic consolidation have been outlined in Chapter 3 by John Ishiyama and, while it is difficult to reach unambiguous conclusions in this area, party development certainly seems to play some part in this process. The process of party system institutionalization in relation to democratic consolidation is, further, carefully explored and analyzed in particular detail in Chapter 4.

In comparative context, surveys of political attitudes as well as social outcomes of public sentiment like organizational membership suggest that the value assigned to contemporary parties remains limited. Equally, both organizational characteristics and election outcomes point to some degree of stability but, even where conditions have been conducive to the process of party development as a whole, to a limited level of party growth and important discontinuities of structure and parliamentary representation.

From another perspective, east European parties continue to show signs of weak institutionalization in terms of their relative lack of autonomy and the general absence of systemness in their organization.[3] They remain open to social and individual pressure, and often show limited organizational staying-power. In conjunction with this, party system institutionalization in eastern Europe is also low in relation to that seen in other new democracies.[4] There is limited stability in perceptions both in the identity of the main parties and of how they behave. As well as the shallow roots parties have in society, their weakly developed organization and the low legitimacy accorded parties and elections, there have yet to emerge clear patterns of party competition. Even where the basic conditions for party development have been met in eastern Europe the process has not necessarily progressed evenly or with great vigour, a pattern best defined as one of *partial institutionalization*. The partial formation at the current stage both of parties and the democratic political system as a whole is summed up in the title of a recent study of the Polish polity – protoparties in a protosystem.[5]

Political Parties and Modern Democracy

The problems of parties in the new democracies of eastern Europe may also be set against a background of related doubts about the efficacy of western democracy and its institutions as national forms of political organization.[6] One reflection of this situation has been the increasingly problematic status of the established west European political party, features of which include falling membership, funding problems and corruption scandals, the decline of traditional ideologies and shifts in fundamental political orientation, growing electoral volatility, declining turnout, and the prominent role played by single-issue politics and more informal social movements. Broad processes of post-industrial change and the marginalization of traditional political structures have been understood to underlie such shifts. In east European terms the operation of a recently restored political autonomy and national sovereignty similarly contrasts strongly with the constraints of global capitalism, to which a new openness leaves post-communist democracy highly vulnerable.

Liberal democracy, it is also argued, has consistently found it difficult and at times impossible (as in the case of fascism) to confront the centrality of antagonism and the importance of elements of hostility in political life, factors which bear critically on the differentiation of social positions and the formation of collective identities. Outbursts of ethnic, religious and nationalist conflict in eastern Europe, it is similarly maintained, cannot be comprehended by those welcoming the universal supremacy of the liberal principles, and they have thus been relegated to the sphere of the archaic or marginalized as a post-totalitarian legacy. The political dimension in modern democracies risks being overly identified with the rule of law, leaving much of the population excluded and available for mobilization by fundamentalist movements or attracted to anti-liberal, populist forms of democracy.[7] Conventional parties from this point of view, like the other institutions of modern liberal democracy, are likely to be unable to cope with the acute tensions and virulent conflicts of post-communism.

But actual experience of the early post-communist period suggests a different conclusion. The pluralist party structures of the leading democratic countries have in fact been sufficiently robust and attractive to the electorate to create effective working legislative bodies and restrict extremist movements to the margins of political life. More concrete analysis shows that organized extremism has not occupied a prominent place in post-communist politics. The fascist Association for the Republic gained limited representation in early Czech parliaments which it lost in the 1998 election, illiberal forces in Hungary only succeeded in taking some seats in 1998 in the form of the Justice and Life Party, while in Poland – following the defeat of the colourful populist Tymiński in the 1990 presidential runoff – representatives of more extreme tendencies have been excluded from the political mainstream altogether.

It is precisely where liberal forces failed to triumph over the communist antagonist and the rule of law was not established, where civil oppositions did not succeed in establishing even a temporary liberal ascendancy, that extremism has had its strongest impact. Milošević retained his dominance as communist party leader and then socialist president of Yugoslavia through to the débâcle of the 1999 Kosovo war; Belarus was left politically marooned by the collapse of the Soviet Union and remained almost wholly untouched by the practices of liberal democracy before Lukashenka took power and mounted an intensified anti-parliamentary campaign to eliminate the embryo party organizations from public life.

Where they have succeeded in establishing themselves, the record of pluralist parties in eastern Europe has been a largely positive one. Experience of the brief post-communist period confirms the perception of parties as the prime political form and a major institutional basis of modern liberal democracy. Despite doubts about their role and the significance of their contribution to contemporary liberal democracy that surfaced in the west during the 1970s, too, the prime role of political parties has also survived relatively unscathed in established democracies and there are no real alternative ideas of how modern democracies might operate without them. They continue to play a major role in organizing political activity, channelling participation and providing the means to make it effective. Professionally organized parties are still essential to the establishment and continuity of a liberal democracy; in most practical senses, 'democracy in the modern world is representative democracy, and the contribution made by political parties is central'.[8]

Party systems effectively determine levels of citizen participation, the activities they sponsor in legislative and electoral arenas exercise a major influence on the nature and stability of political leadership, and the dynamics of party systems have a profound impact on prospects for political stability, the survival of particular regimes and the avoidance of social turmoil.[9] Neither does there seem to be much doubt about the importance of parties and their activities in the course of democratization and the consolidation of new democracies. The mark of a genuinely consolidated democracy, it is argued, is the degree to which the alternation of parties in power is regular and accepted, while the creation of strong parties is one of the main components of a civil society.[10] But there are still serious questions to be raised about the nature of the political party and the range of functions it performs in the established democracies of the developed world.

A comprehensive list of the functions traditionally performed by parties in a democracy is an extensive one, although not all possible tasks have been carried out by all parties. Apart from their basic function of structuring the vote and linking that process with broader forms of opinion structuring, parties also: help to integrate citizens within the broader community and mobilize the public for political participation; facilitate the recruitment of political leaders; organize government; shape public policy by influencing public discussion, formulating programmes and bringing pressure to bear on the incumbent government; and aggregate social interests in ways that can range from simply noting their existence to the purposive structuring of social behaviour.[11] Clearly the range of functions and the intensity with which they are performed has varied over time, as has the importance of the different levels of party organization – modern parties being far more leadership dominated than their predecessors and correspondingly less inclined to perform historically important mediating functions.

Recent discussion, indeed, links the growing dominance of party leadership with changes that have taken place within political parties during the 1990s in response to what has been termed a 'fourth wave' of democratic party-building originating in eastern Europe. In this conception four major party functions are outlined: the identification of goals (ideology and programme), articulation and aggregation of social interests, mobilization and socialization of the general public, elite recruitment and government formation. Only the second of these, it is argued, cannot be performed by an individual party leader.[12] The functional range of the political party has certainly been slimmed down and it has become more specialized as an institution, ceasing to play such a pivotal role in the democratic process as a whole. But while changes in the overall role, structure and function of parties have occurred, they have not as institutions become as irrelevant to the central processes of modern democracy as many maintained during the 1970s and 1980s.

Much of the discussion about the apparent decline of the party on closer examination concerned the increasingly limited relevance of the mass party, whose roots lay very much in the nineteenth century.[13] The emergence of parties with hundreds of thousands of members, an extensive national organization and a well-developed internal structure represented an important contribution to the early formation and operation of contemporary mass democracies, but the conditions that gave rise to them soon began eroding and the consequences of this process were well recognized by the 1960s. On the basis of experiences during the 1990s, and from the perspective of developments during the first decade of post-communist politics, it is more accurate to conclude that the nature of the political party has changed not so much in isolation but in association with the broader transformations of modern democracy.

In terms of political functions, this means that the modern party is:

• less prominent as an agency of societal *integration* – the enormous expansion of the electronic media and the overwhelming impact of television on politics and society over recent decades means that party organizations are now relatively minor agencies for integrating the citizen within the greater community, while modern media and electronics-based campaign techniques are equally decisive for the electoral success of individual parties;[14] political integration is achieved by the manipulation and projection of diffuse but often powerful symbols rather than the organization of concrete activity around specific goals, while individuals relate more directly to the centres of power in modern society and exercize any influence they command primarily as consumers rather than on the basis of any organized civic identity.

• correspondingly less capable of *mobilizing* the population for political participation in terms of enrolling them as party members and securing their formal or informal support on any kind of permanent basis; voter turnout has declined during elections and volatility has increased to the extent that some parties have little in the way of a core base of electoral support on which to count and, in more extreme cases, may rapidly coalesce and become major political forces only to fade away and lose all electoral momentum prior to the next vote; thus of the three 'faces' of party organization it is primarily the 'party on the ground' made of the members who provide the party with potentially loyal voters that can most accurately be said to be in decline (the party in public office and in central office make up the other 'faces').[15]

• less able also to perform the pivotal *mediating* role it has traditionally played in twentieth century politics and appear as the key bonding mechanism or buckle that holds state and civil society together in some kind of stable relationship;[16] in association with a diminished membership base, the weak structure it is able to develop in many contexts gives the party little capacity to act either as a powerful representative of social forces or as an autonomous force with regard to the state. Although common tendencies in most democracies this, like other features, is particularly prominent in the recently liberalized regimes of eastern Europe. Even where political pluralism has put down stronger roots, its institutional development has been limited. The early 'overparticization' of the political process was intimately linked with the paucity of the parties' social ties and an overall organizational deficit.[17]

The diminished capacity of these aspects of the modern party has had particular implications for the new democracies of eastern Europe. Greater fluidity of party structures and the particular weakness of their electoral base in post-communist regimes affect the steering capacity of their governments, a condition that gives rise to a paradoxical emphasis amongst both electors and the elite on political leadership while creating poor conditions and a limited capacity for the actual performance of leadership functions in society as a whole. The strains of post-communist change in social and economic as well as political areas create a demand for stability and need for security that the whole current of liberal-democratization runs counter to. The resistance of those contemporary east European power-centres with strong links with the communist regime to democratic change and the development of party pluralism is quite understandable under these conditions, and there is considerable support for this response amongst the broader population.

In the countries (predominantly of east-central Europe) where democracy has put down stronger roots and party pluralism is most developed, what is most significant is not the sporadic outbreaks of political extremism and the elements of populism that impinge on the parliamentary arena but the relatively minor part they play in the political process as a whole. Parties with a slender social base and few organizational resources maintain not just a sizeable parliamentary presence and access to government power but also a reasonably strong capacity for responsible political behaviour and surprisingly high levels of commitment to democratic norms.

The Nature of Contemporary East European Parties

The growing distance of the mass party from the realities of party politics in modern democracies raises further questions about how the parties that increasingly dominate east European political life are best understood. Several models have emerged in the context of the changing conditions of modern party politics. The weakening link of parties with particular groups (especially the declining attraction of socialist parties for the working class, itself far less homogeneous and considerably diminished in size), the reduced prominence of ideology and growing reliance on the mass media and commercial public relations techniques all contributed to the idea of the catch-all party.[18] On the basis of observations of similar trends, further analysis directed attention to the professionalization of party organization and led to the formulation of ideas of the electoral-professional party.[19] More recently, observation of the lengthy stability of most established democratic party systems, the regular alternation of most parties in government and their growing dependence on state resources has been responsible for the emergence of the concept of the cartel party.[20]

Debate continues about such theoretical proposals and their respective merits in helping to grasp the essentials of the modern party as a generic form. The novelty of the cartel party and questions concerning the level at which the concept might best operate (at system level or in relation to the individual party) are particular issues that have been aired in connection with the most recent formulation.[21] The models referred to above also derive primarily from analysis of west European party developments and have generally been limited in their historical and territorial relevance. Some clearly relate only partially to North American experience (which never saw the development of tightly organized mass parties and have not permitted state support of party activity). Their relevance to east European developments must also be demonstrated rather than assumed if they are to be accepted as useful tools for empirical analysis. Several chapters in this volume have directed attention to the relevance of these models to recent east European developments. The varying capacity of post-communist parties to develop as catch-all organizations was discussed in Chapter 3 – and the likely capacity of such parties to make a particular contribution to democratic consolidation was also argued for. Attention was paid in Chapter 5 to the idea of Polish parties developing as electoral-professional organizations, while issues of cartelization were raised in the context of Slovenian party development in Chapter 6.

On the face of it, the models discussed in the western party literature seem to fit eastern Europe quite well. Some have argued that the eastern developments reflect a more general transformation of European parties, and that 'parties of a new type' have been emerging on this basis in established democracies.[22] Arguments for this kind of influence are not very convincing, though. The implication of the discussion so far has been that patterns of party representation in eastern Europe in fact quite closely resemble that of the west, and that lower levels of institutionalization and party development in the post-communist context tend to replicate characteristics of the relative decline detected in western parties and reflect features of their weakening in established democracies. The *trajectory* of party development is nevertheless different and, while parties may share characteristics and seem to occupy similar positions within a political system, this may be for very different reasons.[23]

Many contemporary parties employ a catch-all electoral strategy but, while in the west this is largely a function of established parties' responses to changing class structures, in eastern Europe it is more a matter of poorly defined party identity and lack of certainty about a target electorate.[24] Early attempts to define the characteristics of the emerging catch-all party also turned out to be rather inconclusive. 'Professionalization' of party activity may appear to be a prominent feature in the absence of a mass membership and extensive rank-and-file involvement in eastern Europe but, as Aleks Szczerbiak argues in Chapter 5, there are few signs that such technical values really determine party activity and (on a very practical basis) there are just no funds to sustain professionalization as a general process. Its influence on any individual party is unlikely to be a strong one. Individual parties may, further, show characteristics of different party types. In Poland, the original Social Democracy could be characterized by its features both as a catch-all organization and a mass party; the Freedom Union equally appeared to be a cadre and a catch-all party.[25]

As well as individual organizational characteristics, it is also important to link political development with the changing external conditions of party activity, as these are likely to have a strong effect on the nature of the evolving party system as a whole. The influence of historical and political context is always important for the analysis of any single party or party system as a whole, but in relation to the cartel party differences in the political role and power of the state are particularly significant factors. In view of the fundamental consequences of the collapse of the communist state and integration within an increasingly globalized world system, this will count no less in the post-communist east European context than in that of recently democratized west and south European parties.[26] The reliance of the newly identified western cartel parties on state subventions equally strikes a ready chord with analysts of eastern Europe, who rightly identify this factor with the acute weakness of most new parties and their similar reliance on the resources of the post-communist state.[27]

Others have also seized on this apparent identity to argue more directly for the emergence of the cartel party as the dominant new form of east European political organization. There has, contends Ágh, been a very rapid shift in east-central Europe from loose movement parties to 'rigidly organized cartels as power parties, expressing a new separation of parties and society'.[28] But contrasting views have also been expressed on the applicability of the cartel concept, particularly in terms of its assumption of a 'fixed menu' of well-established parties with mutual interests and a smoothly functioning working relationship.[29] The context of radically changing state–civil society relations is indeed an important one, but it is a framework that needs analysis in terms of specific east European developments and the characteristics of both post-communist state and society. There is, to be sure, little disagreement about the central role played by the state and its diverse agencies in the development of east European parties. But this is not a sufficient condition for the existence of fully fledged cartel parties in the sense recently proposed for western Europe.

Eastern Europe shows little in the way of the 'fixed menu' of parties deemed to be a major characteristic of the cartel model.[30] In terms of the monopolization of power by a narrow elite and the access of post-communist politicians to state resources, it is precisely where party development is less advanced and the political process more resistant to the activities of openly organized political associations that establishment privilege is more deeply entrenched. It is also in countries like those of the Balkans and the FSU, where this tendency is most commonly observed, that civil society is at its weakest. While shifting relations between state and society are indeed of critical importance for the nature of the modern party, and the dependence on state resources that characterizes many parties seems to be increasing throughout Europe, it is rather the relative weakness of new parties against a background of a similarly impoverished civil society that is the most salient feature of party politics in the east.

The problematic social conditions of contemporary eastern Europe and its perceived lack of civility provide a weak basis of party development as a whole rather than fostering any specific kind of party in the way that the proponents of cartelization argue. The imperfect party democracy that has emerged in eastern Europe is closely linked with the conditions of what has been termed a minimal civic society.[31] The parameters of this situation in terms both of conditions for continued democratization and for future party development in eastern Europe remain unclear. While broad patterns of western democratic practice and west European models of party development offer some guidance they by no means provide a universal template. The focus of attention on relations between parties and state, too, important though it is, is only one part of the story.

The weak social base of party politics in eastern Europe and the tenuous links of party leaders with identifiable social groupings are important factors in eastern Europe in ways closely analogous to patterns of development in the west over recent decades. But the context of post-communism and the broader cultural context of eastern Europe cannot be ignored. General discussion of 'civil society' masks important analytical differences within the region between the impact of domestic society and the emergence of political society in a more sharply defined sense.[32] The emergence of different models of party in western Europe is also linked with shifting configurations of society in general and more distinctive conceptions of a modern civil society.[33] The role of civil society, or different aspects of it, in undermining and seeing off communist rule in eastern Europe remains unclear, and it is hardly surprising that the relationship of the new parties with a rapidly changing post-communist social formation emerges as a highly ambiguous one. What is less uncertain is that pluralist parties are steadily developing in most countries of the region, and that the prospects of continuing democratization are strongly conditioned by the effectiveness of the party government they sustain.

NOTES

1. This account draws on my discussion in *Political Parties in Post-Communist Eastern Europe* (London: Routledge, 2000).
2. S. P. Huntington, *Political Order in Changing Societies* (New Haven: Yale University Press, 1968).
3. A. Panebianco, *Political Parties: Organization and Power* (Cambridge: Cambridge University Press, 1988).
4. S. Mainwaring, 'Party Systems in the Third Wave', *Journal of Democracy*, Vol.9 (1998), pp.67–81.
5. E. Nalewajko, *Protopartie i protosystem? Szkic do obrazu polskiej wielopartyjnoœci* (Warsaw: Instytut Studiów Politycznych PAN, 1997).
6. D. Held (ed.), *Prospects for Democracy* (Cambridge: Polity Press, 1993), p.37.
7. C. Mouffe, *The Return of the Political* (London: Verso, 1993), pp.1–6.
8. P. Burnell, 'Democratization and Economic Change Worldwide – Can Societies Cope ?', *Democratization*, Vol.1 (1994), p.3.
9. G.B. Powell, *Contemporary Democracies* (Cambridge, MA: Harvard University Press, 1982), p.7.
10. J.A. Hall, 'Consolidations of Democracy', in Held, *Prospects for Democracy*, pp.282–3.
11. A. King, 'Political Parties in Western Democracies', in L.J. Cantor (ed.), *Comparative Political Systems* (Boston, MA: Holbrook Press, 1974), pp.303–6.
12. K. von Beyme, 'Party Leadership and Change in Party Systems: Towards a Postmodern party State?' *Government and Opposition*, Vol.31 (1996), p.135.
13. P. Mair, 'Party Organizations: From Civil Society to the State', in R.S. Katz and P. Mair (eds.), *How Parties Organize* (London: Sage, 1994), p.2.
14. S. Mainwaring and T.R. Scully, *Building Democratic Institutions: party systems in Latin America* (Stanford, CA: Stanford University Press, 1995), pp.471–2.
15. Mair, 'Party Organizations', p.4.
16. N. Bobbio, *Democracy and Dictatorship* (Cambridge: Polity Press, 1989), p.25.
17. A. Ágh, *The Politics of Central Europe* (London: Sage, 1998), p.105.
18. O. Kirchheimer, 'The Transformation of the Western European Party System', in J. LaPalombara and M. Weiner (eds.), *Political Parties and Political Development* (Princeton, NJ: Princeton University Press, 1966), pp.177–200.
19. A. Panebianco, *Political Parties: Organization and Power* (Cambridge: Cambridge University Press, 1988).
20. R.S. Katz and P. Mair, 'Changing Models of Party Organization and Party Democracy: the Emergence of the Cartel Party', *Party Politics*, Vol.1 (1995), pp.5–28.
21. R. Koole, 'Cadre, Catch-All or Cartel? A Comment on the Notion of the Cartel Party', *Party Politics*, Vol.2 (1996), pp.507–21.
22. von Beyme, 'Party Leadership and Change', p.135; S. Padgett, 'Parties in Post-Communist Society: The German Case', in P.G. Lewis (ed.), *Party Structure and Organization in East-Central Europe* (Cheltenham: Edward Elgar, 1996), p.184.
23. P. Mair, 'What Is Different About Post-Communist Party Systems?', in *Party System Change: approaches and interpretations* (Oxford: Clarendon Press: 1997).
24. S. Roper, 'The Romanian Party System and the Catch-All Party Phenomenon',

East European Quarterly, Vol.27 (1995), pp.518–32.

25. Nalewajko, *Protopartie*, p.212.
26. Koole, 'Cadre, Catch-All or Cartel?' p.520.
27. A. Ágh, 'The End of the Beginning: the Partial Consolidation of East Central European Parties and Party Systems', *Budapest Papers on Democratic Transition*, No.156 (1996), pp.9–10.
28. *Politics of Central Europe*, p.109.
29. Lewis, *Party Structure and Organization*, pp.12–14; Koole, 'Cadre, Catch-All or Cartel?', pp.508, 514, 520.
30. Katz and Mair, 'Changing Models of Party Organization', p.21.
31. K. von Beyme, 'Parties in the Process of Consolidation in East Central Europe', *Budapest Papers on Democratic Transition*, No.256 (1999), p.22.
32. G. Ekiert, 'Democratization Processes in East Central Europe: A Theoretical Consideration', *British Journal of Political Science*, Vol.21 (1990), pp.285–313.
33. Koole, 'Cadre, Catch-All or Cartel?' pp.511–14.

Abstracts

---

1. Introduction: Democratization and Political Change in Post-Communist Eastern Europe
PAUL G. LEWIS

A prominent aspect of democratization in eastern Europe has been the sequence of elections held since beginning of the end of communist rule in June 1989. They have played a major part in marking the different phases of political change, as well as structuring the process of party evolution and facilitating party development. Four electoral phases can be distinguished during the decade of post-communist change and, in the light of a relatively intensive period of electoral activity between 1997 and 1999, clear signs of democratic party development can be seen in the more advanced countries of the region. Different aspects of this process are examined in the chapters that follow, and political developments are charted both in the democratic leaders and some of the less advanced countries.

2. Towards a Soviet Past or a Socialist Future? Understanding Why Voters Choose Communist Parties in Ukraine, Russia, Bulgaria, Slovakia and the Czech Republic
SARAH OATES, WILLIAM L. MILLER and ÅSE GRØDELAND

This chapter uses public opinion data from 1995 to 1998 to examine why people vote for communist parties in five post-communist countries: Russia, Ukraine, Bulgaria, the Czech Republic and Slovakia. Analysis of the data finds that communist voters are better at picking parties than supporters of other party types and are more committed to voting. In addition, survey data show that communist voters are older and less well-educated, in a cleavage that cuts across country borders. Communist voters are also ideologically consistent, with a heightened dislike of a market economy or joining either NATO or the EU.

3. Sickles into Roses: The Successor Parties and Democratic Consolidation in Post-Communist Politics
JOHN ISHIYAMA

In recent years much attention has been paid to the political resurgence of the former communist parties, as well as to their recent electoral declines. This article investigates how the communist successor parties have contributed to the process of democratic consolidation in new democracies (or not). It addresses three questions: (1) To what extent have the communist successor parties drawn their electorate, and especially the 'losers' of the transition, into acceptance of the democratic rules of the game; (2) Are the supporters of more electorally successful communist successor parties more likely to embrace democracy than supporters of less successful successor parties; (3) Does the level of support for democracy among supporters of the communits successor parties vary across different organizational types of parties? It was found that the degree to which a communist successor party appears to have a positive impact on democratic consolidation depends on the kind of party its has become and whether that party enjoyed some degree of success early on in the democratic transition.

4. *Party System Institutionalization in New Democracies: Poland – A Trend-Setter with no Followers*
RADOSLAW MARKOWSKI

The aim of this chapter is to explain the development of the Polish party system and related processes of institutionalization. Links are drawn between two phenomena believed to be causally related: party system institutionalization and democratic consolidation. Political science approaches tend to see parties and party system institutionalization as a necessary but not sufficient prerequisite of democratic consolidation. And even though the intensity of the claim varies considerably, the general expectation is that the 'appropriate' sequence of development is as indicated above. In this chapter an attempt is made to convince the reader that the Polish case proves to be to the contrary. In a way this represents 'bad news' for institutionally oriented political scientists – the institutionalization of parties comes last, as the *finale* of other consolidating changes, not as their precondition. The sequence of events in Poland shows that the macro-economic success occurred first, this being followed by its positive subjective evaluation, then by an increase in satisfaction with democracy and – more importantly – in growth of diffuse political support, and only finally by party system institutionalization. The latter phenomenon should not, however, be confused with the institutionalization of parties themselves – this process is still ahead of us.

5. *The 'Professionalization' of Party Campaigning in Post-Communist Poland*
ALEKS SZCZERBIAK

This chapter considers whether or not there is a process of 'professionalization' of party campaigning in post-communist eastern Europe by examining the new parties that have emerged in Poland since 1989. Most parties employed a tiny number of 'bureaucrats' in their party headquarters and there was some evidence that they were utilizing 'professional' advisers and consultants. However, this was confined mainly to election campaigns and motivated mainly by personal and political sympathies. Given the new parties' extremely weak financial bases, together with a lingering suspicion of Western professional communication advisers, there is also no realistic prospect that such 'professionals' will develop as a substitute for weak party bureaucracies as envisaged in the electoral-professional and cartel models.

6. *Party and State in Democratic Slovenia*
ALENKA KRAŠOVEC

Political parties are organizations with several functions, and they play many roles in society. In carrying them out parties need different (financial, human, media) resources. The costs of party activity have rapidly escalated over the last few years, and parties (especially parliamentary ones) now receive the largest share of their costs from the state. Slovenian parties have from the beginning been almost completely dependent on the state, although parliamentary parties have been in a privileged position because only they have been entitled to continuing direct and indirect public subsidies. Whenever this position has been at stake, they have acted as a relatively homogeneous bloc trying to retain (or increase) all of their privileges. In these two respects, Slovenian parliamentary parties fit into the category of cartel parties.

7. *Institutions and Party Development in the Baltic States*
VELLO PETTAI and MARCUS KREUZER

This chapter presents some initial hypotheses and research results concerning the effect of representative institutions on party development in the post-communist Baltic states of Estonia, Latvia and Lithuania. The research is part of a longer-term project which aims to test institutionalist propositions against the backdrop of what is arguably an ideal natural experiment: while the three ex-Soviet republics share a common recent past and political legacy, they have each adopted very different representative institutions, which we expect will have very distinct effects on the formation of disciplined, cohesive political parties. A wide-ranging survey of Baltic politicians concerning their electoral and political behaviour will be conducted on the basis of some of the research questions presented here. Combined analysis should yield important contributions to the understanding of electoral institutions, party formation and democratization.

8. *Slovakia Ten years After the Collapse of Communist Rule*
GORDON WIGHTMAN

Following the relatively smooth first phase of a transition to democracy within the frame-work of a unifed Czechoslovakia, the nature of Slovak development became more prob-lematic under the dominant but politically ambiguous domininance of Vladimír Mečiar and his party, the MDS. They exerted a strong influence over the political and economic transformation of the country from the period preceding the breakup of the federation in the second half of 1992 until the elections of 1998, which saw the victory of an anti-Mečiar coalition. Continuing problems of political fragmentation and the polarization of public opinion within Slovakia nevertheless raised serious questions about the prospects for consolidation of the country's post-communist democracy.

9. *Perspectives on Democratic Party Development in Belarus*
ELENA A. KORASTELEVA

Contradictory tendencies in party development in post-communist Belarus are identified and discussed. The republic moved from a proliferation of independent parties in the early 1990s to a decline in their salience by the tenth year of transition under conditions of growing authoritarianism. The parties that survived, however, acquired some degree of legitimacy and public support. Social cleavages provide a measure of potential structural continuity between the pre- and post-Soviet periods in Belarus, and thus constitute a further source of stability. But any emerging pattern of party activity has been overridden by the president's reimposition of strengthening authoritarian tendencies. His actions have produced a major cleavage in the political system as a whole that supersedes emerg-ing dimensions of party competition and generally marginalizes party development.

ABSTRACTS

10. *Strands of Conservative Politics in Post-Communist Transition: Adapting to Europeanization and Democratization*
KENNETH KA-LOK CHAN

The political economy of post-Communist transition has been centred on what might be called a US-style ideological conservatism discourse that, in turn, helped successive governments to legitimize neo-liberal, monetarist policies. The aim of this chapter is to examine the formation of a multitude of ideological tendencies against the backdrop of marketization, democratization and European integration of the region. The basic premise of this preliminary study is that, contrary to the rhetoric that there is no alternative to the neo-liberal economic model, post-Communist transition has generated a distinctive ideological competition between socialist, neo-liberal and traditional concerns. The analysis sheds light on the conditions for the emergence and re-orientation of the various ideological tendencies at the level of political practice, and on the prospects of consensus politics from the ideological perspective.

11. *Patterns of Europeanization and Transnational Party Co-operation: Party Development in Central and Eastern Europe*
GEOFFREY PRIDHAM

This article explores the theme of comparing party systems in Central and Eastern Europe (CEE) with ideological patterns of established party systems in the European Union. After looking at party development in the first decade of post-Communist democracies and at possibilities for Europeanization, it concentrates on transnational party co-operation as a mechanism for testing the validity of categorizing party families in CEE. Such co-operation can be influential in party development and provides real pressures to conform to familiar ideological patterns or 'standard parties', but there are limitations to its influence deriving from domestic politics. Transnational party links have developed more intensively with countries in East-Central Europe than in other parts of CEE due to greater compatibility of party systems in the former but also to their more successful transitions to democracy. This trend is reinforced by these countries' better chances for accession to the EU.

12. *Conclusion: Party Development and Democratization in Eastern Europe*
PAUL G. LEWIS

The progress of democratization across eastern European falls into a relatively differentiated pattern. After ten years or so of post-communist change, democratic institutions and processes have become quite well established in the countries of east-central Europe and the Baltic states. Progress has been less marked in the Balkans and core countries of the former Soviet Union. Party development in terms of institutionalization has been one of its key features. In the face of pessimistic predictions about the future of liberal democracy in general and the capacity of post-communist regimes more particularly, the performance of the party systems in the more advanced east European countries in coping with the turmoil of post-communist change has definitely been a positive one. The range of functions performed by the modern party has nevertheless changed in association with the transformations of contemporary democracy more generally, and this has also impinged on the particular links that can be drawn between party development and democratization in eastern Europe.

215

Notes on Contributors

Kenneth Ka-Lok Chan received his D.Phil. in Politics from Nuffield College, University of Oxford in 1998 and is currently Assistant Professor of European Studies at the Hong Kong Baptist University. He has also taught at Warsaw University and Gdansk University, Poland. His interests include post-Communist politics, democratization, British politics, European Union studies and Hong Kong politics. He has published articles in *Europe-Asia Studies, Electoral Studies, Party Politics, Oxford International Review, Studia Polityczne* (in Polish) and *Hong Kong Journal of Social Sciences* (in Chinese).

Åse Grødeland is a Senior Analyst for the International Crisis Group in Central Asia. Dr Grødeland, who served as co-director for a DFID/ESRC project on corruption at University of Glasgow from 1996 to 1999, has published several works on post-communist Europe. She is an expert on environmental issues, public opinion and elections in the former Soviet Union.

John Ishiyama is an Associate Professor of Political Science at Truman State University in Kirksville, Missouri, USA. He is co-author of the book *Ethnopolitics in the New Europe* (Lynne Rienner, 1998) with Marijke Breuning, and editor of a volume entitled *Communist Successor Parties in Post Communist Politics* (Nova Science, 1999). He has also written a number of journal articles on party politics in Eastern Europe and the Former Soviet Union that have appeared in such journals as *Comparative Politics, Comparative Political Studies, Europe-Asia Studies, Political Research Quarterly, Political Science Quarterly, Democratization, Party Politics, Communist and Post-Communist Studies* and *Nations and Nationalism.*

Elena Korasteleva is a Ph.D. student in the Department of European Studies at the University of Bath, and is Research Network Coordinator for an INTAS project on 'The Comparative Analysis of Charismatic Political Leadership in Russia, Ukraine and Belarus'.

Alenka Krašovec is a Ph.D. student and an Assistant in the field of Political Science at the Faculty of Social Sciences and also a Research Assistant at the Centre for Political Research of the University of Ljubljana, Slovenia.

Paul G. Lewis is Reader in Central and East European Politics at the Open University, UK. He is the author of *Central Europe Since 1945* (Longman, 1994) and *Political Parties in Post-Communist Eastern Europe* (Routledge, 2000), as well as the editor of and contributor to a number of other books. He has also published articles in a range of journals including *The British Journal of Political Science, Democratization, Europe-Asia Studies, Government and Opposition, Journal of Communist Studies and Transition Politics,* and *Party Politics,* particularly in the area of democratization, east European party development, and central and east European political development.

Radoslaw Markowski is head of the Electoral Studies Division at the Institute of Political Studies, Polish Academy of Sciences, and Director and Principal Investigator of the Polish National Election Study since 1995. His main areas of interest are: electoral behaviour, party systems, democratic consolidation, as well as comparative politics more generally. His most recent book in English is, as co-author, *Post-Communist Party Systems: Competition, Representation and Inter-party Cooperation* (Cambridge University Press, 1999) and, in Polish, *Wybory parlamentarne 1997: system partyjny – postawy polityczne – zachowania wyborcze* [Parliamentary elections of 1997: party system – political attitudes – electoral behaviour: Ebert & ISP PAN, 1999].

William L. Miller is the Edward Caird Professor of Politics at the University of Glasgow. Professor Miller has published extensively on public opinion, elections and the media, including his work on corruption, officials and public opinion in Eastern Europe. His most recent book (with Åse Berit Grødeland and Tatyana Y. Koshechkina) is *A Culture of Corruption? Coping with Government in Postcommunist Europe,* (Central European University Press, 2001).

Sarah Oates, a lecturer in the Politics Department at the University of Glasgow, studies post-communist parties, elections and the media. She wrote her doctoral dissertation at Emory University (Atlanta, USA) on the Russian parliamentary elections and is working on a book on the role of the media in Russian campaigns. She has written several articles on post-communist elections and is co-editor of *Elections and Voters in Post-communist Russia* (Cheltenham: Edward Elgar, 1998).

Vello Pettai is Lecturer in Political Science at the University of Tartu. He specializes in comparative ethnopolitics and is completing his dissertation at Columbia University on nationalist collective action frames in Estonia and Latvia. He has published previously in *Post-Soviet Affairs, East European Politics and Society* and *Journal of Democracy.* His co-author **Marcus Kreuzer** is an assistant professor at Villanova University. His work focuses on representative institutions in inter-war Europe and contemporary Eastern Europe. He is author of *Institutions and Innovation – Voters, Politicians and Interest Groups in the Consolidation of Democracy: France and Germany 1870–1939* (Ann Arbor: University of Michigan Press, 2001).

Geoffrey Pridham is Professor of European Politics and Director of the Centre for Mediterranean Studies at the University of Bristol, UK. His main research field is comparative democratization, on which he has published widely, and is currently working on a project looking at EU enlargement and domestic politics in post-Communist accession countries. Recent book publications include *The Dynamics of Democratization: A Comparative Approach* (Continuum, 2000) and *Experimenting with Democracy: Regime Change in the Balkans,* edited with Tom Gallagher (Routledge, 2000).

Aleks Szczerbiak is Lecturer in Contemporary European Studies at the Sussex European Institute, University of Sussex. He specializes in central and east European politics and his current research interests include party development and electoral politics in post-communist Poland.

Gordon Wightman is Lecturer in the School of Politics and Communication Studies at the University of Liverpool. He is the author of a number of articles and book chapters on politics in the Czech Republic and Slovakia, and is editor of *Party Formation in East-Central Europe* (Edward Elgar, 1995).

Index

Albania 5–7, 9, 41, 44–5, 163, 193

Balcerowicz, Leszek 80, 82, 84, 168, 170
Belarus 2; Accord 144, 147; Agrarian Party
144–7, 149; authoritarian rule 9, 149–50;
Belarussian Christian Democratic Party 143,
147; Belarussian Labour Party 144–5;
Belarussian Peasant Party 145–6;
Belarussian Popular Front 144–6, 149, 163;
Belarussian Socialist Hramada 142–3;
Christian Democratic Union 143, 145, 147;
Communist Party of Belarus 146–7;
communists 141–2, 144, 149;
democratization 12, 141, 149; elections 5,
141–2, 144, 149; Liberal Democratic Party
145–6; nationalism 141–4, 146–7; party
development 12, 141–2, 145–6, 149, 200;
Party of Communists of Belarus 145, 147,
149; presidential power 13, 146; relations
with Russia 143–5, 149; Social Democratic
Party 145–6, 149, 163; suspension of
parliament 12, 141–2, 145–6, 149, 200;
United Civic Party 145–6, 148
Benes, Edvard 136–7
Bosnia-Herzegovina 5, 8–9, 42, 163
Bulgaria 5; Bulgarian Socialist Party 18–19,
22, 24, 29–30, 44–5, 167, 172; Communist
Party 16, 19, 22; communists 16, 20, 22–3,
27–9; elections 5–6, 8, 19–20, 172–3;
legislature 41; satisfaction with democracy
44–6, 48; Union of Democratic Forces 157,
172, 180, 193

Civil Liberties 9, 34, 93, 141, 161
Communists 16, 18, 21, 23–30; anti-communists
5–8, 126, 156–7, 160, 180; antipathy towards
EU and NATO 16, 26–7; attitude towards
market economy 16, 27; communist
conservatism 13, 157–9, 174; support for
democracy 33, 43, 47, 49; successor parties
32–3, 37, 40–44, 47–9, 167, 199
Conservatism 13, 136, 152–61, 168–9, 171–2,
174, 181, 186
Croatia 5–6, 9, 163, 187, 193
Czechoslovakia 5, 127, 134–8, 180, 199
Czech Republic 2–3; Christian Democratic
Union 3, 163, 172; Civic Democratic Party
3, 10, 23,163, 170, 172, 181; Communist
Party of Bohemia and Moravia 3, 11, 16, 19,

22, 44–5, 49, 167–8, 172; communists 16,
20, 22–4, 26–9; Czech Social Democratic
Party 3, 22–3, 163, 167–8, 172, 181;
elections 3, 10, 19, 61, 168, 172, 203;
Freedom Union 3, 163, 172; legislature 41;
satisfaction with democracy 44–6, 48

Democratization 1–2; Belarus 141;
conservatism 152–3, 158-9, 161–2, 170–72,
175; democratic consolidation 11, 14, 32–5,
37–8, 41–3, 47–9, 55–6, 58, 61, 65–6, 68–9,
73–4, 76, 114, 122, 124, 126, 199, 201, 207;
democratic institutionalization 56, 114;
democratic transition 6, 48, 114, 126, 196;
elections 6; FSU and the Balkans 200; party
activity 203; party development 13, 107,
179–80, 183, 194, 199–200; Poland 75;
popular support for democracy 34–5, 3809,
41–8, 65, 68; prospects for 209; Slovenia 93;
stabilization of political class 56
Dubcek, Alexander 138
Dzurinda, Mikulas 132, 136, 139

Elections 1–6, 8, 34, 37, 41, 61–2, 115, 130,
141, 155, 162, 166, 170, 180, 186, 195, 199,
205; electoral volatility 8, 10, 56, 200, 202
Estonia 4; elections 4–6, 10, 109, 114, 118,
122–4; electoral system 108–13, 115–21,
123; Estonian Coalition Party 4, 164;
Estonian Democratic Labour Party 44–5;
Estonian Reform Party 4, 164; legislature
41; Moderates 4, 164; party consolidation
114–15, 124; party development 12, 124;
satisfaction with democracy 44–6, 48
Ethnic minorities 69, 157, 161, 182, 193, 200,
202
Europeanization 13, 136, 153, 159–62, 170,
172, 179, 183–4, 196; transnational party
cooperation 13, 162–5, 179, 184–6, 193–6
European Union 5, 154, 157–8, 161–2, 171–2,
183-6, 193, 195–6, 199; attitudes to joining
EU 26–7, 128, 132, 139, 159, 168, 175, 183,
194; Christian Democratic International
163–5; European Democratic Union 162–5,
184–5, 193; European People's Party 162–5,
184, 186, 194; European Union of Christian
Democrats 163–5, 169, 186, 193; Liberal
International 162–5, 185, 193; Socialist
International 162–6, 168, 185, 195